D1713832

essentials of general speech communication

McGRAW-HILL SERIES IN SPEECH

Glen E. Mills
Consulting Editor in General Speech

John J. O'Neill
Consulting Editor in Speech Pathology

Aly and Aly: *A Rhetoric of Public Speaking*
Armstrong and Brandes: *The Oral Interpretation of Literature*
Baird: *American Public Addresses*
Baird: *Argumentation, Discussion, and Debate*
Baird, Knower, and Becker: *Essentials of General Speech Communication*
Baird, Knower, and Becker: *General Speech Communication*
Carrell and Tiffany: *Phonetics*
Gibson: *A Reader in Speech Communication*
Hahn, Lomas, Hargis, and Vandraegen: *Basic Voice Training for Speech*
Hasling: *The Message, the Speaker, the Audience*
Henning: *Improving Oral Communication*
Kaplan: *Anatomy and Physiology of Speech*
Kruger: *Modern Debate*
Ogilvie: *Speech in the Elementary School*
Ogilvie and Rees: *Communication Skills: Voice and Pronunciation*
Powers: *Fundamentals of Speech*
Reid: *Speaking Well*
Reid: *Teaching Speech*
Robinson and Becker: *Effective Speech for the Teacher*
Wells: *Cleft Palate and Its Associated Speech Disorders*

FOURTH EDITION

A. Craig Baird
Department of Speech and Dramatic Art
University of Iowa

Franklin H. Knower
Department of Speech
The Ohio State University

Samuel L. Becker
Department of Speech and Dramatic Art
University of Iowa

ESSENTiALS of GENERAL SPEECH COMMUNiCATiON

McGRAW-HILL BOOK COMPANY

New York St. Louis San Francisco Düsseldorf Johannesburg
Kuala Lumpur London Mexico Montreal New Delhi
Panama Rio de Janeiro Singapore Sydney Toronto

Essentials of General Speech Communication

234567890BPBP7987654

Library of Congress Cataloging in Publication Date

Baird, Albert Craig, 1883–
    Essentials of general speech communication.

    (McGraw-Hill series in speech)
    First-3d eds. published under title: Essentials of general speech.
        1. Public speaking. I. Knower, Franklin Hayward, 1901–   joint author. II. Becker, Samuel L., joint author. III. Title.
PN4121.B314 1973   808.5   72–6641
ISBN 0-07-003252-1

This book was set in Theme by Allen-Wayne Technical Corp. The editors were Walter Maytham, Robert Weber, and Helen Greenberg; the designer was Betty Binns; and the production supervisor was Joe Campanella.
The printer and binder was The Book Press, Inc.

CONTENTS

pREfACE

The fourth edition of *Essentials of General Speech Communication*
is designed for the first college-level course in speech communication. We assume that generally it will be a one-term course with
limited credit, though the book is easily adaptable to a longer or
more intensive course.

Our aim is to meet the communication needs of all college students, whatever their major, whether they are enrolled in a four-
year liberal arts college or a community or junior college. We have
assumed that the student's work in speech communication will be
integrated with his work in literature, history, ethics, economics,
natural science, psychology, business, and the other disciplines
from which the communication situation emerges. This integration
will contribute to the student's becoming a more effective communicator, just as his work in speech communication will aid him in
his study and practice of these other disciplines.

Essentials of General Speech Communication covers the major
principles and techniques of effective communication in the contemporary world. It focuses on the communicative environment
(Chapter 1), the range of roles which the communicator must play
(Chapter 2), audiences and communicative situations (Chapter 3),
materials for the development of messages (Chapter 4), analysis
and structure of messages (Chapter 5), verbal and nonverbal symbol systems (Chapter 6), channels of communication (Chapter 7),
and the typical speaking situations, including discussion, and
informative, and persuasive discourse (Chapters 8 through 12).
Four exemplary speeches can be found in the Appendix.

This textbook balances the traditional rhetorical paradigms with
contemporary, practical communicative experiences. The values

of traditional rhetoric are retained, but are articulated with the insights gained from the behavioral sciences, linguistics and semantics, and the multiplying experimental studies of communication. Neither the humanities nor the sciences have a monopoly on truth. Both are useful and important approaches to an understanding of communication processes and, combined with wisdom and creativity, can contribute to a student's skillful participation in these processes.

Though *Essentials of General Speech Communication* does not minimize formal speaking, it enlarges its scope to focus on a variety of the communication experiences which a student will encounter in the postacademic world. These include informal conversations, dialogues, problem-solving discussions, panels, and every sort of presentation of information and ideas—planned and unplanned—with family or friends, professional colleagues, salesmen, reporters, or the general public. This practical approach to the communicator in all of his roles, including his role as audience, is the key and aim of this student-oriented textbook. We hope that this book will help the student to realize his maximum development as a person.

The authors have prepared a *Teacher's Manual* to accompany this edition of *Essentials of General Speech Communication*. This manual contains course outlines, suggested projects, examination questions, and other teaching aids.

> *A. Craig Baird*
> *Franklin H. Knower*
> *Samuel L. Becker*

ESSENTIALS of GENERAL SPEECH COMMUNICATION

your
communication
environment

Twentieth-century man lives in a pressure cooker of communication; everyone and everything are pushing him in different
directions. The media are telling him to buy a car, cigarettes, and
deodorants, to wear an auto seat belt, to vote for the party of his
choice, to support our military efforts, and to demonstrate against
war. His children are asking him to play with them or to give them
money for the movies or to buy them a car, while his wife is pushing him to mow the lawn but to take it easy and to fix his tie.
Those above him at the office are telling him to work harder, and
those below him are telling him to stop making *them* work so
hard. All of this pushing is done through communication.

We are pushed by our television sets, radios, newspapers, magazines, billboards, handbills, memoranda and, most of all, by the
old-fashioned open mouth which is often so uncomfortably close
to our ear. We are pushed through not only verbal communication,
but nonverbal as well. We are attacked not only at supraliminal
levels, but also at the barely liminal and even at the subliminal.
We cannot escape this barrage of communication. As one writer
has said, the world is a "blooming, buzzing, confusion."

The problem for you in this busy field of stimuli is how to make
your own messages stand out and how to pick out the messages

you need to notice. Actually, when you look at our contemporary environment, it is amazing that any effective communication takes place at all.

Meanings of communication

Before going further, we probably ought to define what we mean by "communication." What does it mean to you? Is any sort of talk, writing, or display of signs communication? We suggest that the answer to this question is "no." We suggest also that one of the problems that many people have in communicating results, at least in part, from too simplistic a conception of communication. Too many people define communication as something akin to shooting spitballs. Shooting spitballs requires only some sort of material that can purposefully be changed through wetting and wadding — and then shot out. If there is someone to aim it at, that's fine; but whether he is hit or not has little effect on whether one is shooting spitballs. (As a matter of fact, if our spitball misses, we can always say our target moved.) In communication, too, one begins with some sort of material whose form can be purposefully changed through manipulation or translation. Again, you shoot it out. However, if it fails to hit the target, there is no communication. If there is no perception by a receiver, there has been no communication. On the other hand, if the message de-coded by the receiver has little similarity to the message intended by the sender, there is communication, but the sender has failed. Whether the message is verbal or nonverbal, whether it is a radio commercial, a poem, a poster, a speech, or a piece of sculpture, the problem is the same. *"Communication" is the symbolic inter-action of two or more persons.* If communication is to occur, some stimulus must be *received*, the potential receiver of the message must give it his *attention*, and the message must be *intelligible*. It may or may not be correctly understood, but it must make sense.

Goals of understanding and skill

In order to have some control of your communication environment
and its effects upon you, you must learn to understand as completely as possible how it works, and you must develop maximum
skill at affecting it.

Though you have been talking and listening, saying things with
facial expressions and gestures and watching the facial expressions
and gestures of others for a good part of your life, it is a safe bet
that the communication which went on was often not as efficient
or effective or satisfactory as it might have been. Shakespeare may
well have been commenting upon our feeble efforts in *Romeo and
Juliet* when he had Romeo say, "She speaks, yet she says nothing."
The sad fact is that we, like Juliet, usually go right on in our usual
way unaware of what is going on about us — unaware of our failures
as sources and receivers of messages. Though most of us learned to
talk and to hear the talk of others about as easily as we learned to
walk, the difference between normal talking or listening and skillful
communication is as great as the difference between walking and
accomplished ballet dancing. Effective communication requires
sensitivity and skill that can come only from careful study of communication processes and an awareness of what you and others are
doing as you communicate. It also requires a great deal of understanding of other people. As a matter of fact, learning to communicate effectively means, in large part, learning to understand
what causes other people to behave as they do. Whenever we talk
in this book about choosing a subject, finding materials, organizing
your message, or using appropriate language, we are really talking
directly and indirectly about factors which affect human behavior.
You do not ordinarily select a subject, choose materials, organize
your message, or deliver it in a certain way solely because of your
personal needs; you make these choices in part because of the
needs of those with whom you are communicating.

Communication as social mold and bond

Communication both shapes society and holds it together. Ours
is a social world; whatever you do, you are involved with other

people. You live among your family, your friends, and your co-workers. You need to understand and be understood by them. You need to shape your behavior to some extent because of others, and you need to help others to shape their behavior because of you. In other words, society can exist only through interaction and mutual adjustment among people. Conflicts arise and society tends to disintegrate when there is a breakdown in this interaction — when adequate adjustments do not occur. That is to say, only adequate communication can create and maintain the sort of society that we want.

The more skilled at communication are the people whose goal is a just and good society, the greater the chances that we will have that sort of society. As one, presumably, with that goal, you have the responsibility to develop to the maximum your abilities to communicate in order to help your society toward that goal. This is true whether your society is made up of two persons, of the persons in a college, of a total community, or of an entire nation. It is only through the various and continuing processes of communication that men are able to adjust to each other and to work together for individual and mutual goals.

Cultural determinants of communication

Communication not only shapes society, it is also shaped by society. We use the language of our fellows. We accept similar if not identical value systems. We play similar roles. We seek similar goals. Such matters make for stability of a culture. On the whole, a *culture* operates in a state of *balance,* or equilibrium, primarily stabilizing, yet reaching out as in hope for a better world tomorrow. Communication works both to preserve the old and to generate the new.

Law and *formal policy* are communicable ideas that stabilize and unify human behavior. The *mores, customs,* and *norms* of a culture are types of unwritten law. Some difficulties in communication arise from the fact that different groups in a culture often have different norms, or that different groups accept changing norms or mores at varying rates. The so-called generation gap, for example, is probably caused to some extent by the readier acceptance by young people of changing norms of what is acceptable language in "polite society."

Subcultures within a major culture often have people with vastly different *images* of what is desirable in communication, different *attitudes* toward communication, different *value systems* in some respects, and different *habits* of communication. Differences between subcultures account for such phenomena as the conflicts between urban and rural regions, or among conservatives, liberals, and radicals, and manifest themselves in different life-styles and goals. Since the same fact, the same communication stimulus, may be perceived differently by people with such differences, misunderstanding is almost inevitable. But this is not to say that to be different is bad. Maturity in our culture is marked by a tolerance of differences. To condemn others simply for being different is a mark of ignorance and conceit.

Social purpose in communication

The sort of communication with which we are primarily concerned in this book is purposive communication. People become involved in a communication situation for a specific reason — they want to find out something, or decide what to think or do or, perhaps, be entertained. On the other hand, their purpose may be to help someone else learn something, decide something, or be entertained. In order to achieve any one of these goals, each individual involved must constantly make decisions or predictions about the best thing to do next. In a very real sense, the processes of communication are largely a continual set of predictions and testing of predictions. When you seek information or advice, whether conscious of the process or not, you are predicting where or from whom you can get it. As you listen to a person, you are constantly making predictions about what he means by what he is saying and what he will say next.

As you give information or advice to another person, you make predictions about the information he already has, about the language with which he is familiar, and about the order of presentation which will be easiest for him to understand or which will influence him most. Both seeker and giver constantly check their predictions through observation of the responses of the other. Thus, there is mutual effect. In this sense, all who are involved in a communication situation are both senders and receivers of messages and, sometimes more important, one is doing both simultaneously. Therefore, some theorists consider it somewhat inaccurate to categorize some people in a situation as sources and others as receivers. In many communication situations, each individual is simultaneously source and receiver most of the time.

Though we are concerned primarily with oral communication in this book, it is important to recognize that oral communication works within a context of all forms of communication, nonoral as well as oral, nonverbal as well as verbal. Though we will not go into these other aspects in as great detail, we hope that we can give you enough knowledge about what they are and how they operate so that you can continue to develop further sophistication on your own or in other courses.

We hope that this book will help you to learn what sorts of communication processes are fruitful for various purposes. For example, evidence is clear that formal public speeches have little likelihood of changing votes in a national political election. Informal communication among friends, on a one-to-one basis, is more effective for this purpose. On the other hand, the enthusiasm of party workers is apparently best created with mass meetings and speeches to the party faithful; informal conversations are less useful for this purpose. The mass media are most effective at introducing knowledge of new ideas; interpersonal communication seems essential for most people to change "knowledge of" to "practice of."

This book is not prescriptive. Our purpose is not to help you learn a set of rules on the "correct" way to communicate. Rather, it is to give you some method for analyzing any communication situation and making intelligent decisions about the communicative behaviors you should adopt for that occasion. In most communication situations, there is an audience of one or more persons in a state of need or drive (which either existed before or is induced by a communicator through his structuring of stimuli), and the goal of the communicator is to suggest what the audience can do to reduce that state.

As regards the needs of the audience and the demands of the situation, we will discuss many functions which communication can serve:

1 Reinforcement of existing attitudes or tendencies to behave in certain ways. Whipping up the enthusiasm of the already persuaded is an extreme example of this phenomenon.

2 Dissonance reduction. When members of the audience are torn between conflicting attitudes or between a particular attitude and contradictory knowledge, communication can help to direct the way in which people will reduce that dissonance — whether they will move in one direction or the other, or try to reconcile both attitudes or the attitude and the cognition.

3 Providing information or ideas for opinion leaders to use in their interpersonal communication.

4 Increasing salience for an issue so that it is talked of more, or so that people are more aware of it.

5 Self-adjustment — testing one's position. As someone has said, "How can I know what I think if I don't say it?" More important, how can one know how sound or useful his opinion or knowledge is unless he tries it out on others and sees how it works? In this way, communication is not only a means of influencing others but also a means of adjusting oneself to others. One speaks, notes the responses, adjusts, speaks, notes responses, etc.

6 Social functions — making and keeping friends and

acquaintances; maintaining one's position within a group of friends or acquaintances.

The ultimate test of communication is whether it serves the desired functions well.

Clearly a speech or any other communication form functions differently when it concerns an issue on which an audience has received no or few other messages than when it concerns one for which the audience has gotten many other messages.

An effective communicator must be sensitive to all these factors which affect the processes of communication. An effective communicator, above all, is one who has acquired the ability to place himself in the shoes of those with whom he is interacting — one who understands their needs and the other forces acting upon them and who can, therefore, predict the responses they will make. An effective communicator is sensitive to the conflicting needs and purposes of the various individuals in the communication situation. He assumes major responsibility for the "success" of any given communication encounter. He does not shift blame to others if he is misunderstood or if he does not understand them. He assumes major responsibility for both being clear to others and understanding what others are saying, no matter how complex or confused their messages. (As a student, have you ever found yourself blaming the teacher when you failed to understand something? As a member of a family or other group, have you ever thought others were stupid because they did not understand you?)

Principles of learning

You may be convinced that you have no talent for communication and that you will never be very good at it. On the other hand, you may have been comparatively successful at communicating up to this point in your life without much effort. Perhaps you've been told you have talent, and you have some trophies or certificates to prove it. Don't let either attitude discourage you or lull you into complacency. You will find that the in-depth study of communication is complex and challenging, but not impossible. To become first-rate, you have much to learn, and you'll do it only if it's something you want very much. *If you can accept and develop the desire to learn, you have taken the first step.* At times you will believe that you have no ability, that you started the race too late, but, if it's something you want to do, don't let that worry you.

Don't let anyone fool you into believing he has simple answers to the problems of communication. If you accept those simple answers, sooner or later you'll learn that you have been misled. Understanding communication means the development of personal insight into a long and complex interacting set of factors. *The study of communication is an intellectual endeavor of the highest order.* You will need to learn how to differentiate communication from noncommunication, how to describe, analyze, synthesize, explain, and evaluate all aspects of communication.

Multidisciplinary sources

What other studies may help you become a better communicator? The most important is a general or liberal education. You will need to communicate with many people whose specialty is different from your own. Your general education provides a bridge, a basis for reaching them. An expert communicator needs to be a liberally educated man, just as a liberally educated man should be expert in communication.

Most communication involves a language, and communication scholars utilize many disciplines in the study of language, such as linguistics and general semantics.

The study of some aspects of psychology is helpful in understanding communication. Psychologists have made contributions to our understanding of learning, perception, memory, thinking, judgment, and personality. They have taught us about man's motivations, emotions, feelings, moods, and attitudes, and many other variables important in communication.

Sociologists have contributed to our understanding of the social nature of communication and how it works in groups, organizations, and institutions. They are concerned with group norms and variabilities, with mores, social sanctions, and taboos, and with the diffusion of innovation.

The study of communication involves variables also studied in philosophy. Philosophers, as well as psychologists and linguists, have added to our knowledge of symbolic behavior. Philosophers are concerned with the logic of analysis, inference, ethics, and aesthetics.

We can learn things about communication from many other arts, sciences, and technologies. We should note especially the fields concerned with other forms of communicative behavior: arts such as painting and graphics; technologies such as broadcasting and journalism; management; salesmanship; and teaching.

Excellent communication is complex

A factor which makes communication more difficult and skill at communication more essential is that many of the messages or ideas with which we must deal today are far more complex than they were in the past, while the human organism has stayed pretty much the same. Thus, to increase your skill at communicating, you must learn to use more and more abstract symbols effectively—relatively simple stimuli which carry a great deal of information. Symbols help us to communicate more efficiently. They also help us to organize, to put into perspective, the fragmented, almost random flow of data by which any man is bombarded. Symbols help us to structure and make "sense" out of our environment, whether that "sense" has any relationship to "reality" or not. If we do not structure these data from our environment, we cannot operate. As a skilled communicator, you can learn to organize data in fruitful ways for your purposes and help others to do so; in a very real sense, you can provide key symbols for others.

You can also help in ensuring more systematic diffusion of critical information. Clearly, among the many serious problems faced by this and any other country is the diffusion of *facts* which people need to vote intelligently on local, state, or national issues, or to eliminate prejudice toward minority groups, or to do something about the crowded cities; and the diffusion of *ideas,* such as new ways of teaching, farming, raising children, or operating a college or university.

The context of communication

Communication is complex in yet another sense. Any single communication in which you participate is not an isolated event. What happens in the situation depends in large part on forces outside the situation, and what follows the speech also depends on an ongoing stream of forces. Your message will never be the first influence on anyone else's behavior or knowledge. It is not truly possible to pick an initial influence, because all prior experiences interact with the stimuli in your speech to affect each member of the audience, and your speech becomes part of that process of change and development. So it is important for you to think of communication as a process or set of processes in which there is constant change of each involved individual; in which each individual's responses of any sort affect each of the other individuals in the situation; and in which perceptions of these responses interact with each individual's total experiences in the past and present.

If you look at speaking or any other form of communication in these ways, you will learn to be sensitive and respond more fruitfully to the fact that a great deal besides speech is going on while one is speaking — the speaker is changing in the process of speaking, the audience is changing, the situation is changing — and that much will go on afterward.

Democracy demands participation

Another problem which communication skill can help resolve is the need in our country for indigenous leadership and widespread participation by individuals in various groups and communities. It is generally recognized, for example, that many of the problems of minority groups cannot be resolved until such leadership and participation develop. Similar problems and needs exist in many other countries. Participatory democracy is essential to the kind of society that most of us want, and widespread communication must occur between and among all the people in a society before such a condition can exist.

You may think that you, as an individual, can have little impact on these widespread national or international problems. However, ample evidence from recent history shows that a single person can have a great impact. Consider Senator Eugene McCarthy, who in 1968 was largely responsible for bringing foreign policy questions to the attention of the American public, or Ralph Nader, who in the late sixties and early seventies focused the nation's attention on automobile safety. These men, in different ways, spoke to the entire nation. However, not all communication, to have an impact, need be directed at or involve the so-called mass public. Sociologist David Riesman has noted that if we are to live long enough to imagine and, hopefully, to create a utopian society, our imperative need "is for ideas and for small audiences for them — ideas which are not immediately cut short or truncated by the need to make them appealing to a mass audience. . . . We must have the courage to experiment with ideas among ourselves and within each of us — ideas which cannot immediately be sloganized or sold."[1]

Ethics and relativity

Another important attribute of the effective communicator is ethics. But what is "ethics"? What communicative behaviors are "ethical"? Early philosophers viewed the universe as absolute, with all issues firmly resolved. They theorized confidently about a

[1] David Riesman, "Private People and Public Policy," *Shenandoah*, 10:63-64, Autumn 1958.

unified world. They thought they had penetrated to the heart of this universe and revealed "truth" through their speculations.

The rise of science undermined this absolutism. The nineteenth- and twentieth-century scientific advances called for more tangible methods of determining knowledge and truth. Pragmatists, such as William James, determined truth by its consequences. The idea was true if it was useful. This meant that knowledge constantly changed; there were no certainties, no final definitions, no permanent "facts."

It appears now that the pendulum may be swinging back the other way. Questions are being raised increasingly about whether we have depended too much on scientific thought alone, whether we need to consider more humanistic values and humanistic "truths."

Brembeck and Howell suggest that the most useful ethical standard for communicators is "social utility."[2] By this they mean the degree to which individuals or groups are benefitted. If, as is often the case, some individuals are injured while others benefit from the communication, you must weigh those outcomes and estimate whether the good overbalances the bad.

Ethics and standards

Though no universal agreement concerning what is right in a given case can be dogmatically pronounced, we have within reasonable limits the benefits of cumulative experiences that suggest standards for our choices. All world cultures have provided a social context for desirable behavior within their frameworks. Experience, and reactions to environment and cohesion to communal life, become the customs, laws, cultural inheritance, traditions, and practices of a tribe or a race.

The standards of Western civilization developed similarly. The cultural sentiments of Aristotle and other classicists have been mingled with those of the later thinkers. They are strongly rein-

[2] Winston L. Brembeck and William S. Howell, *Persuasion*, Prentice-Hall, Inc., Englewood Cliffs, N.J., 1952, p. 455.

forced by Judeo-Christian morality and its guides for conduct. The ethical standards that confront us are thus flexible and change with each new generation and its experiences. But they have a large degree of stability because of their social utility.

Although we cannot find an ethical yardstick satisfactory to all, the generally accepted principles of social behavior and the analysis of specific appeals in relation to audiences provide a sound guide for your ethical speaking. You who communicate can be "good men and women skilled in speaking and writing." Your position may be that of Socrates: "When you strive for noble ends, it is also noble to endure whatever pain the effort may involve."[3] There is still hope for our society if most of us continue to strive in this way.

Ethics and the responsibilities of the communicator

The major debates and most important questions in the United States these days involve great ethical issues as well as political, philosophical, economic, military, social, or educational questions: should a program of birth control be adopted by the federal government? Should state legislatures liberalize their abortion laws? Should the federal government enact legislation to prohibit cigarette smoking in the United States? Should sex education be taught in all public schools? Should state governments outlaw DDT? Should negotiation and settlement replace strikes in major American industries? Should the federal government establish a policy of price and wage controls? Should the United States withdraw all armed forces from Southeast Asia immediately? Should college and university students who engage in campus violence be immediately expelled? Should marijuana be legalized? Should the U.S. Post Office be turned into a government-owned corporation? Should the military draft in the United States be discontinued?

[3] Plato, *Phaedrus, Ion, Gorgias,* and *Symposium,* tr. Lane Cooper, Oxford Press, New York, 1938, p. 64, quoted in A. Craig Baird, *Rhetoric,* Ronald Press, New York, 1965, p. 115.

Each of these questions, regardless of its immediate arguments, involves basic issues concerning the welfare of society and of individuals. Such important national controversies call for broad philosophical and ethical discussions which should increase the probability of wise and just action.

Making ethical choices would be a simple matter if one could simply choose between right and wrong, good and evil. Unfortunately, one must generally choose among *relative* goods or *relative* evils. For example, one cannot simply choose between what is good and bad for the individual; one must often choose between what is good for the individual and what is good for the society. It is certainly "good" to advocate every individual's right to associate or not associate with whomever he pleases, but it is also "good" to advocate that no one be excluded from a country club because of his race or religion or sex. We assume you believe that if someone owns a house he ought to be permitted to sell it to whomever he pleases. However, we assume you also believe that no one should be prevented from buying a house because of his race, religion, sex, or any other feature. On such issues, you cannot have it both ways. You must make a decision about the greater good, and this is not always an easy thing to do.

Another difficult ethical choice that a communicator often must make is among means to a good end. We must often face the issue of whether good ends justify unethical means. If you are certain that what you want others to do is "right" and "for their own good," are you justified in withholding information which might cause them not to do it? Are you justified in falsifying evidence? We believe that you are not. We believe that in a democratic society, the *means* by which decisions are made may well be as important in the long run as the decisions themselves. Democracy, like communication, is a process, not a product, and it is important that the process be an ethical one. Since the processes of communication are essential parts of the democratic process, they too must be ethical.

An often neglected ethical issue in communication has to do not with what you might say, but rather with what you might not say.

Too often, when there are important issues to be determined, when people are needed who will take a stand, we remain silent rather than speak out. Too often, for example, we see a wrong in our society — someone discriminated against or someone who needs help — and we fail to speak out because of our timidity or fear of becoming involved or even harmed. We believe that such timidity, such failures to fulfill our responsibilities as citizens and as human beings, are as unethical as anything that we might do.

We assume that you, as a communicator, have no special wisdom that will enable you alone to set the goals for society, but you do have a responsibility to help in setting them and to acquire a sophisticated knowledge of existing goals and needs and to make your communication consistent with them. This is not to say that your responsibility is necessarily to serve the status quo or to aid your society to achieve goals which you believe to be destructive. But it is to say that your responsibility is to help in the development and attainment of those societal goals which are just and which serve mankind.

The best communicator is sensitive to the needs of those with whom he communicates and tries to serve their needs rather than his own. For example, in a discussion, it is essential that you be concerned more with achieving the group goal and helping others in the group to make their maximum contribution than with displaying your superior knowledge. In teaching, it is more important to discover what each learner already knows and needs to learn and to help him learn it than to deliver a series of preset lectures, no matter how perfectly organized and beautifully delivered. In other words, the art of communication is "other-directed," not "inner-directed." If you consider the truly great speeches of recent times — Franklin Delano Roosevelt's speeches during the depths of the Depression, Winston Churchill's speeches during the darkest days of World War II, Martin Luther King's speeches at the height of the civil rights movement that he led — you will see that the speakers did not begin with their personal needs and purposes; they began rather with the needs and purposes of their audience and the larger society. And so should you.

PROJECTS AND PROBLEMS

1 Keep a communication diary for a day, describing as precisely as possible the kinds, amount, and purposes of the communication in which you engage. Include all speaking, writing, listening, and reading. What do you infer from this diary about the importance of these various forms of communication for you?

2 List all the definitions of communication that you can think of. What inferences can you draw from the differences or commonalities among them?

3 Someone once asked, "How can I know what I think if I don't say it?" In what sense or senses might that strange question be meaningful? Consider, for example (though not exclusively), the possible relationship between thought and language and the relevance of feedback to thought.

4 In this chapter, we listed six important functions or purposes of communication. What other functions can you think of?

5 Read the introductory chapter in one or more of the references suggested at the end of this chapter and report to the class on what you have read. Try to relate your thinking about what communication is to the explicit or implied definition of communication that you find in your reading. Invite and answer questions from the class.

6 Hold a class discussion about personal experiences in communication which were successful or unsuccessful, or communication experiences in which you encountered difficulty. Consider what generalizations you can make about communication as a result of the experiences which various members of the group have had.

7 Develop a list of the kinds of experiences which should help you to improve your ability to communicate. Which have already worked for you? How can you make them work better? How could you go about trying some of the others that you list?

8 Develop a list of your experiences with problems, barriers to, and breakdowns in communication. Ask others to share their difficult communication experiences with you. As a class, discuss and make a list of the apparent reasons for these difficulties. With the help of your instructor, try to find at least one way to work on solving what you believe to be the major problems.

9 Read one of the references at the end of the chapter and discuss its application to the problem of understanding cultural influences on communication. What aspects of communication are most influenced by cultural differences?

10 Hold a class discussion on subcultural differences in communication within the United States. How many kinds of cross-cultural differences within our country can you identify? What can you suggest for overcoming these differences?

11 In his paper cited in the bibliography at the end of this chapter, Franklyn S. Haiman discusses what he labels "the rhetoric of the streets." Is it useful to consider these phenomena communication, or are they so different in purpose and means that we only confuse matters by lumping them together with other phenomena we label communication? Defend your position in a class discussion on this topic.

12 Discuss the theory that freedoms of speech, press, and thought are essential for democratic government.

13 Comment on: "The enemies of all liberty flourish and grow strong in the dark of enforced silence," or "There is a logic of discourse, the goal of which is the attainment and protection of personal liberty."

14 Discuss: Should there be any limits on freedom of speech? If so, under what conditions? If not, why not?

15 One of the criteria of the ethics of communication noted in Chapter 1 is whether communication or a series of messages produces social gains for those involved. Should we take this to mean that good ends may justify any means? Why or why not?

REFERENCES

Barnlund, Dean C. (ed.), *Interpersonal Communication: Survey and Studies.* Boston: Houghton Mifflin, 1968.

Berlo, David K., *The Process of Communication.* New York: Holt, Rinehart and Winston, 1960.

Binkley, Luther J., *Contemporary Ethical Theories.* New York: Philosophical Library, 1961.

Boorstein, Daniel J., *The Image.* New York: Harper Colophon Books, 1961.

Boulding, Kenneth E., *The Image.* Ann Arbor: University of Michigan Press, 1961.

Campbell, James H., and Hal W. Hepler (eds.), *Dimensions in Communication: Readings,* 2d ed. Belmont, Calif.: Wadsworth, 1970.

Crane, Edgar, *Marketing Communications.* New York: John Wiley & Sons, 1965.

Haiman, Franklyn S., "The Rhetoric of the Streets: Some Legal and Ethical Considerations," in *A Reader in Speech Communication,* ed. James W. Gibson. New York: McGraw-Hill, 1971, pp. 5-24.

Heider, Fritz, *The Psychology of Interpersonal Relations.* New York: John Wiley & Sons, 1964.

Johannesen, Richard L. (ed.), *Ethics and Persuasion: Selected Readings.* New York: Random House, 1967.

Keller, Paul W., and Charles T. Brown, "An Interpersonal Ethic for Communication," in *A Reader in Speech Communication,* ed. James W. Gibson. New York: McGraw-Hill, 1971, pp. 43-49.

Matson, Floyd W., and Ashley Montagu (eds.), *The Human Dialogue: Perspective on Communication.* New York: Free Press, 1967.

Mowrer, O. Hobart, *Learning Theory and the Symbolic Process.* New York: John Wiley & Sons, 1960.

Murphy, Richard, "Preface to an Ethic of Rhetoric," in D. C. Bryant (ed.), *The Rhetorical Idiom.* Ithaca, N.Y.: Cornell University Press, 1958.

Nilsen, Thomas, *Ethics of Speech Communication.* Indianapolis: Bobbs-Merrill, 1966, Chaps. 1 and 3.

Oliver, Robert T., *Culture and Communication.* Springfield, Ill.: Charles C Thomas, 1962.

Rivers, William L., and Wilbur Schramm, *Responsibility in Mass Communication.* New York: Harper & Row, 1969.

Schramm, Wilbur, *The Science of Human Communication.* New York: Basic Books, 1963.

Sereno, Kenneth K., and C. David Mortensen (eds.), *Foundations of Communication Theory.* New York: Harper & Row, 1970.

Smith, Alfred G. (ed.), *Communication and Culture.* New York: Holt, Rinehart and Winston, 1966, pp. 103-118.

Staats, Arthur W., *Learning, Language, and Cognition.* New York: Holt, Rinehart and Winston, 1968.

you the communicator: a complex of roles

2

We mentioned in Chapter 1 that whenever you are involved in a communication situation, you are both a sender and a receiver virtually all the time, even though one of these roles may dominate at any given moment. In addition, consciously or unconsciously, you are constantly evaluating both your own performance and the performance of those to whom you are listening or with whom you are interacting. In this chapter, we want to discuss some of the major elements involved in all three of these roles. We believe it is fruitful to discuss them together because, in a sense, they are different aspects of the same phenomenon and because you must generally play all these roles simultaneously. Learning to listen better and to evaluate the messages of others more intelligently should help you learn to speak and to evaluate your own messages better.

We will be talking primarily about oral communication in this chapter — speaking and listening — though most of what we will say applies equally to reading and writing or any other transmission and reception of information and ideas. It applies not only to formal speeches or lectures but also to discussions and conversations, as well as to clear "reading" of feedback from others when you are speaking and clear sending of feedback to others when they are speaking.

In attempting to improve our ability to communicate, most of us concentrate almost totally on our sending skills. This is unfortunate, because our skills at receiving and evaluating are at least as important. Listening, for example, is not only one of the best ways of learning new information and ideas, it is also one of the best ways of learning about people — those to whom you listen. As any sound book on how to win friends and influence people will tell you, more friends are won and people influenced by those who listen well than by those who speak well. People appreciate others who care enough about them and their ideas to listen carefully to what they say. Nothing can create more trouble among friends or in a family or business than people who just do not bother to listen to anyone else.

A recent study showed that the average adult spends more than a third of his waking hours listening.[1] The majority of people report that they get most of their information from radio and television or from other people. Hence, good listening is essential for each of us.

Though there has been considerable research on communication and its effects, speaking, listening, and evaluating communication are still largely arts, rather than sciences. This is especially true of evaluation. As a critic, you are — and should be — heavily influenced by your set of values and by an intangible reflective pattern. There is no meaningful formula for weighing the relative importance for any particular situation of content, organization, language, delivery, and all the other elements of communication. You must judge them in relation to the total impression or effect of the communication *in the particular situation in which it occurs.*

Because the situation is so important, you as a speaker, listener, or critic must be knowledgeable of the social and political context in which the communication is taking place. You must immerse yourself in contemporary issues, such as ecology, foreign policy, the economy, and the relevance of higher education. To deal with dis-

---

[1] Larry A. Samovar, Robert D. Brooks, and Richard E. Porter, "A Survey of Adult Communication Activities," *The Journal of Communication,* 19:301-307, 1969.

course on economic questions in the 1970s, for example, you must understand the problems of inflation, recession, and unemployment; you must be familiar with monetary restraints, the cost-of-living index, the International Monetary Fund, and "paper gold." You must know the historical background which the participants bring to the discussion of the issue.

Attention: the base for effective communication

Effective communication is work. If you think of the word "attention," it will help you to remember the two key parts of good communication: "at," or focus — what you attend to — and "tension" — the energy you put into that focusing. To be a good speaker, for example, you must learn to release sufficient energy to be at least moderately aggressive. Neither a shy, retiring person nor an extremely aggressive one is apt to get the fullest response from his audience. The former is simply not given attention; a conversation with the latter is avoided. This is not to say that any single energy level is appropriate for all occasions, but rather that adaptation to many communication situations calls for the ability to speak forcefully when the occasion calls for it. We are speaking here of the force of enthusiasm, persistence, and painstaking thoroughness. It is possible, of course, to be too highly motivated. The communicator who is overanxious, tense, easily angered, or speaks in hate or out of fear may be less credible than the person who can "keep his cool."

Listening, like speaking, is not a passive skill. Not only must you maintain a level of tension and focus on the relevant cues in the message, you must also understand the ideas presented, evaluate the implications of each, select those you find worth remembering, and organize them in a way which will aid recall and maximize their usefulness. In short, listening is not merely a matter of placing yourself within earshot. It is not merely waiting until you can get in your word. Many, if not most, persons listen with the attitude that it is the responsibility of the speaker alone to put across his ideas. This attitude can destroy potentially useful communication and reduce your self-control. If you make listening an energetic, thoughtful, critical process, you control your own thinking; if you do not listen carefully and critically, you are little more than a sponge, and often not a very good one.

Some causes of ineffective listening

Despite — or perhaps because of — the inordinate amount of time that we spend listening to parents, teachers, fellow students, and all sorts of other speakers on radio and television and in face-to-face situations, most of us are very ineffective listeners. For evidence of our failure, replicate one of the "rumor" studies some time. Tell a detailed story to one person, especially a story that is contrary to the attitudes and expectations of most people. Have him tell it to another person who has not heard it before, have him tell it to another, etc. By the time the story or "rumor" has gone through five or six persons, it is often almost unrecognizable. Much of the distortion which occurs in rumor transmissions is due to the fact that most of us are overly influenced by the habits or *set* we bring to the communication situation and the attitudes or expectations created by the situation. All of these phenomena affect our perceptions of the speaker and his message, especially when the message contains ideas which are new or with which we disagree. They tend to disrupt our comprehension and retention of the message. We find it too easy to tell ourselves that the room is too hot or the seats too hard, or that the speaker is not worth listening to, that he is hard to hear or understand, that his delivery is bad, or that he is obnoxious or unsure of himself. Too often we are thinking about what we will say next, rather than listening first to what others are saying. We fail to become sufficiently involved with other persons and what they are trying to do or say. We are too easily distracted by other things going on, and we rationalize by saying that the speaker is not interesting enough.

Improving attention

You can develop your ability to control your focus, energy level, and span of attention for both speaking and listening, but it takes conscious practice. Practice speaking and listening in a variety of situations which demand different sorts of adjustment. As a listener, learn to adjust to different speaking rates or different rates at which ideas are thrown at you, just as you learn to adjust your own speaking rate and number of ideas you present to meet the needs of different audiences and situations. Practice keeping a level of tension which will help your concentration. As a listener, or "reader," of feedback, this generally means *increasing* your level of tension. As a speaker, this generally means *reducing* your level of tension so that it does not distract you from what you are trying to say and those to whom you are trying to say it. Learn not to lose focus because of distractions: unexpected dress or irrelevant behavior of the speaker or a member of the audience, unusual or foul language, unexpected topics that arise, ideas that arouse your emotions, or any other unusual or irrelevant aspect of the situation.

Attend to the total communication situation

As a speaker, listener, or critic of communication, you must attend to all the means and modes by which we inform and influence one another. A given communicative act involves an interplay of message (facts, evidence, and amplifying materials, organized in some way and presented through language and other means), an audience or audiences (with particular backgrounds, purposes, and communication skills), a speaker or speakers (also with particular backgrounds, purposes, and communication skills), and a situation (which includes a social and cultural context).

Nonverbal stimuli

"Communication," as we use the term in this book, means not only creating and attending to aural stimuli, but paying close attention to visual and other cues as well. In Chapters 6 and 7 we will present detailed ideas on nonverbal communication and the various channels through which we communicate. We would only note here that you must learn to focus upon nonverbal as well as verbal cues. They can tell you something about the speaker's confidence. Also, they often indicate something about the speaker's attitude toward what he is saying. Be careful, though, not to mistake nervousness or inexperience for insincerity or something else. It is extremely helpful if you know the speaker well, so that you are aware of the nonverbal cues to expect under normal conditions. In some cases, the inflections, pauses, and physical movements of the speaker are as relevant to focus on as what he says.

Effects of attitude on communication

When we are involved in communication, we are generally conscious of and concerned with the effects of what we perceive upon our attitudes. We should be equally conscious of and concerned with the converse — the effects of our attitudes upon what we perceive — for these attitudes can easily interfere with and bias our critical or accurate listening. Listening expert Ralph Nichols calls them "emotional filters" and warns us against letting our attitudes about a topic or our opinions of a speaker or his appearance filter out what the speaker is saying.

Understand the factors which can cause you to be influenced in a communication situation without your complete awareness. Your need for consistency, your reference groups, and reinforcement — all of which we discuss in greater detail in Chapter 3 — can affect your response to communication. An understanding of the way in which these phenomena affect people will help to inoculate you against being overly persuasible. This knowledge will operate similarly to the awareness that comes from hearing a persuasive speech in which the speaker reminds the audience that they will be hearing arguments on the other side or even tells them what some of those arguments are. This type of inoculation helps the members of the audience build their defenses against these counterarguments. Just so, an awareness of the psychological factors in persuasion will help you to build your defenses against these factors so that you are in more conscious control of your own decision making.

This is not to say that you should never change your attitudes or other behaviors; this to say that you should be conscious of various kinds of appeals and their probable effect upon you so that you are in control of that effect, rather than being in the control of others more sophisticated in the processes of communication.

The speaker as message

In one sense, the speaker is part of his message, even before he utters a word. The interpretation and effect of a message can be influenced as much by who speaks as by any other variable. Therefore, it is important that you understand the ways in which you and other speakers can affect the communication process, independently of anything you say. This understanding should help you to be a more effective communicator and a more effective evaluator or critic of other communicators.

One quality of a speaker which can influence audiences was labeled by classical rhetoricians as "ethos" or "ethical quality." Aristotle said that there are three dimensions of ethos: intelligence, character, and goodwill. Many contemporary communications scholars label this quality "credibility" rather than ethos. Their behavioral research also seems to indicate that it has only two important dimensions rather than three; these are trustworthiness and expertness — whether the audience believes the speaker is honest and knows what he is talking about.

In planning your communication efforts, or in trying to understand the communication efforts and effects of others, be aware that there are two classes of factors which influence your credibility, or ethos. One is the reputation which you bring to the communication situation; the other is what you do during the communication situation to alter that reputation. These are sometimes called *extrinsic* and *intrinsic* factors.

Extrinsic factors in credibility   Since those with whom you communicate usually have some knowledge about you and, hence, some expectations of your trustworthiness and credibility, they will be predisposed to respond to what you say in a particular way. If what they have heard about you or their prior experience with you has caused them to expect you to know what you are talking about or caused them to perceive that you are interested in helping them, they will have a higher probability of accepting what you say. On the other hand, if they expect that you do not care about them or that you do not know what you are talking about, they will have a lower probability of accepting your information and arguments.

Intrinsic factors in credibility   What you do during your speech will also alter your credibility and, hence, your effectiveness. The audience's perception of the ideas you present and what you seem to know about the topic will affect their perception of your credibility. Their perception will also be altered by the confidence with which you speak, by your attitude of interest or disinterest, by the language that you use, and by whether you listen to them when they speak or ask questions. If you speak condescendingly, your credibility and your chances of achieving your purposes are reduced. If your comments are disorganized, the audience will assume that you are not a very good thinker. There is ample evidence of the way in which speech qualities such as delivery, organization, and use of evidence enhance credibility.

Confidence and stage fright

Part of the message that we get from many speakers is that they have no confidence in what they are saying. In fact, the problem may really be that they have no confidence in themselves and their ability to communicate. This is a very common phenomenon, and quite serious at times. It can occur even to those who at one time or another say it is not a problem. The reported instances of stage fright may be an inadequate index of its frequency, for some people are so embarrassed about their nervousness that they will not admit to it.

Our main concern is that many people do not understand such reactions in themselves or others. They feel confused and upset by such a reaction and even do things about it that are self-defeating and damaging. It does no good to run away and refuse to speak. A person who runs away not only loses the opportunity to serve others, he may also reinforce his negative reactions and make them worse in the future. The first step is to understand this nervous reaction.

The symptoms of stage fright are all typical fear responses. They can be understood as parts of one's organismic reaction in fright. They apparently have survival value in adapting to physical dangers. They do not have survival value in speaking. The intensity of the experience changes with time. If you are bothered by stage fright try the following kinds of adjustment:

Study human emotional behavior; learn what causes the various signs of nervousness and how common they are.

Stop and think about what it feels like to be nervous. This may cause the nervous feeling to disappear.

Talk about your nervousness to family and friends.

Don't memorize or read your speeches; have an outline developed with concrete materials, perhaps from your personal experiences. Arrange these materials in a sequence easy to remember. Try to get off to a good start.

Use relaxation techniques.

Have notes available for self-prompting in case you need them.

Develop attitudes inconsistent with nervousness, such as a sense of humor, great concern, conviction. It is almost impossible to be nervous and have a sense of humor at the same time.

Prepare carefully.

Use cues to stimulate your memory and thoughts.

Understand communication well enough so that you know when you are doing reasonably well.

Set reasonable goals, a step at a time.

Watch for and adapt to feedback.

Anticipate and plan for the unexpected.

There is a point in the range of motor responses called "optimum tonicity." This state is neither highly relaxed nor highly tense. If you are plagued with overtension, you can achieve relaxation by voluntary production of tension and release. Deep breathing also facilitates relaxation. Learn to use up the energy-producing tension with controlled activity. Let your total physical being reflect and express the ideas of your message.

Listening to aid the speaker

We said before that the way in which others perceive you — your credibility — is affected by whether you listen to what they have to say. When you look at a speaker and act alert and attentive, an essential message is communicated to him — the message that you are considerate and respect him and what he has to say. It gives him confidence in you, and almost any speaker is most communicative with those in whom he has confidence.

Through your listening behavior, without ever uttering a word, you can control many speakers to a very great extent. Not only can you give the speaker confidence and facilitate his speaking, but, with other sorts of visual cues, you can cause him to slow down, repeat, rephrase, or become more lively.

It will also help the speaker and you if you keep your mind open to new ideas until you at least hear him out. You might take a cue from physicist Robert Oppenheimer, who talked about the fact that, in the contemporary world, we cannot sanction ignorance, insensitivity, or indifference.

When a friend tells us of a new discovery we may not understand, we may not be able to listen without jeopardizing the work that is ours and closer to us; but we cannot find in a book or canon — and we should not seek — ground for hallowing our ignorance. If a man tells us that he sees differently than we, or that he finds beautiful what we find ugly, we may have to leave the room from fatigue or trouble; but that is our weakness and our default. If we must live with a perpetual sense that the world and the men in it are greater than we and too much for us, let it be the measure of our virtue that we know this and seek no comfort. Above all, let us not proclaim that the limits of our powers correspond to some special wisdom in our choice of life, of learning, or of beauty.[2]

To put Oppenheimer's point another way, learn to put yourself in the shoes of the speaker, to get a sense of what he is trying to say and why.

Effective listening is always a creative, as well as a re-creative, activity. It is never more so, though, than when listening for enjoyment. Not only is empathy important at such times, but also imagination. In viewing a play or listening to a poem, for example, the creative act is incomplete until the receiver does his part by "filling in" and interpreting the work in terms of his own experience and understanding.

Listening with a purpose

There is no single "right" way to listen, just as there is no single "right" way to speak. You must adapt both to the purpose of the

[2] Robert Oppenheimer, "The Open Mind," Fund for Adult Education's *News Digest*, Feb. 1, 1960, p. 1.

moment. If you are listening to Walter Cronkite on television in order to get ideas on how to speak well, you will attend to different things than if you are listening to get information for a report on world affairs. If you are listening to someone reading Keats or Allen Ginsberg, you will listen in still other ways. Therefore, *be conscious* of what you are listening for and adjust your mental and physical set accordingly. However, do not fall into the habit of hearing only what you want to hear, whether it has been said or not. Wishful listening is as harmful a psychological habit as wishful thinking.

Your listening will be most successful if you are specific about your purpose in listening. If you are evaluating a speech, for example, are you evaluating it in order to decide whether to accept the speaker's proposals? Are you evaluating it to determine whether it will be effective with some particular audience? Are you evaluating it to help the speaker become more effective in moving people or in making a favorable impression on certain kinds of auditors? Or are you evaluating it to discover why it was or wasn't effective at fulfilling its purpose? Perhaps you are evaluating a group of effective speeches in order to develop or refine a set of principles about what makes various types of contemporary communication effective. Or you may be evaluating or analyzing a speech to find out why the speaker said and did what he did. By deciding on your specific purpose or purposes, you will be able to listen more intelligently and to select appropriate methods and criteria for your evaluation. You should also consider the ways in which your criteria might differ when you evaluate a more or less formal speech, discussion, conversation, debate, or other type of discourse. Knowledge of the standards of criticism or evaluation of communication which have been developed over time by various scholars will also be helpful to you.

If you are listening to a speech in order to evaluate it, you should take into consideration the purposes of the others besides yourself who are involved in the communicative situation — both the speaker and the members of the audience. Is the speaker merely trying to give the audience some information, or is he attempting to persuade them to accept some particular position? Is he trying to get the listeners to do something, or is he merely trying to keep them awake and interested? Whatever his purpose and the purposes of the audience, you as a critic should recognize them and decide whether they have been achieved to a reasonable degree.

With a knowledge of the speaker's purpose, the audience's purpose, and your own purpose, you have a basis for assessing what he says and does in terms of relevance to these purposes, usefulness, adequacy, and bias.

Structure your listening

Structuring your listening is most important when your purpose is the acquisition of information and ideas. In addition to detecting the major purpose of what is being said, you must try to determine the central theme, the main ideas, and the important relationships among the ideas and between the ideas and the theme. Discriminate between facts and opinions. As you listen, evaluate ideas just as you evaluate material in planning one of your own speeches. Examine each idea for clarity, accuracy, logic, and relevance to the theme and to your purpose. Take cognizance of the source of the ideas. Weigh the evidence carefully as you hear it. See whether parts of the speech are appealing to your motives or attitudes in a way which is irrelevant to the issue.

When you are evaluating a speech, attend closely to its organization. Organization is no mere mechanical detail; it reflects the speaker's thinking. In some cases he may use a precise outline — with a formal opening, seriatim treatment of related topics, and conventional appeals at the end. In other cases he may resort, equally effectively, to some other means of achieving unity. As a critic, you will note which ideas and materials are included, as well as those which are omitted; you will note the relationship of organization to audience needs and interests; and you will note the percentage of time and space allotted to each idea.

You will learn to structure your listening more effectively if you practice predicting what is going to be said in the message and what it is that you are to learn or understand or believe. If you predict correctly, in effect you get the point twice. If you predict incorrectly, you can compare what the speaker did with what you predicted, which will give you a good start toward the analysis of his speech. Listen for those parts of the message which cue your attention: sentences which forecast what is coming, which show development or a relationship, indicate a transition, or summarize. Listen for the message "between the lines." Ask yourself what the speaker has *not* said that is relevant. Make applications, provide examples, and reorganize what you hear into the most useful shape for your purposes. This use of prior knowledge will help you to decide not only which ideas are relevant and useful but also whether they are true.

Just as a speaker can speak or write a speech more easily if he has an outline of what he wants to say, so you as a listener can grasp and store what a speaker says if you have some fair notion beforehand of what he is likely to say and how he will say it. Clearly, you must be careful not to let your preconceptions mislead you. As we indicated earlier, there is a real danger of hearing what you expect to hear. On the other hand, intelligent expectations can aid listening and learning. Your expectations will generally be most accurate if you know as much about the speaker as possible, have a fairly clear notion of how he perceives you and others in the audience, and understand his purpose in speaking.

With reasonable expectations, you will not be forced into attempting the impossible task of trying to focus on everything, or trying to outline everything, or, the extreme, trying to copy down everything that the speaker says.

Your purposeful listening will be helped if you interpret what you hear in terms of your own experience, as well as your purposes and those of the speaker. The important way to test the accuracy of what you hear is to relate it to what you already know.

You will also find it helpful to acquire the habit, after listening to a speech or participating in a discussion, of reviewing what you have heard and seen.

Evaluate ideas and evidence

You must consider what the speaker's ideas are. How original are they? How consistent? How sensible? How are they related to other ideas that you know about? How clearly are they expressed? How acceptable are they to you and to other members of the audience? Most important, how well do they meet your needs or the needs of other audience members?

Analyze the speaker's supporting evidence and reasoning. Even in a short speech, concrete support for the central idea or ideas should be presented — hypothetical or actual cases, anecdotes, analogies, definitions, cause-to-effect illustrations, and similar material. In your examination of these materials, you will need to become something of a logician. You must apply tests of acceptable definitions, inference, alleged "fact," analogy, reasoning, generalization from cases, authority, and refutation. In short, you must determine whether the speaker's thinking is sound. A logical appraisal of any speech is difficult, but necessary.[3]

You must also evaluate the motivational appeals in speeches that you hear. Effective communicators appeal to audience attitudes and needs. They appeal to motives of self-preservation, a desire to acquire goods and comforts, personal and social satisfactions, or beliefs in duty and justice. We noted earlier that you must be a logician of sorts to analyze the speaker's reasoning. To recognize and analyze these motivational appeals, you must be something of a psychologist.

Evaluate language

Communicative effectiveness depends much on language skill. Whether planning your own messages or evaluating those of others, you must be constantly aware that the effectiveness with which ideas are transmitted is dependent largely on language. One's com-

---

[3]For further details on the logical appraisal of a speech, see Chapter 11.

positions must be accurate, clear, appropriate, and interesting. Ambiguity or vagueness, floridity or general dullness, and triteness must be avoided. A good speaker needs a sufficiently large vocabularly both to maintain interest and to adapt to a variety of different types of topics, occasions, and listeners. At the same time, his vocabulary must remain within a range which appears natural for him so that he doesn't seem to be trying to impress listeners with his erudition or, conversely, talking down to them.[4]

Avoid propaganda

In recent years, the term "propaganda" has fallen into disrepute with many communication scholars. However, we believe that it is a label for an important idea for which we have found no other suitable label. By propaganda we do not mean any persuasive messages with which we or you disagree, which is the way the word has been used too often. By propaganda we mean, rather, any persuasive message which is *deceptive* either because its origins or sources are veiled, the interests or purposes of the sources are hidden, the persuasive methods are misleading, or the effects which will occur if the message is successful are intentionally concealed. Deception or concealment is the key element in propaganda, and if this element is present, the message is propaganda whether a foreign government is sending it to us or we are sending it to them, whether it is advertising or education, a call for a return to fundamental capitalism or a call for revolution. Any message is propaganda if it attempts to misdirect the thinking of its audience.

As a speaker, avoid being a propagandist. As a listener and critic, learn to recognize it and to counteract its influence on your thinking. This recognition will be aided if you keep in mind the two paths that a propagandist tends to follow.

He may, in the first place, concentrate on exploiting all the pitfalls that human reasoning is susceptible to —

[4]Language is discussed in much further detail in Chapter 6.

building up generalizations on inadequate or misperceived data; applying the wrong generalization to a specific instance, and reaching a false conclusion; misinterpreting the sequence of two events or their coexistence in terms of a cause and effect relationship; or transferring an estimate of an event one is familiar with to a new, apparently similar one. He may, on the other hand, follow the other path. Instead of attempting to misdirect a person's thought, he may try to obstruct it, to neutralize it. This he can do by flooding the mind with such an uncontrollable flow of emotion that the individual's thinking mechanism bogs down.[5]

Consider the audience

In Chapter 1 we discussed the social nature of communication, the fact that any communication involves and affects more than one person and that, to be a good communicator, you must be sensitive to the behavior of others. Sensitivity involves the ability to perceive social issues as others see them and to experience a sense of concern for others. As every speech is of its time, so is it of the immediate audience. When communication is effective, the differences among those involved seem to melt. Fusion seems to occur. If you are the speaker and are successful, you take "sovereign possession of the audience," but the audience also takes possession of you.

As a speaker or a critic, try to understand something of the similarities and differences among members of the audience, their biases, mental habits and attitudes, politics, occupations, traditions, economic level, sex, age, etc. These factors furnish a profile which can aid you in planning your speech or in judging the effects of your speech and the speeches of others. In many cases, of course, it will not be possible to find out as much as you might like about the audience — for example, when you perform on radio or television.

[5] Michael Choukas, *Propaganda Comes of Age*, Public Affairs Press, Washington, 1965, pp. 123, 125.

In such cases, you must fathom as best you can, with the aid of the press and existing surveys, the probable makeup of the listeners.

Final judgment of communication

In this chapter and in other chapters of this book, we have discussed many of the elements which contribute to effective communication. In order to evaluate the qualities of a speech, however, as we said at the beginning of this chapter, you cannot simply put these various factors into some sort of formula and calculate a value. First of all, there is too much that we do not yet know about communication processes to make this feasible. Even more important, there are many elements involved that do not fit a measurement model. Foremost among these is the moral or ethical judgment which you must make, correlative with your intellectual appraisal. Perhaps the best test of whether communication is "good" or "bad" is whether the behavior of those who were involved or who were exposed to the communication is changed in positive or negative ways. As students of communication and critics of our own speaking and the speaking of others, we must judge the worth of a speech or set of speeches by its impact on other individuals and on the society. No communication can be judged good or worthwhile except as it makes some positive difference in the lives of people.

The difference that communication makes is often difficult to detect. We cannot judge it solely by its immediate impact, though the immediate impact may provide clues concerning the long-range influence. Most speakers hope for immediate approval of their performances, whether their aim is to entertain or to inform or to change the attitudes and conduct of their listeners. They look for some applause, or at least nods of approval or remarks that indicate audience endorsement. If the speaker is a student, he hopes that his instructor will give him a laudatory critique; if he is a politician, he hopes for favorable letters and telegrams and increased campaign contributions. The result that the politician wants in the long run, though, is to cause the majority of the people to vote for him. The result that the student probably wishes for in the long run is to cause his professor to give him a high grade — though we hope he is also concerned with other, more important, long-range effects.

Clearly, long-range impact is the most important criterion by which communication should be judged. Just as clearly, because any one speech — or even rather extended communication — occurs within the sort of complex communication environment in which all of us exist, its impact is impossible to pinpoint precisely. Nonetheless, if you are to be a good critic or an able communicator, you must learn to pin it down as precisely as you can — to separate the communication influences from all the other influences on human behavior, and the influence of one speech or set of speeches from others. You must learn to deal with levels of *probability* as opposed to *certainty*. With practice, intelligence, and all of the knowledge of human behavior that you can gather, you can reach a high level of probability indeed.

PROJECTS AND PROBLEMS

1   In the Campbell and Hepler chapter noted in the bibliography at the end of this chapter, the authors argue that all communicative activity is directed to changing behavior. Do you agree or disagree? Justify your response.

2   It has been said that communication and neutrality are contradictory, that the very act of communication on a topic is non-neutral. In what senses, if any, do you believe this to be true? Explain.

3   To what extent should you as a speech critic assume social usefulness as a criterion for every speech? If, in evaluating the effect of a particular speech, you observe the unethical use of data or devices, how shall you deal with such a matter in your evaluation?

4   Prepare a paper in which you set forth what you believe to be the fundamental differences between oral and written composition.

5 Prepare and present orally in class an evaluation of a speech recently given by an important national leader.

6 Collect five specimens of speech criticism found in newspapers and periodicals. Try especially to secure a number of reports by editorial writers and columnists on speeches of major importance. Comment on each criticism.

7 Differentiate between impressionistic and judicial speech criticism.

8 To what extent should the literary considerations of permanence and beauty enter into your judgment of a speech?

9 Make a list of what you consider to be your strengths and weaknesses as a listener. Be as specific as possible. Discuss this list with your instructor or the class.

10 At your next classroom or other campus lecture, everyone in the class should take notes and concentrate closely on the speaker, according to the suggestions in this chapter. Before coming to class, each individual should determine what the major points and purposes of the speaker were. Compare notes in class to see whether all of you agree on these major points and purposes. If you do not, try to determine in your class discussion why you failed to perceive the speech in the same way. Were there things the speaker could have done to make his points better? Were there things that you as listeners could have done to comprehend and remember better?

REFERENCES

Biddle, Bruce J., and Edwin J. Thomas, *Role Theory.* New York: John Wiley & Sons, 1966.

Borden, George A., Richard B. Gregg, and Theodore C. Grove, *Speech Behavior and Human Interaction.* Englewood Cliffs, N.J.: Prentice-Hall, 1969.

Brown, Charles T., and Charles Van Riper, *Speech and Man.* Englewood Cliffs, N.J.: Prentice-Hall, 1966.

Campbell, James H., and Hal W. Hepler, "Persuasion and Interpersonal Relations," in *Dimensions in Communication: Readings,* eds. James H. Campbell and Hal W. Hepler, 2d ed. Belmont, Calif.: Wadsworth, 1970, pp. 130-137.

Cathcart, Robert, *Post-Communication.* Indianapolis: Bobbs-Merrill, 1966.

Choukas, Michael, *Propaganda Comes of Age.* Washington, D.C.: Public Affairs Press, 1965.

Duker, Sam (ed.), *Listening Readings.* New York: Scarecrow Press, 1966.

Goffman, Erving, *Behavior in Public Places.* New York: Free Press, 1963.

——— *Strategic Interaction.* Philadelphia: University of Pennsylvania Press, 1969.

Hillbruner, Anthony, *Critical Dimensions.* New York: Random House, 1966.

Johnson, Wendell, *Your Most Enchanted Listener.* New York: Harper & Row, 1956.

Katz, Elihu, and Paul F. Lazarsfeld, *Personal Influence.* Glencoe, Ill.: Free Press, 1955.

Kretch, David, et al., *Individual in Society.* New York: McGraw-Hill, 1962.

Nichols, Ralph G., and Leonard A. Stevens, *Are You Listening?* New York: McGraw-Hill, 1957.

Payne, Donald E. (ed.), *The Obstinate Audience.* Ann Arbor, Mich.: Foundation for Research on Human Behavior, 1965.

Sanford, Nevitt, *Self and Society.* New York: Atherton Press, 1966.

Thonssen, Lester, A. Craig Baird, and Waldo W. Braden, *Speech Criticism,* 2d ed. New York: Ronald Press, 1970.

Toch, Hans, and Henry Clay Smith, *Social Perception.* Princeton, N.J.: D. Van Nostrand, 1968.

Whyte, William H., Jr., *Is Anybody Listening?* New York: Simon and Schuster, 1952.

your
audience
and
situation

3

Adaptation to your audience is one of the most important aspects of communication. Communication is a social activity. In general, people do not talk simply to be talking or write simply to be writing. Rather, they communicate largely to help themselves adjust to each other and to their environment.

There are various ways in which one can adapt to an audience. Too often, we adapt by simply finding the arguments which will persuade that audience or the language which will make our ideas most clear so that our purposes are served. Although this is clearly important, it is not as important as serving the needs or purposes of the audience. To put this another way, in most communication situations which you will encounter, you ought to be thinking not only or primarily of how to move the audience according to your desires, but also of how to change yourself — how to change your communication behaviors to meet the needs and desires of the audience. This means that you must understand those with whom you talk. You must become sensitive to their needs because your effectiveness as a speaker will depend on far more than your ideas alone. It will depend to a very large extent on the identification of your listeners with you and your message.

If you are to understand fully the processes of communication and learn to adapt to various audiences and situations — and thereby become an effective communicator — you must understand the forces which cause people to behave as they do, make them say what they do, and respond to what others say as they do. In other words, you should understand some of the laws or generalizations about human behavior that scholars of communication and other forms of human behavior have established.

Below are three major generalizations about human behavior with which you should be familiar. We will state each one briefly and then discuss the way in which each applies in communication situations.

1 When a response is reinforced, it is more likely to recur.

2 Our behaviors are affected by our reference groups — groups to which we look for models of how to behave and groups from which we seek reinforcement.

3 There is pressure within an individual to achieve and maintain consistency among what he knows, what he believes, and what he does.

Reinforcement

The principle of *reinforcement*, often called the "law of effect," is probably the most consistent finding from all educational research. It has been found again and again that if reinforcement — some reward, some satisfaction — accompanies a response which a learner makes, he will learn that response faster than others not accompanied by reinforcement. Thus, in teaching, it is important to find ways to reinforce the responses which you want your audience to make. This reinforcement does not always need to be some sort of reward. It has been found, for example, that simply the knowledge that one is making the "correct" response is reinforcing to most individuals.

An obvious implication of the law of effect is that, when communicating, you must plan your messages, your responses, and the rest of the communication situation in such a way as to give the others involved some sense of satisfaction or other reinforcement if they learn or do what you believe they ought to be learning or doing during or following your speaking with them. At certain times, it is possible to provide immediate reward or satisfaction. At other times, reinforcement occurs because of future reward of which people are made aware. For example, your audience might be made aware that they can increase the probability of achieving one of their long-range goals — such as happiness, satisfaction, money, or love — through learning or doing what you are suggesting.

In short, those with whom you communicate will not be moved simply because you indicate that you wish them to be or even because it is "right"; they will be moved if they are aware that it is in either their short-range or long-range interest to do so. And it is part of your job as a communicator to ensure that awareness.

Reference groups

Another consistent finding of research on human behavior is that what people believe and do tends to be consistent with what is believed and done by their *reference groups,* that is, by other persons with whom they have pleasant contacts or with whom they would like to have pleasant contacts, or by individuals or groups with whom they are motivated to gain or maintain acceptance. We judge our own behavior and beliefs with reference to those individuals or groups from which we seek reinforcement, hence the term. It is difficult for any of us to be convinced to agree with something when those with whom we associate disagree, especially those whom we regard as authoritative or closely related to the issue. Consciously or not, we feel guilt or uncertainty concerning any action which runs counter to the expectations of our reference groups.

The fact that each of us has many reference groups complicates this matter and makes things more difficult for the communicator. Often some of our reference groups have conflicting expectations of our beliefs and behavior. You have probably experienced this conflict at times. Perhaps your family and your close friends had different expectations of your behavior in some situation. Perhaps you have encountered conflict because one group of your friends has one belief about American foreign policy and another group has an opposing belief. Generally, at any given point in time, for any given action, one of our reference groups is more dominant; we tend to respond more strongly to its press. A communicator can have some influence here by reminding an audience of its reference group whose norms are most consistent with the point of view he is advocating.

Knowledge of reference groups is important to you not only as a communicator so that you can maximize the influence of those groups whose press is consistent with yours and minimize those whose press is inconsistent. It can also help you to predict the beliefs and patterns of behavior which your audience members bring to the communication situation.

Roles

Closely related to the notion of reference groups is the idea of *roles*. Just as an actor on the stage behaves differently when he is playing different types of roles, so all people act differently when they are playing their different roles — student, boyfriend, son, club president, etc. A knowledge of the expected behaviors for people in their various roles can help you to understand and to predict better their behaviors in communication situations. Careful observation of a variety of individuals in typical roles will help you to predict the ways in which people play the role of student in a college class and the ways in which they play the role of college sport at a football game. It will help you to understand and predict how a person's behavior will vary when he is at a political precinct caucus and when he is discussing politics at a party. To put all of this another way, our reference groups have not only accepted behaviors or norms for their members but also somewhat different behaviors which they accept from those who are playing different roles.

Consistency

One of the most recent theoretical ideas in the behavioral sciences
is that of the press within individuals toward *consistency*.[1] The
theory, based on evidence from many studies, indicates the existence of strong pressure within individuals to make the things they
know, believe, and do consistent within themselves and with each
other. Thus, if you believe that college professors do not care
about students and you observe a professor going out of his way to
help his students, you will feel pressure within you to either (1)
change your belief about professors, (2) perceive the professor's act
as in some way not really helpful but perhaps only self-serving, or
(3) combine the two, i.e., become somewhat more favorable toward
professors and yet still not perceive the professor's action quite as
positively as a student with an initially positive attitude toward the
faculty. In a speaking situation, if you mention that the governor
of the state favors an increase in tuition at the state colleges and
universities, the response of an audience member will depend upon
his initial attitudes toward the governor and toward the proposed
tuition increase. If he is more favorable to the governor than unfavorable to the increase, he will tend to improve his attitude
toward the increase. On the other hand, if he is only slightly favorable toward the governor but very much against the increase, it
probably will not affect the latter at all and make his attitude
toward the governor more unfavorable.
  Consistency theory provides an additional reason for learning what
it is that your audience knows and believes, because this knowledge
will enable you to predict how that audience will perceive and respond to various messages which you might prepare for them. If
an audience member's initial knowledge and attitudes are quite different from yours, the way that he perceives and integrates your

[1] Behavioral scientists use various terms for their descriptions of this phenomenon — "dissonance theory," "balance theory," the "congruity hypothesis," "congruence theory" — but the basic principle remains the same.
For a concise description of some of the research on each, see Chester A.
Insko, *Theories of Attitude Change*, Appleton-Century-Crofts, New York,
1967.

message will be quite different from the way that you would perceive and integrate it. Thus, *it is more important that you create your messages with the background and purposes of the audience in mind than with your background and purposes completely dominating what you do.*

Perception and "reality"

Most of us go through life firmly convinced that we perceive the world around us as it "really is." When we perceive a house, we *know* a house is really there; when we perceive someone displaying prejudice, we *know* prejudice is really there; when we perceive someone listening, we *know* that he is really listening. Anyone who doubts the reality of these things must be "blind" or "deaf" or "stupid." We become upset if this reality is questioned. We fail to realize that statements about what we perceive are statements of *belief*, rather than statements of *fact*. They are in large part statements about ourselves, rather than statements about the world. Walter Lippmann, in his famous book *Public Opinion,* was one of the early scholars of communication to talk about the ways in which people respond not to the "world out there," but to the "pictures in their heads."

To be an able communicator, or to understand the process of communication, it is very important to understand the difference between your perceptions and the world out there. It is also important to recognize that this same phenomenon occurs among all of those with whom you communicate. The picture in each of their heads is different, and all are different from the picture in your head. Each of us gives a slightly different form and meaning to the stimuli from the world out there because each of us has had different past experiences which are relevant to a perception. In any given instance, our needs or purposes at that time and our expectations or beliefs about the world affect what we perceive. From the infinite number of stimuli in our environment we selectively receive those which are consistent with our needs and beliefs, our purposes and expectations. This behavior, though it creates communication and other problems at times, is not stupid; it is necessary for survival in a complex world.

Each new experience further shapes our expectations about the world. We know "for sure" those things with which we have had many consistent experiences. Thus, we are able to make decisions; we are able to act.

Audience analysis

The communication problem that these factors in perception create is that, too often, we make false assumptions about the perceptions of those with whom we are communicating. We assume greater homogeneity of past experience and, hence, greater homogeneity of perceptions and meaning than in fact exist. This is not to say that there is no similarity in the past experiences of most people. Clearly there is similarity, or there could be no communication at all. The commonality of our experiences makes it possible for us to communicate adequately for many purposes. We get into trouble when we assume that our successes at communicating about the price of eggs, the size of shoes, the color of a house, or the score of a basketball game assure equivalent successes at communicating about beauty, love, foreign policy, and the economy. For such complex topics, it is essential to adequate communication that each of us consider more the experiences, expectations, and purposes of those with whom we are communicating.

Once you know something about the experiences, expectations, and purposes of those with whom you are communicating, you can use your knowledge to help you select examples, illustrations, arguments, and evidence. It can even help you to select the very language in which you couch these examples.

Perception seems to be most clearly explained by the consistency theory which we described earlier. Many of the findings on perception indicate that individuals structure sensory impulses in such a way as to make their perception most consistent with what they already know, what they already believe, and the way in which they already behave. The problem for you, as for any communicator, is to find ways to overcome those forces which lead to a misperception of your message or to use that pressure for consistency in such a way that it increases, rather than decreases, the probability of your message being perceived correctly.

Using the results of audience analysis

Knowledge of these theoretical notions about human behavior and sensitivity to what the audience knows and believes can help you not only to determine what to say but also to organize what you say. For example, if you are convinced of your audience's need for some particular bit of knowledge or their need to take some action, but you know that the audience is unaware of its need, you ought to begin your speech by establishing that need. On the other hand, if the audience is already aware of the need, it would be better to go directly to the information or ideas that will help them to satisfy their need.

Sensitivity to the audience *and* the situation will also help ensure that the language you use is appropriate to both. We do not need to tell you that what is appropriate among your friends may be quite inappropriate among your fellow workers, and vice versa. For many of us, the language that is appropriate among our friends is inappropriate in school. Some studies in the ghettos, for example, have shown wide variances between "home talk" and "school talk." If a ghetto child attempted to use school talk consistently among his friends, he would not be a very effective communicator. In fact, he would soon have no friends. This is an extreme example of what can happen to you in your speaking. You will sharply reduce your effectiveness as a communicator if you fail to adapt your language to the audience and the situation. This is not to say that you must be a "phony" and try to impress a sophisticated audience or talk down to an unsophisticated one. It is to say that you must be sensitive to the appropriate language to use for a given group in a given situation.

Sometimes, in order to discover the knowledge, ideas, and needs of your audience, you must do some systematic research on the audience as well as on the topic. When you are speaking with people whom you know quite well, the need for such research is minimal — though careful observation of even this audience is important, both before, during, and after your interaction with them, to be sure that you have assessed the situation accurately. When you are going to speak with people whom you do not know very well, there is clearly the need for more systematic study of them. This does not usually mean a formal survey, though it may in rare instances. It may simply mean a few inquiries directed at people who are more familiar with them than you are. It may mean attempting to discover what they have said or written on the topic. One of our students, who was going to be interviewed for a job, went to the library and found some articles which had been written by some of the men who would be interviewing him. The knowledge thus gained was invaluable to him in that important communication situation.

Feedback

Audience adaptation of the sort that we have been talking about does not function solely to help in the *planning* of your speech. It is something that goes on *while* you are speaking and during all of your communicative interaction with others. In most communication, there is a give and take; you are listening at least as much as you are talking. You need to adjust what you say, and even how you listen or what you listen for, to what you hear and see. While you are speaking, even if it is a formal speech, you should be receiving messages from your audience to which you adapt. These messages may be in the form of frowns, laughter, quizzical looks, heads nodding in agreement or shaking in disagreement, or perhaps people falling asleep. These messages coming to you from your audience should serve as a check on how you are doing; they should provide cues to what to do more of or less of or differently.

An extremely important part of the communicator's job is this constant evaluation of his effect. Just as a good teacher constantly assesses what a class is learning so that he can adjust his teaching accordingly — repeating a unit when necessary, speeding up, trying to teach the unit in a different way, etc. — so a speaker must constantly assess the responses of his audience to see whether to adjust his communication plan. Does the audience seem interested? Do they seem to be getting the point? Are they responding to the point as you hoped they would? You cannot assume that the meaning of the nonverbal messages that you get from the audience will always be immediately clear. You must learn to "read" them.

Messages coming back to a communicator, whether the facial expressions of the audience, or grunts, or groans, or movement, or even verbal statements, are often called "feedback." This is a useful way to think of them. However, it may be even more useful not to think of yourself as a speaker sending messages to an audience, which in turn sends feedback to which you can adjust. It may be better to think of yourself and everyone else involved in any communication situation as both sending and receiving messages all the time. Thus, even when you are giving a formal speech, you are as much an audience as the people who are sitting and listening to you, and they are "speaking" to you loudly and clearly even though they may utter no sound. Just as they must learn to understand your verbal messages, you must learn to understand their messages, both verbal and nonverbal. Clearly, the same is true when only you and one other person are involved in the communication situation.

It is important for you as a communicator to be aware of the sensing of feedback and to practice improving your ability to sense and interpret it. Clearly, this means understanding the type of person with whom you are talking, for the cues a listener feeds back to a speaker vary widely. To take an obvious example, you must know the listener well enough to know whether, if his eyes are closed, he is listening carefully or is asleep. Awareness of this sensing of feedback and practice at improving your ability to sense and interpret it are essential for optimum communication. The effective communicator is constantly adjusting what he says and does to this feedback. The effective communicator, in his receiving role, is also constantly adjusting the visual and auditory cues he gives the source in order to shape that source's behaviors to his needs.

Another major implication of the interdependence of sender, receiver, and situation is the effect which these interactions have upon you. Have you ever thought about the extent to which you lose control of your own behavior because of the feedback from a receiver of your message? For example, how is your behavior affected when you address someone by name and he growls, "Yeah, what do you want?" To what extent does your reaction affect the probability of your communication goals being achieved? You must become aware of the fact that you are often affected by feedback without even knowing it. Learn to be sensitive to feedback, but at the same time, learn to control your responses to it.

Steps in audience analysis: a summary

There are five aspects of an audience which you should keep in mind when you are planning a speech or any other form of communication. These are knowledge, interests, beliefs or attitudes, prior behaviors, and the number of persons who will be in the group.

People differ widely in the amount of *knowledge* they possess, and so they certainly will differ in what they know or understand about your subject. You will need to make some educated guesses about how much your audience knows. You will want to save time and maintain interest by not dwelling at length upon those aspects of your subject already well known to your audience. And of course you will need to relate the new and unknown to the known.

A major reason for adapting to audience *interests* is to enable you to get the listeners' attention. Unless we can get attention, not just for its own sake but attention to some important aspect of our message, the communication cannot succeed.

We are all interested in meeting our biological needs, yet we also possess strong interests in meeting these needs in conformity with the mores and conventions of our culture. If we experience dissonance or anxiety or intense motivation, we are interested in carrying on some activity which will reduce this unpleasant state of affairs. We are interested in things which bring us satisfaction and in maintaining our rights and privileges in society, but we are also interested in gaining social acceptance and approval. Such interests as these are common. Any communication in which we engage should be shaped in light of such interests in the audience.

What are the *attitudes* and *beliefs* of the listeners toward your subject? What political, religious, economic, aesthetic, and other prejudices are they likely to have? Their group affiliations, needs, and desires will determine their prejudices. In planning a speech to influence the attitudes of these listeners, you should consider why their preliminary attitudes are as they are. Have they read widely and discussed this subject? Have they had firsthand experience with it? Are they following the lead of some person or some group they admire?

What if most of them, at the start, are opposed to your topic? You will need to unfold your ideas by beginning with ideas they will accept and leading them by successive steps from preliminaries to the final conclusions.

Since you will sometimes speak to persuade people to action, you need to know something about *the way they have behaved or are able to behave* about your subject. Have they performed similar acts in the past? Do they have the resources, including knowledge and skill, to do what you are asking? Do you know of any reservations or doubts which must be dispelled before you can get the desired response? Can you give them adequate reasons for action? Can you dwell upon these motives to create and release the energies necessary for action?

The *size of the audience* is an important dimension because the magnitude of the response will depend in some ways on the number of people involved.

There are many other dimensions of audience behavior you may need to consider at times. For example, what do they expect of you in the occasion and situation? What are their capacities and talent? They have certain organizational roles, identities, physical

characteristics, and attainments. In general these features will result
in differences in their interests, information, attitudes, and other behaviors which we have suggested earlier.

Meeting the demands of the occasion

Analysis and adaptation to the audience is closely related to the
analysis and adaptation to the occasion. An important aspect of
your audience analysis must be concerned with understanding why
the audience or others involved in the communication situation
with you are there. Why are you there? What factors gave rise to
this situation? What relevant things happened prior to this? What
is the purpose of this encounter? What needs to be done?

Many of the great speeches in man's history have grown out of
crisis situations — war, economic depression, natural disaster, severe
racial conflict, political upheaval, etc. Even lesser crises call for adjustments which only communication can help to bring about — a
sales slump in a business, a misunderstanding between husband and
wife, parent and child, student and teacher, or among friends.

But it is not only crisis situations which create demands for communication. Almost every situation in which we find ourselves
calls for a certain amount and kind of communication. Each particular occasion — the time, the place, the social milieu, what has
gone before, what will probably follow, the others who are involved — places certain demands on you as a communicator. In
some ways, the occasion limits the kinds of speaking that you can
do to be effective. In other ways, if you understand the occasion,
it can open special communicative opportunities for you. A form
of speaking which is extremely effective in the context of one
time and place is totally ineffective in other times and places. For
example, the kind of speech which will be effective at a partisan
political rally is totally out of place in a discussion designed to enlighten uncommitted young voters about the major factors to consider in deciding for whom to vote.[2]

[2]For an interesting analysis of the importance of the situation in communication, see Lloyd Bitzer, "The Rhetorical Situation," *Philosophy and Rhetoric*,
1:1-14, 1968.

One of the reasons that analysis of the occasion and analysis of the audience are closely related is that the nature of the occasion affects the audience that will be present. The audience at that political rally just mentioned will tend to be voters who are already committed to the party and so have their minds made up. They will also be people who are almost certain to vote. On the other hand, if you get into a political discussion at a party or in your rooming house or dormitory, those with whom you are talking will probably be far less partisan; some will probably not even be very interested or involved with politics.

People also have different norms or customs when they are in different situations. These affect the expectations which those with whom you are communicating will have of you — their set.

The occasion affects the other messages which they get before and after yours and, perhaps, even while you are communicating. To cite an obvious example, if you are the sole speaker, you can operate differently than if you are sharing the platform with other speakers and may be the fourth or fifth person to talk on a particular topic.

Some types of occasions have such specific demands that special kinds of speaking have been developed for them. One example is the occasion in which someone must present an idea for the approval of others — a new design for an office building, a new method of teaching a course, a new budget, a proposal for a political campaign, a plan for marketing a product in a different way. A recently published book, in fact, deals with speaking for the occasion in which a presentation must be made.[3]

Occasions vary so much that it is difficult to present precise ideas on means for analyzing and adapting to all of them. All that we can suggest is that you try to be sensitive to the peculiar demands of each situation in which you find yourself. Be aware of the expectations and needs of that situation, what is happening at the moment, and what led up to that moment. This sensitivity will increase the probability of your coming up with the right idea at the right place —that idea, as they say, whose time has come.

[3]William S. Howell and Ernest G. Bormann, *Presentational Speaking for Business and the Professions*, Harper & Row, New York, 1971.

PROJECTS AND PROBLEMS

1 Select an issue which interests you and then think of a group of persons whom you are sure have clear attitudes on this issue. It should be a group with which you are familiar — perhaps a club in which you are a member, the members of this or some other class, the people in your housing unit, or the people in your neighborhood in your hometown. Analyze the group to determine as well as you can the probable reasons the members hold the attitudes that they do toward the issue you selected. In a five-minute speech to the class, describe the group, its attitudes, and the probable reasons for those attitudes.

2 Select someone with whom you communicate sometimes. Describe in as great detail as possible the ways in which your attitudes and views of the world differ and the problems or potential problems these differences create for your communication together.

3 Discuss and evaluate each of the kinds of feedback the teachers in your various classes give to you and the kinds you give to them. Be as specific as possible. Include in your discussion suggestions for improvement for you and for your teachers.

4 Read chapter one of Walter Lippmann's *Public Opinion.* Report to the class on instances in which you have observed that "the world outside" and certain people's "pictures in their heads" differ. Discuss also the implications of these observations for communication.

5 Read the introduction to Erving Goffman's *The Presentation of Self in Everyday Life.* Speak to the class on the relevance of Goffman's major points regarding communication or on your experiences that confirm or contradict his points.

6 Discuss the ethical problems of adapting your communication, especially the kinds of arguments you use, to your audience. Are there dangers here? If so, what are they and how might they be avoided or minimized? If you see no ethical problem or danger, present a convincing case to the class for this point of view.

7 Describe your major reference groups. In what ways do you believe that some of your attitudes and behaviors are affected by some of these groups? Be as specific as possible.

REFERENCES

Becker, Samuel, "Research Findings in Broadcasting and Civil Rights," *Television Quarterly*, 5:72-82, 1966. An example of an audience analysis on one specific issue.

Berelson, Bernard, and Gary A. Steiner, *Human Behavior.* New York: Harcourt, Brace & World, 1964.

Borden, George A., *An Introduction to Human Communication Theory.* Dubuque, Iowa: William C. Brown, 1971.

Clevenger, Theodore, Jr., *Audience Analysis.* Indianapolis: Bobbs-Merrill, 1966.

Ellingsworth, Huber W., and Theodore Clevenger, Jr., *Speech and Social Action.* Englewood Cliffs, N.J.: Prentice-Hall, 1967, chap. 5.

Gergen, Kenneth J., *The Psychology of Behavior Exchange.* Reading, Mass.: Addison-Wesley, 1969.

Goffman, Erving, *The Presentation of Self in Everyday Life.* Garden City, N.Y.: Doubleday, 1959, Introduction.

Holtzman, Paul D., *The Psychology of Speakers' Audiences.* Glenview, Ill.: Scott, Foresman, 1969.

Lippman, Walter, *Public Opinion.* New York: Macmillan, 1960. There are many reprintings of this classic, which was first published in 1922. There is much wisdom here for someone attempting to understand audiences.

McLeod, Jack M., "The Contribution of Psychology to Human Communication Theory," in *Human Communication Theory,* ed. Frank E. X. Dance. New York: Holt, Rinehart and Winston, 1967, pp. 202-235.

Scheidel, Thomas M., *Persuasive Speaking.* Glenview, Ill.: Scott, Foresman, 1967. See especially chap. 2, "Antecedents to Persuasive Speaking."

Smith, Henry Clay, *Sensitivity to People.* New York: McGraw-Hill, 1966.

Tagiuri, Renato, and Luigi Petrullo, *Person Perception and Interpersonal Behavior.* Stanford, Calif.: Stanford University Press, 1958.

YOUR MESSAGE, PURPOSES, AND MATERIALS

4

"What shall I talk about?" This question, almost as old as human association, also confronts the college student, perhaps especially those in speech classes. What shall be the theme for your presentation? Your topic may be assigned to you, such as "What am I and why do I need charisma?" (You will at once adjust the title!)

Some of you find little inspiration in addressing only your fellow students. Others of you chafe at the restrictions of some of the speaking assignments or other rules that you believe make classroom oral exchange artificial.

As we write this chapter, the air is filled with such topics for conversation, discussion, and debate as, How does a policy of wage and price controls affect my budget? How can we get complete equality for males and females? What is good and bad about gay liberation? What are the implications of "future shock" for our careers? Which party will most of the new eighteen-year-old voters favor?

In our discussion of speech it will be helpful to think of the message as the essence of your entire communicative activity.

The message: its purpose

A message rises out of the experiences and needs of a human being to establish contact with others. A person may succumb to fright and utter sounds to aid his own and his mates' survival. Or he may be stirred to improve his own or others' physical, social, or material well-being. The drift of your thinking and oral participation may include the giving and receiving of knowledge; the give-and-take of controversial inquiry; the utterances of admonition, approval, eulogy; or just chatter which has no purpose other than maintaining contact with another human being.

The message and you

The content and direction of your message are colored by your personality and experience as you relate to your world. You will constantly draw on your experiences and observations. For example, if you have lived in Yarmouth, Maine, you are familiar with clam digging and lobster fishing, the use of kelp as fertilizer, and down-East speech. If you have lived in certain sections of metropolitan Chicago, you are familiar with urban traffic, museums, the downtown business world, pollution, substandard housing, and people of varied backgrounds living close together.

What is your perception and opinion of political, educational, social, or religious ideas and movements? Are you concerned with the problem of the hydrogen bomb, American astronauts, further moon ventures, drug laws, permanent wage and price controls, graduate versus undergraduate studies in universities, teaching by television, reforming prisons, making the Supreme Court more conservative, sexual freedom, more rigid automobile driver tests, pop art, black power, obsolescence of picket lines, law and order, expansion of hospitals, limiting Medicare costs, a minimum wage of $2.25 per hour, abortion laws?

Your audience and the message

Ask yourself, "What does my audience want to hear about? What are their needs? What controversial issues confront them?" If they are concerned only with such matters as dating and tomorrow night's basketball game, how can you enlist and hold their attention when you introduce topics representing wider concerns?

In choosing topics and messages, most students of communication are self-centered rather than audience-centered. It is harder to answer the question "What are others interested in?" than the question "What means much to me?" You should be continually alert to the activities, opinions, vocations, and avocations of your audience. Your mental and emotional projection into the minds and personalities of your listeners will provide you with subjects that both appeal to and help them.

Your message and the contemporary scene

The scene and occasion of your talk will, in many cases, suggest your message. You may have the good fortune to engage in an informal radio discussion with other students on the subject "Larger student participation in college government." You may take part in a campaign to raise funds for the Red Cross or increase the budget for a student union. In any case, you will be sensitive to the requirements of the hour — including the nature of the occasion, time of day, audience, and specific aim of the group.

General characteristics of the message

Your message may be very brief or quite extensive. It may be a single radio commercial or an entire series of speeches and newspaper articles on a major issue. Even within one speech you may, in one sense, have a number of different messages. Your message may be an answer to an inquiry, or the stimulus for responses from others. It may be part of a debate or your end of an informal dialogue in class, in your rooming house, or over the local radio station. The message may originate with you alone, or it may be the joint expression or production of a group.

You may think of your message as the ideas or meaning being communicated to your audience. Though there is obviously a relationship, a message is not synonymous with ideas and meaning. We believe that it is more fruitful to conceive of the latter two as a function of the interaction between your message and those who receive it. (This conception of meaning is developed more fully in Chapter 6.) Clearly, though, the meanings and the ideas which you want to stimulate in the minds of your listeners are important considerations as you plan the content of your message. Those meanings and ideas will be stimulated not only by the literal content of what you say but also by the language with which you express that content, by the way in which you structure the language and content, and by the way in which you deliver it. All of these, in fact, are part of the message which you present to your audience.

Limit the subject

Since it is impossible to deal adequately in a brief speech with all the arguments or information about any subject, you must fit your topic to the time allotted you. If, for example, you propose to talk about the attitudes of incoming students on American campuses, discuss one phase, such as "My reaction to this campus." Or, if your subject is professional football, you may limit it to "Strategy in football," or even more specifically, to "George Blanda's kicking of a 50-yard field goal in yesterday's game." Your listeners will be much happier if you whittle out a segment that you can develop concretely, with illustration and summary.

The suggestions above are also applicable if you are in a small group discussion.

Your purpose in oral communication

If your communication is to be effective you must plan it with a specific purpose in mind. Ask yourself especially what your aim is with the particular audience. What do you wish your listeners to do? Add to their knowledge? Accept your point of view? Your purpose may be any one or combination of the following:

1 To inform the listeners (add to their facts and ideas, increase their wisdom, strengthen their judgment, and enlarge their ways of looking at problems), primarily through expositional devices ("How the copying machine in my office works").

2 To interest or entertain them, chiefly through narrative, dramatic, and descriptive devices ("My one day of house-to-house selling").

3 To arouse them to praise or blame, usually through your tribute to an individual, institution, idea, or attitude ("Why Independence Day is obsolete").

4 To convince them of the truth or falsity of an idea or attitude ("One suggestion for retaining your individual freedom and personality in a mass society").

5 To stimulate them to reflective thinking on a problem ("How can we solve the problem of downtown parking?")

6 To persuade them to follow a given course of action ("Vote for my candidate in the coming election").

7 To achieve some combination of these motives.

It is almost impossible and certainly unwise to confine your materials to one of these purposes exclusively. They support each other. To be sure, you must have a primary aim, such as to inform. But even a short talk will generally be more effective if it has elements which interest, inspire, and even convince.

Testing the subject

To test the skill with which you have selected a subject, you may ask yourself several questions:

1 Is the subject suggested by the interests, knowledge, attitudes, and needs of my hearers?

2 Is the subject appropriate to the occasion?

3 Is the subject timely?

4 Is the subject important?

5 Does the subject add to the listener's knowledge?

6 Does the subject grow out of my experience, interests, observations, or knowledge?

7 Do I have genuine enthusiasm for the subject?

8 Have I properly limited the subject?

9 Does the subject result from my purpose to explain, entertain, impress, convince, persuade, or deliberate with an audience?

You can also check the success of your topic selection by a post-mortem examination of the speaking performance itself.

Techniques for securing materials for your messages

How can you find materials that are appropriate and interesting?
When you have selected your purpose and topic, you have automatically determined the main idea or ideas of your communication. Your next task is to find materials which will expand or explain these ideas. Five principal techniques or skills will help you in finding these materials: thinking, recalling personal experiences and observations, listening, talking (including interviewing), and reading (including note-taking).

Thinking

Size up your topic mentally. Students often distrust their own ideas; in the presence of faculty or other experts, the inexperienced student may minimize the value of his own judgments. Speech improvement, like other forms of learning, depends much on the exercise of independent thinking.

Ask yourself about the importance of your subject to your audience. Is this subject timely for them, interesting, worth talking about?

Ask what the subject means. Consider the clarification of terms and ideas beyond specific dictionary definitions. An entire talk can be developed from the question "What are withholding taxes?"

Decide what problem is involved and what probable causes and results accompany it. This approach is somewhat like that of the chronological method, but it is more typical of the "problem-and-solution" procedure of persuasive and discussional speaking.

John Dewey has described the basis of thought or reflection as perplexity and conflict. With no perplexities, Dewey would say, man is thoughtless. "Men do not, in their natural state, think when they have no troubles to deal with, no difficulties to overcome." Just as change brought about by personal problem solving has its beginning in a state of doubt, uneasiness, and conflict to be resolved, so communication intended to produce change must give attention to that dissonance in the listener's thinking which is perhaps necessary to get him to give any attention to your argument. The mental grappling with the problem and the more systematic examination of the way out are the essence of fruitful thinking.

Thoughtful reaction to perplexity and conflict is supplemented by an attempt to decipher the relatively unknown. This movement from the known to the unknown, the leap in the dark, is reflective inference. The representative modes of reasoning or inferring are (1) reasoning from specific instances and details to generalization, (2) analogy, (3) causal relations, (4) authority, and (5) other types. (For a more detailed discussion of logical methods, see Chapter 11.)

Listening

Stimulating ideas and facts are borne in upon you by speakers all through your waking hours. Consider these oral communicative situations that you experience constantly: lectures (in classrooms or elsewhere), student colloquies or organized panels, committee meetings, give-and-take exchanges with others as you come and go, radio and television broadcasts, business conferences, sermons, political campaign speeches, and all sorts of other talks.

Review the sections of Chapter 2 which discuss ideas for the improvement of listening.

Conversation and discussion

If attentive and thoughtful listening informs and stimulates you, then you will benefit from conversation and informal discussions. Franklin D. Roosevelt often revised his speeches after discussion with his colleagues, as did Winston Churchill, John F. Kennedy, Adlai Stevenson, and Richard Nixon.

You too can test your thinking and the effectiveness of your presentation in informal discussion with others. Try it, for example, with the ideas you plan to present in your next speaking assignment for this class.

Interviewing

For sources of your talks, you will become an inquiring reporter. Such a role will be worth your while in proportion to your preparation for it and your orderly management of the information you seek.

Reading

If we have had a New Deal in speechmaking and listening since the advent of radio and television, we have also had a golden age of miscellaneous reading since the invention of the linotype machine and since elementary school education has become universal. Lincoln, in his Indiana and Illinois youth, had comparatively few books. He studied the *Kentucky Preceptor,* Murray's *English Reader,* Weems' *Life of George Washington, Indiana Statutes,* Scott's *Lessons on Elocution,* and a few great classics, including the Bible. We today have access to the classics, but in addition, because of the public and school libraries and the proliferation of paperbacks, we can pick and choose from an endless variety of more recent published matter.

Using the library

In preparing your talks, be sure you can find your way easily and efficiently about the library. Know the most important books of reference, and how to find and make use of the appropriate magazines and newspapers. Have some idea of how to get at the immense fund of information in government documents. Be alert to the possibility of using the many pamphlets issued by nongovernmental organizations. Know where to find bibliographies, how to make convenient lists of references, how to read efficiently, and how to take notes. Don't hesitate to consult the librarians.

The general steps described below constitute the procedure you should follow in getting library results for your proposed talk.

Standard references   In the reference section of the library are encyclopedias, handbooks, and similar books of general and special information. They provide an excellent starting point for research on almost any subject. In order to acquaint yourself with the wide variety of useful reference works, study Constance Winchell's *Guide to Reference Books.* This is the most complete guide to reference works available. Between editions, it is kept reasonably up to date with supplements.

Here is a small sample of the reference works which can be useful.

1 *Encyclopedias.* First use the standard encyclopedias. Students sometimes search vainly for elementary material on a specific theme, forgetting that there is often ample

information readily available in general encyclopedias such as the *Encyclopaedia Britannica* or *Encyclopedia Americana.*

2 *Special encyclopedias.* Special encyclopedias provide information in various fields. You may obtain helpful information from Seligman's *Encyclopedia of the Social Sciences* (fifteen volumes). For religious or philosophical material, you may refer to the *Catholic Encyclopedia,* the *Encyclopedia of Religion and Ethics,* or the *Jewish Encyclopedia.* Try the *Encyclopedia of Educational Research.*

3 *Yearbooks.* You will also find on the reference shelves a collection of yearbooks which will supply up-to-date information on your subject. *The Americana Annual,* for example, gives a dependable survey of current events and biographical items for each year. Similarly useful are the *Britannica Book of the Year* (since 1917), the *New International Yearbook* (since 1907), and the *World Book Encyclopedia Annual* (since 1931). The *World Almanac* (since 1868) also has an astonishingly varied fund of information and an excellent index at the front.

4 *Directories and biographical dictionaries.* You will frequently want to identify the authorities in the field in which you are working. Or perhaps you are planning to interview a member of your college faculty. Often you will find such people listed in *Who's Who in America, Who's Who in American Education, Leaders in American Education, American Men of Science,* or the *Directory of American Scholars.* For prominent Americans of other years, see *Who Was Who in America* or the excellent general biographical source, the *Dictionary of American Biography* (1928-1937, twenty volumes), or the *National Cyclopedia of American Biography* (twenty-six volumes, since 1892). *Current Biography* gives biographies of people featured in the current press. See also *Webster's Biographical Dictionary* and *Biography Index; A Quarterly Index to Biographical Material in Books and Magazines.*

5 *Special references on current problems.* An important source for materials on current problems is the *Reference*

Shelf Series, in which about ten issues appear each year.
Included in this series is *Representative American
Speeches,* an annual collection.

6 *Bibliographies of bibliographies.* Often, one of the
most efficient means for locating the basic writings on a
topic is to use one of the reference works which lists
bibliographies. The most comprehensive bibliography
of bibliographies published in English is Theodore Bester-
man's *A World Bibliography of Bibliographies.* Another
excellent one for recent topics because it is published
semiannually is *Bibliographic Index: A Cumulative
Bibliography of Bibliographies.*

Journals In the field of education the *Speech Teacher, American
Scholar, School and Society, English Journal,* and many others
will prove helpful. In economics and business, the *American Economic Review, Barron's Weekly, Financial World, Monthly Labor
Review,* and *Nation's Business,* to mention a few examples, are in
most libraries. In sociology, *Survey Graphic, American Journal of
Sociology,* and many others are available. In the fields of government, law, and current history there are such magazines as the
*American Political Science Review, Annals of the American Acad-
emy of Political and Social Science, Current History,* and *Current
Events and Foreign Affairs.*

Newspapers Although a considerable number of mediocre newspapers exist in America, there are many papers of high merit and
good reputation. Some of these you will consult both for recent
news and for background information, which are often contained
in feature articles. The *New York Times,* for example, contains a
great deal of information, as its index shows. Other important
papers are *Christian Science Monitor, Washington* (D.C.) *Post, St.
Louis Post-Dispatch, Louisville Courier-Journal, Des Moines Reg-
ister, New Orleans Picayune, Minneapolis Star, Omaha Bee, Denver
Post, San Francisco Chronicle,* and *Los Angeles Times.*

Government documents Either through your library or, in some
cases, by direct correspondence with the Superintendent of Documents in Washington, you can obtain various kinds of government

reports and speeches providing accurate and authoritative materials. For example, the *Statistical Abstract of the United States*, published annually by the U.S. Bureau of Foreign and Domestic Commerce, is a "summary of authoritative statistics showing trends in trade and industry, as well as social progress." It presents figures on area, population, education, finances, wages, and a wide range of other subjects. The *Commerce Yearbook* gives detailed information about business conditions in the United States. *Commerce Reports* and the *Monthly Labor Review* are useful monthly surveys. There are many kinds of congressional documents, including reports of congressional committee hearings, which are useful for many political and current affairs subjects. You may need the help of your librarian in finding such reports in your library or in ordering them, but the *Monthly Catalog of United States Government Publications* with a cumulative index published every ten years should be helpful.

The most important government document for speech students is, without question, the *Congressional Record*, which presents the proceedings of the House of Representatives and the Senate. It is issued daily, with fortnightly indexes.

From all these reference works you will develop a working bibliography specifically for your needs. We assume that you who study speech will know how to use the library card file and how to find your way to the sources pertinent to your topic.

Prepare a list of references

If you intend to spend at least several hours reading in preparation for a speech, discussion, or some other form of communication, make use of bibliographical sources, including indexes, in order to avoid hours of probably wasteful, random rambling through stray books and articles. Using these sources, prepare a short working list of references. Your list will be selective though thorough within the limits of your subject, and accurately recorded. You should include important books, magazines, pamphlets, reports, and newspaper and encyclopedia articles.

List your references systematically, using cards or slips of paper; place only one item on each card. Classify them by type, such as newspapers or magazines. In citing books and pamphlets, include the author's last name, his first name or initials, the exact title of the work, the number of the edition if there is more than one, the publisher, and the place and date of publication. For example:

Toffler, Alvin. *Future Shock*, Random House, Inc., New York, 1970.

For periodicals and newspapers, list (for convenience in the order here suggested) the author's name, title of the article, title of the periodical, volume, pages, and date. For example:

Crockett, George W., Jr. "Reflections of a Jurist on Civil Disobedience," *The American Scholar*, 40:584-591, Autumn 1971.

Use a file box with suitable guide cards in which to store your references. Aim at accuracy and order in your references so that you can quickly and easily find what you want. Debaters often cooperate in drafting and using such references.

Note-taking

The final step in collecting ideas and information for your speaking is taking notes of what you read and jotting down your own original ideas. Do not become one of those who eschew the whole mechanical process of note-taking as a bore and a waste of time. On the other hand, also avoid becoming one of those ultraconscientious copyists who put down almost everything. Complete reliance on memory is insufficient if you wish to classify many details. Voluminous reproduction without discrimination is useless. A more sensible procedure is generally as follows:

1 Aim to get the gist of an idea or an article. Read discriminately.

2 Use cards or papers of a uniform size. Notebook

recordings are inconvenient because they limit your freedom to shuffle the items into various orders.

3 Place one fact on a card.

4 Tag each card at the top with the topic or division under which the statement or date may fall.

5 Cite at the bottom the exact source. Be accurate and complete in the citation. You will later appreciate your meticulousness here.

6 If you quote, quote accurately, but avoid long quotations. Use quotation marks where appropriate so that you can tell later which are the words of the author and which your own.

7 Get facts rather than broad opinions.

8 Start out with a general scheme for your reading and for the classification of your notes. Later you can modify it.

PROJECTS AND PROBLEMS

1 Interview a faculty member on a special topic chosen by you. Make up a five-minute classroom talk in which you give the essence of that interview.

2 Present to the class a brief summary and interpretation of a book which you have recently read on a contemporary problem.

3 Using the reference works cited in this chapter, or other analogous reference works, locate ten articles or books on a topic which interests you. *Use at least five different reference works.* List your ten articles or books in proper bibliographical form and indicate, in each case, the reference work through which you located it.

4 Present a three- to five-minute talk using specific facts and figures as the backbone of the presentation. Develop an outline for your speech and cite on the margins the exact sources of your figures. For statistical examples, consult the bulletins of learned societies (e.g., *Speech Monographs* for data on the effect of various communication variables), government reports such as *Statistical Abstracts of the United States,* or other appropriate sources. Possible subjects for this speech:

   a The trend in unemployment will probably be upward (or downward).
   b We are in for a period of inflation (or recession).
   c Colleges discriminate against women.
   d Eighteen-, nineteen-, and twenty-year-old voters will have a major impact on the American political scene.
   e Students should have a nonprofit, cooperative store at which to buy books and other necessities.
   f The pollution of our environment is increasing

5 Present a speech based primarily on comparison and contrast (including analogies if you wish).

6 Present a speech which incorporates as the main elements either incidents, anecdotes, questions, authorities, or some combination of these. Be sure to limit the subject. Possible subjects for this speech:

a The spirit of intolerance is rising in the United States.
b American cities 100 years from now.
c If I were president of this college.
d Americans are succumbing to the "mass mind."
e Our society needs radical overhauling.
f The need for a religious faith was never greater than it is today.

7 Using as a guide the criteria for "testing the message" suggested in this chapter, test the message used in one of the talks you have made in this class.

8 Proceed as in project 7. Test the message in one of the speeches in the Appendix.

REFERENCES

Aldrich, Ella V., *Using Books and Libraries,* rev. ed. Englewood Cliffs, N.J.: Prentice-Hall, 1946.

Bettinghaus, Erwin P., *Message Preparation.* Indianapolis: Bobbs-Merrill, 1966.

Jeffrey, Robert C., and Owen Peterson, *Speech: A Text with Adapted Readings.* New York: Harper & Row, 1971. See especially chap. 4, "Analyzing Subjects," and chap. 5, "Gathering Materials."

Mills, Glen E., *Message Preparation.* Indianapolis: Bobbs-Merrill, 1966.

Monroe, Alan H., and Douglas Ehninger, *Principles of Speech Communication,* 6th ed. Glenview, Ill.: Scott, Foresman, 1969. See especially chap. 6, "Supporting the Point."

Newman, Robert P., and Dale R. Newman, *Evidence.* Boston: Houghton Mifflin, 1969.

Terris, Walter, *Content and Organization of Speeches.* Dubuque, Iowa: William C. Brown, 1968. See especially chap. 5, "Research: The Sources."

Walter, Otis, "Creativity and the Rules of Rhetoric," in *A Reader in Speech Communication,* ed. James W. Gibson. New York: McGraw-Hill, 1971, pp. 139-145.

orqanizAtioN
ANd
outLiNiNq

5

The organization of ideas in the speech message serves two basic functions. First, having a pattern of organization helps you to shape your materials. Second, appropriate structural design will help your listeners to understand and better appreciate your message. Much of the meaning we would communicate, as well as the meaning others derive from our communication, involves categorizing our thoughts. One sequence of main ideas can convey a different meaning from another.

Your categories of ideas must represent the essence of your subject. Your organization provides an opportunity to pretest your logic, for it can help you to see the relationship of the details you select to your purpose. It can also help you to control the relative amount of time devoted to each part of your speech. Organizing gives you a chance to consider psychological implications and to select points and lines of development in light of probable audience interpretation. It is also a time to make decisions about the style of your speech. The style to be used may determine your organization.

A clear framework will aid you in recalling your ideas and thus will increase your fluency. It may also enhance your credibility as a speaker. Audiences generally respond better to speakers and speeches that are carefully organized. The well-structured speech holds attention and helps listeners to comprehend more easily. The less motivated the audience, the more important is organization, according to the communication research which has been done on organization. For an unmotivated audience, it is important to arouse their interest and their need for the information immediately. It is also important that the speech be easy to follow.

So important did the classical rhetoricians regard organization (*dispositio*) that they stressed it as one of the five major components of oral communication: *inventio* (invention), *dispositio*, *elocutio* (style), *memoria* (memory), and *pronunciatio* (delivery).

To Cicero, *dispositio* was the adapting of the product of invention to a particular situation. He discussed the grouping of ideas in the natural order but stressed that the construction of each speech should be determined by the specific audience problems involved.

Concept of organization

Systematic steps in organization will guide you to an effective pattern for the presentation of your ideas.

1 Decide upon the objective of your speech—the audience reaction you hope for.

2 Express your purpose in a topic or thesis sentence.

3 Divide your subject into a few main points.

4 Organize your material so as to ensure unity, the massing or emphasis of the points, and audience adaptation.

5 Organize the introduction to ensure orientation of your subject and the interest and attention of your audience.

6 Organize the main body so that you move forward from one aspect of your subject to another in a way that will be logical to your audience.

7 Organize the conclusion so that it reinforces your initial speaking purpose.

Selection

Selection, the process of choosing the ideas and their supports for the message, is the most difficult of the steps effecting satisfactory division or organization. The starting point here, as in dealing with other aspects of communication, is that of audience analysis. Your identification with your audience and the occasion becomes a major determinant of what should be included and what excluded or expanded.

Selection is also aided by a clear-cut thesis or statement that embodies both your overall idea and your more specific informative, persuasive, or entertainment purpose. Your thesis should be sufficiently definite to guide properly every step in preparation.

Proportion

The aim of proportion is to set out the most important ideas and parts so that the listener or reader can properly appreciate their relative importance and react, presumably favorably, to your purposes. The rhetorical aim is to secure impressiveness and better retention.

Proportion, as a principle of structure, is partly a matter of position. What is presented at the beginning or end is generally more easily remembered than what is included elsewhere in the message. The trained speaker will place at the beginning ideas or information of major importance to his theme.

The other half of proportion is space. We tend to be most impressed by what a good speaker talks chiefly about. What is held before the attention longest should penetrate further than what is briefly revealed. Thus repetition of ideas through explanation, illustration, logical detail, comparison, contrast, and other methods will help these important concepts to be relatively impressive.

Obviously, as we have implied, selection and proportion are interacting and overlapping processes. What is important enough to be included and which of the included ideas need the most space and the best position are problems that concern adjustment to the needs and behavior of the audience.

Order or arrangement

What is the best order, in general, for a speech to follow?

Speeches, as teachers often have reminded us, should have at least three well-defined divisions or parts: an introduction, a main body, and a conclusion. Plato, in the fourth century B.C., stated not only that a speech should have a beginning, middle, and end but also that it should be put together like "a living creature."

First, you will introduce yourself and your ideas to the group (gain attention, establish need); elaborate on your ideas so that they are established and emphasized; and, finally, climax the whole with a summary or appeal. The creation of goodwill for you and your thinking is the aim of the introduction. The successive marshaling of the ideas to be implanted is the work of the main body. The effort to consolidate these impressions makes up the conclusion.

John Dewey proposed the problem-solution approach to organization. To him, the pattern included, in successive steps: attention getting, statement of the problem, possible solutions, the best solution, and action to implement the solution. This formula is helpful both in preparing for persuasive communication and, with some modifications, in almost every other type of speech communication.

Alan Monroe developed a similar plan of organization: the motivated sequence, which has been widely applied by students of communication. It was based on five parts: gaining attention, showing the need, presenting the solution, visualizing the results, and requesting action or approval. It reflected the salesmanship method in which the need step is enforced by fulfillment or satisfaction and the "closing of the sale."

Specific methods of arrangement

Organization should stem from careful analysis of the audience and of your topic. Knowing how you will organize your speech will be especially helpful in the selection, classification, and proportioning of materials as you assemble them into an orderly whole. The organizational patterns presented below reflect this analytical approach. The use of any one of them depends much on the purpose of the speech, the character of the audience, the occasion, and to a considerable degree the type of content. The patterns are not independent, of course, and you may find it valuable at times to use a combination of patterns in a single speech.

Time order   In the time-order pattern, the message items are arranged in chronological sequence—past to present or present to future. In some cases a reverse time order may be appropriate.

Topographical, or space, order   Topographical, or space, order means that the materials are arranged according to some pattern of space—from near to far, local to national, bottom to top, front to rear, inside to outside, and so on. This method is more often used in descriptive narrative than in argument or exposition. During the flight to the moon of Apollo 14 in July 1970, the daily accounts were largely those of successive distances traversed to and from the earth, each step including the lapses.

Classification order   The classificational, or topical, pattern calls for grouping under some meaningful set of categories. For example, speech is highly important in contemporary American life. It promotes political cohesion and progress. It facilitates social intercourse and experiences. It stimulates economic activities. Thus, a speech about speech could be organized on the basis of these topics, with a section devoted to expanding upon each of the reasons that oral discourse is important.

Causal sequence   The causal order or development traces causes and/or results to a given agent, situation, or condition. Most argumentative talks use some variation of the causal sequence. The Dewey analysis, mentioned above, focuses on the conditions calling for a change (the bad situation and the possible disastrous results if unchecked, and the beneficial results if a given solution is presented).

Problem-solution The problem-solution pattern is practically identical with the causal. It simply puts more emphasis on the comparison of possible solutions and the advocacy of one. In addition, it may include an analysis of the conditions that threaten sound solutions.

The psychological method Here the organization is governed mainly by the speaker's analysis of the motivations of the hearers. All discourse, as we have stated repeatedly, should be guided by the nature and needs of the audience. The psychological treatment, however, is more obviously adjusted directly to the fears, hopes, self-interests, and other drives and attitudes of those who listen. The unity and organization to be found in the speech are determined chiefly by this attention to dominant motivations.

Refutatory method One other method of speech development is that of almost pure refutation. The seasoned debater, for example, will make mental or other notes during a speech to which he is to reply. Then, during his rebuttal, he will restate those sections that he believes are especially vulnerable.

The introduction

How long or short should be the introduction? As we have indicated, such questions can be answered only by a careful analysis of the given audience, the immediate situation, including time limits, and the character and purpose of the discourse. For a brief talk (three to five minutes) or one in which you find yourself part of an extemporaneous dialogue or panel, you will obviously hope to

(1) establish goodwill between your auditors and yourself, (2) explain what your subject is or involves, and (3) make clear your theme and purpose. Your subject and purpose may on occasion need to be inductively and tactfully unfolded to audiences hostile to your proposed conclusions.

Your initial job, as in all communicative situations, is to enlist the attention and cooperation of the audience. This need applies equally to a face-to-face group and a radio or television audience. At the start, your listeners may be preoccupied with other thoughts or activities, or they may be curious momentarily about you as an unknown talker. They may be bored with or indifferent to your topic, or they may be prejudiced against you because you are a North Irish Protestant or a sophomore recently jailed for participating in an illegal New Left demonstration. Cicero's advice to the young men of Rome was to "render auditors well-disposed, attentive, teachable."

1 You may begin by announcing your topic and outline of your talk. Note the opening words by Bernard Berelson, president of the Population Council:

My assignment this morning is two-fold: first to describe the current trends in world population, and second to account for the allegedly limited progress toward population control (whatever that may mean, and note that there can be several different definitions, from mild to severe).[1]

2 You may begin with a personal reference. Note the personal start, mingled with humor, by Fletcher Byrom, president of the Kopper Company, when he delivered his talk, "Hang Loose," at the International Marketing Congress, American Marketing Association, Atlanta, Georgia, June 16, 1969:

My name, in case you missed it, is Fletcher Byrom. I am 50 years old and I am the chief executive officer of one

[1] *Vital Speeches of the Day*, 37:349, Mar. 15, 1971.

of America's 200 largest corporations. So far as I know, I
am in full possession of all my faculties. My doctor and
my insurance counselor tell me I am in good physical condition. I think I can out-hustle, out-talk and out-work any
man in this room.[2]

3 You may begin by referring to the importance of the
occasion. Senator Edmund Muskie opened his address,
"The Astronauts at the Moon," at Jeffersonville, Indiana,
on July 25, 1969, by referring to the "magnificent adven-
ture of Apollo II."[3]

4 You may begin with a direct defense of your ideas
and yourself. Richard M. Nixon began his nationwide
radio and television apologia, "The Checkers Speech,"
September 23, 1952, as follows:

My fellow Americans: I come before you tonight as a
candidate for the Vice-Presidency and as a man whose
honesty and integrity have been questioned.[4]

5 You may begin with a humorous or mock-heroic
reference. Note the opening of Alfred M. Lilienthal's
address at New York City, Dec. 3, 1970.

Mr. Chairman, Senator Thurmond, Congressman Rarick,
Dr. Rowe, Ladies and Gentlemen: When I was asked to
speak to this distinguished group, I was originally told
that I should try to contain my remarks to ten minutes.
This reminded me of a 1956 winter morning when I was
to address the Los Angeles Breakfast Club and was told
that I could talk about the then Suez Crisis for six minutes, sandwiched in between a Swiss yodeler, and a Sia-
mese dancer.

[2] *Vital Speeches of the Day*, 30:604, July 15, 1969.
[3] *Congressional Record*, July 31, 1969, Appendix *E* 6515.
[4] A. Craig Baird, *Representative American Speeches*, H. W. Wilson Co., New
York, 1952–1953, pp. 74–82.

The only thing that saved me at 7:30 A.M. in California before the five hundred tired businessmen and women was an introductory story told by a genial ex-naval chaplain in introducing me:

Two young men, Jack and Charlie, had gone through high school and college together. Both had good jobs. One morning, Jack called Charlie and said, "They've got me."

"Who's got you?"

"The draft board. But I am going to fool them. I once had a hernia, and I am going to wear my truss."

So Jack, wearing his truss, went down to the draft board. Three doctors examined him, took out his draft card and put down "M. E." Jack said, "What's that?" They said, "Medically Exempt."

Four weeks later, bright and early in the morning, Charlie called Jack and said, "They've got me."

"Who's got you?"

"The draft board."

"Haven't you something wrong—flat feet, bad back, ulcers?"

"No, I am in perfect health, as you know."

"Well then, I'll lend you my truss and you go down and make the usual complaints that you can't lift things, you have intermittent pains, and they will let you off for having a hernia."

"Charlie went to the draft board. The same three doctors examined him and then took out his draft card and put down, "M. E." "Medically Exempt?" asked Charlie. "No," replied doctor. "Middle East. Anyone who can wear a truss upside down can certainly ride a camel."[5]

6   You may begin with a striking question.

7   You may begin by citing a striking fact or by giving a condensed narrative. President Franklin D. Roosevelt, on December 8, 1941, began his appeal to Congress for a

declaration of war against Japan thus:

"Yesterday, December 7, 1941–a date that will live in
infamy–the United States of America was suddenly and
deliberately attacked by the naval and air forces of the
Empire of Japan."[6]

Organization of the body

If the introduction has been well designed and if the division of the
subject, based upon the specific purpose, has been clearly made,
the problem of organizing the main body of the speech is mostly
accomplished. Your job is to state clearly the essential ideas or
propositions that make up your subject division and to relate them
to each other.

First and last, you will continue to select and arrange these
divisions with an eye to their acceptability to your listeners.

Selection of ideas You may wonder, in view of the audience and
the limited time at your disposal, what two or three main points of
your topic you should stress. It may be wisest to talk mostly about
one point and only illustrate others. You should not make the
customary mistake of trying to cover everything in three minutes.

In the body of your talk you will continue to make clear your
specific purpose. You will see that the statements presenting your
division of the subject are clearly enunciated throughout. Furthermore, you will insert enough repetitive, transitional, summarizing,
and topic-introductory sentences to make the listener see the relevance of the materials and the significance of your structure.

Order Arrange your material and subject ideas in the order most
appropriate for securing both logical sequence and audience acceptance. Refer again to your plans of analysis or division, whether
chronological, topographical, definitional, logical, problem-solution,
psychological, or other.

[6] A. Craig Baird (ed.), *American Public Addresses: 1740–1952*, McGraw-Hill,
New York, 1956, p. 266.

Will you proceed from the limited to the more general? It all depends. Often you gain your point by moving from several concrete items to a wider statement of principles until the logical goal is accepted. On the other hand, when you want your audience to accept a belief about a particular case, when your time is limited, and when your audience requires the most rigid logic, your treatment may well begin with the generalization.

The problem of selecting the order for presentation of the topic constantly arises, and the relative importance and appeal of topics must be considered. Always keep in mind that it is impossible to answer the question of most effective order without an understanding of your particular audience and the specific requirements of the meeting.

Organization of the conclusion

The conclusion, like the introduction, may have a function other than that of adding to the listener's knowledge of the topic. The final sentence, or perhaps paragraph, should summarize what has been said, especially if your remarks have been rather complicated. If your subject matter is in special need of repetition, a somewhat longer summary may be in order—perhaps a recapitulation in slightly different language. In general, good advice is for any speaker to stop when he is done.

The function of the conclusion, however, is often more than making clear what has been said. You must also impress your speaking or listening colleagues and inspire them to action. Your conclusion may end with a challenge, an applicable quotation, a summary, a prophecy, an appeal, a series of questions, or other material and techniques to enforce your purpose. Note some of these types of conclusions:

1 *Summary.* Charles W. Eliot concluded his address, "Five American Contributions to Civilization," by restating the five contributions to civilization: peace keeping, religious toleration, the development of man's suffrage, the wel-

coming of newcomers, and the diffusion of well being.[7]

2 *Personal appeal.* Woodrow Wilson concluded his first inaugural address, Mar. 4, 1913, with a personal appeal for support of his national program:

This is not a day of triumph: it is a day of dedication. Here muster, not the forces of party, but the forces of humanity. Men's hearts wait upon us: men's lives hang in the balance; men's hopes call upon us to say what we will do. Who shall live up to the great trust? Who dares fail to try? I summon all honest men, all patriotic, all forward-looking men, to my side. God helping me, I will not fail them, if they will but counsel and sustain me!"[8]

The outline

An outline enables you to survey your case as a unit, to note digressions, to size up the major and minor divisions of your analysis, to evaluate the order of your topics, to gauge more carefully the length of your speech, to take a second look at your definitions, and to inspect your illustrations and other facts, all of which should be inserted in your outline. This blueprint will aid you in developing more easily the talk itself. In short, the outline, if properly used, should make you a better speaker. But you must never feel compelled to follow it slavishly.

For your convenience in constructing the outline, we suggest that you apply standard principles and rules. Your instructor may have decided views about methods of outlining; his advice concerning these mechanics will be important. The suggestions given below can be modified or interpreted to suit your needs. These rules are based upon the experience of many speechmakers.

[7]Charles W. Eliot, *American Contributions to Civilization,* The Century Co., New York, 1897, pp. 34–35.
[8]Baird, 1956, p. 224.

1 *Prefix to the outline a clear statement of your subject.* Be sure that the statement represents a careful limiting of the general field you have chosen for your talk. Be sure that your topic sentence reveals clearly and concisely the content and direction of your discourse.

2 Organize your outline generally into introduction, discussion, and conclusion.

3 Use complete sentences throughout.

4 See to it that your statements of main ideas say exactly what you mean. Be sure that they are the main ideas, that they do not overlap, and that they are arranged in the sequence which facilitates their understanding or support for your purpose.

5 Use suitable symbols and indentations. The customary system of numbering, lettering, and indenting is as follows:

I _____
  A _____
    1. _____
      a. _____
        (1)_____
          (a)_____

6 Where logic is an issue, give each division at least two heads. Where one subpoint is adequate for support or illustration, a single subdivision may suffice. Have few main headings in your outline. Otherwise your division may represent no division at all. Keep the wording short.

7 See that each subtopic is logically subordinate to the topic under which it is placed. See that the entire framework, both in its large elements and in its minor statements, is a logical unit. If you have placed ideas together with care, each subhead will support a more general proposition.

8 Include in your introduction those steps necessary to secure a proper unfolding of your subject. Usually include some of the following: (a) a reason for the speech or other data that identify you and your topic with the audience and the occasion, (b) an explanation of terms, (c) the purpose sentence (often in the form of a question), and (d) a statement of the topics you propose to develop.

9 Include in your conclusion a summary or any other material necessary to reinforce or apply the ideas previously developed.

10 On the margin or in the body of the outline, insert at the appropriate point the exact source of any materials quoted or cited from printed sources.

11 Include the concrete materials composing your speech, motivative as well as logical, but in the outline avoid much personal comment. Make an outline, not an essay.

Types of outlines

Speech outlines are here suggested with some differences in outlining indicated, determined by whether the speech is to inform, entertain, or persuade.

Outline for an informative speech Outlines for the short informative, or expositional, speech are comparatively simple. The subtopics provide further details about the main topics rather than, as in the case of the typical argumentative outline, give reasons for the support of propositions.

Outline for an argumentative or persuasive speech The outline for an argumentative or persuasive speech is more elaborate. Although much exposition is included, the framework of the outline consists of a series of reasons. "For" or an equivalent word is used in such an outline to link main and subideas to demonstrate the reasoning process. Thus:

I. Wider support of educational television is needed for:
A. The claim that educational needs should be handled exclusively by commercial stations is not justified, for
1. Few commercial stations can afford to devote much of their daytime service and best evening hours to nonprofit educational shows, for
a. (Further subtopics)

A full outline of this argumentative type is called a brief.

Outline for a panel discussion   The discussion outline varies somewhat from the expositional or argumentative forms. Its pattern usually includes (1) cause for discussion, (2) definitions, (3) goals to be considered in any solution of the problem, (4) diagnosis or analysis of the problem corresponding to the step that, in the argumentative brief, examines the need for the proposed change, (5) examination of representative solutions, and (6) arguments to support the solution that is chosen by the group.

This individual outline, converted from a series of declarative statements to one made up of impartial questions, then becomes a group outline for use by the members of the panel, who set out to answer these questions.

Outline and the speaker's notes   Once you have assembled a satisfactory outline, should you carry it with you and speak directly from it? Certainly not; it will cramp your speaking style. Should you memorize it as it stands? This would probably not be too helpful. Should you write a full speech from it and recite the results verbatim? You may write the speech, but you will probably not have time to memorize it, nor should you do so. The more practicable procedure is to draft a few speaker's notes from your material — catch phrases that will guide you in the speech itself, if you feel you must have such support   These notes are for you alone.

Your aim in such preparation is still to develop as an extemporaneous speaker. You will make both an outline and speaker's notes; the latter will be much more abbreviated, informal, and private than the former. And you may easily disregard any such "props" in your short speech.

PROJECTS AND PROBLEMS

1 Identify and state the main ideas in one of the speeches in the Appendix which your instructor will assign. Bring this information to class in written form and compare your analysis with the analyses of other members of the class. If there is disagreement, determine the probable reasons for it.

2 To apply the principles of developing a subject by time sequence, prepare and present a five-minute speech in which the two or three main divisions of the topic are arranged in chronological order. Possible subjects for this speech (which you may limit further):

    a The black civil rights struggle since Martin Luther King.
    b The development of intercollegiate football.
    c Country and Western music in the past decade.
    d The early history of the motion picture.
    e The commune as an alternative life-style.

3 To apply the principles of developing a subject by classification, prepare and present a five-minute speech in which the two or three main headings will be classificational or topical. Possible subjects for this speech (which you may limit further):

    a The qualifications of a good speaker.
    b The qualifications of a good listener.
    c The production of a play.
    d The advantages of living in New England (or any other section of the United States).
    e The editing of a film.

4 To apply the principles of developing a subject by logical order, prepare and present a five-minute speech in which the two or three main headings are in logical or cause-and-effect order. Possible subjects for this speech (which you may limit further):

a Limiting the size of cities.
b Reducing the number of automobiles on our streets and roads.
c The relationship of drug use to birth defects.
d Smoking and lung cancer.
e More national scholarships for college students.
f Our antiquated county government system.
g Student power.

5 To study and apply methods of systematic outlining, before presenting one of the speeches suggested in projects 2, 3, or 4 above, prepare a full-sentence outline. Give it to your instructor before the delivery of the speech. At the following class period the outline will be returned, with comments on your method of outlining. At the discretion of your instructor, this assignment will be repeated for some of your later classroom presentations.

6 Test and report to the class concerning the outlining of a speech in the Appendix.

REFERENCES

Bruner, Jerome S., Jacqueline J. Goodnow, and George A. Austen, *A Study in Thinking.* New York: John Wiley & Sons, 1966.

Deese, James, *The Structure of Associations in Language and Thought.* Baltimore: Johns Hopkins Press, 1965.

Hovland, Carl I., et al., *The Order of Presentation in Persuasion.* New Haven: Yale University Press, 1957.

McCroskey, James, *An Introduction to Rhetorical Communication.* Englewood Cliffs, N.J.: Prentice-Hall, 1968, chap. 11.

Thonssen, Lester, A. Craig Baird, and Waldo W. Braden, *Speech Criticism,* 2d ed. New York: Ronald Press, 1970, chap. 15.

Wiseman, Gordon, and Larry Barker, *Speech: Interpersonal Communication.* San Francisco: Chandler Publishing Company, 1967, chap. 4.

symbol
systems:
verbal
and
nonverbal

6

The story is told of the man who went into a large modern drug-store and asked for a small tube of toothpaste. The clerk handed him one marked "Large." The customer returned it and repeated that he wanted the small size. The clerk replied, "That is the small size."
"What's the large size called?" asked the man.
"That's Giant."
"Is that the biggest?"
"Oh, no. Next is King, then Economy, and then the biggest of all—Family!"[1]
This story illustrates one of the many problems we have in understanding and using language well. You might condemn advertisers and others who use or abuse language in this way, but your condemnation will probably have little effect on the behavior of those who do it. If you are to be an effective communicator, it is far more important to try to understand than to condemn. It is far more important to try to understand the way in which language and our other symbol systems work, the variations which we find

[1] Roul Tunley, "The Big Package Flap," *Saturday Review*, Apr. 9, 1966, p. 64.

within our various cultures, and the variety of functions which symbol systems serve.

There are many symbolic systems, but natural languages are the best developed, the most subtle, and the most complicated of all. They are the product of abilities which are unique to man.

What is language?

Before going further, we probably ought to indicate somewhat more clearly how we are using the term "language." Since it is difficult to communicate the many and complex facets of the term with a single definition, we will provide three definitions and then suggest some of their implications. These implications will be further amplified throughout the remainder of this chapter.

One linguist has defined language as "a socially institutionalized sign system . . ., the result of centuries of gradual development and change."[2] Another says language is "a system of arbitrary symbols by which thought is conveyed from one human being to another."[3] A key element for contemporary scholars of language is brought in by the definition of language as a set of symbols with rules of grammar which may be either explicit or implicit. Note the key terms in these definitions. They will help you to understand what language is and how it works. Most important, these understandings should help you to be a more effective user of language—a more effective communicator.

The elements of language

The two basic elements for a language, as these definitions indicate, are a set of symbols and a structure, or a vocabulary and a syntax or grammar.

[2] John B. Carroll, *Language and Thought*, Prentice-Hall, Englewood Cliffs, N.J., 1964, p. 8.

[3] John P. Hughes, *The Science of Language*, Random House, New York, 1964, p. 6.

The first element is the *vocabulary* or *set of symbols*. By a symbol, we mean anything which, by common agreement, stands for something else. Symbols are arbitrary; there is no necessary logical connection between the symbol and the thing symbolized. A particular banner to some persons may be the symbol of their country; but to others it may simply be a piece of cloth for covering the table. Not all symbols are part of a language, of course; not all are verbal symbols. The cross, a flag, a road sign are nonverbal symbols. We will consider these more fully in the latter part of this chapter. Whether verbal or nonverbal, the most useful symbols are those which are most definite, consistent, and universal. They need to be definite or specific so that the intended users know to what each refers. Each needs to be reasonably consistent; its referent must not shift too rapidly, or users of the symbol will confuse each other. It needs to be sufficiently universal so that most members of the language community agree to its referent or referents.

It takes more than meaningful words to make a meaningful sentence, of course. And different arrangements of the same words can result in different meanings. The important element which shapes the meaning of groups of words is the *structure* or *syntax* or *grammar*. Thus any language must have grammatical rules. This does not mean that every speaker, to communicate well, must follow precisely the same rules or that speakers must follow the rules set down in the so-called grammar books.

Despite what many of us may have learned at one time, rules of grammar are not important primarily because they provide a basis for distinguishing between the educated and uneducated, or between the careful and the careless. In itself, grammar is unimportant. It is important only because it makes possible our expression of an infinite variety of meanings through an infinite variety of sentences. It is a powerful means for converting ideas into communicable form. It makes communication and organized, abstract thinking possible.

There is a third element which is important in our definitions of language and which is crucial to our understanding of the way in which language works. Language exists in the *human social context* and is shaped by that context. A language shifts with the life-styles and needs of its users. In a very real sense, whenever someone utters something, anything at all, he is talking about himself. When he says, "That is a large tree," or "He is dull," or "She is a radical," he is saying something about his perceptions, the meanings that he has accepted for those terms, and about his conception of tree sizes, what he finds interesting in men, or his own political orientations. To understand such messages, we must understand the speaker.

Language and thought

Obviously, man not only affects language but is affected by language. He learns and is persuaded by words that he hears and reads. Less obviously, he is also affected by his unconscious assumptions about language. You remember as a youngster accepting the "fact" that certain words were "bad" or "fighting words." If anyone called you one of those, the only thing that you could do was to fight him. Looking back on such thoughts now, they seem silly. Yet, even as adults, we continue to make signal or habitual responses to many words. For many of us some of these words are "radical," "protest," "demonstration," and even "peace." For others of us, some of these words are "conservative," "the establishment," "Americanism," and even "the American flag." Too often, we respond to these terms or labels without thinking, without recognizing, for example, that protest[1] is not protest[2] and protest[2] is not protest[3], just as conservative[1] is not conservative[2] and conservative[2] is not conservative[3]. These kinds of responses undoubtedly contributed to the senseless persecution of German-Americans during World War I and Japanese-Americans during World War II in the United States, to the mass slaughter of Jews in Nazi Germany in the 1930s, and to the ill-treatment of nonwhites through most of our country's history.

The importance of nonverbal communication

Language is obviously important in communication. However, reliance on words alone, or even on words as the dominant element, can result in inefficient or ineffective communication. Consider, for example, explaining to someone how to drive a car without nonverbal aids, or describing the appearance of a person, or teaching someone how to pluck and dress a chicken, or instructing a class in swimming. This consideration should make obvious the fact that much communication, to be effective, cannot rely solely upon words. In fact, if you become sensitive to the varieties of communication going on about you, you will discover that there is a great deal of nonverbal communication in our society, though much of it is unplanned.

This is not to say, of course, that nonverbal communication is always or necessarily more effective than verbal communication. The overgeneralization of the cliché "One picture is worth a thousand words" can be made immediately obvious by asking what picture will explain the way to make out a federal income tax form. The important thing is to develop an understanding of nonverbal forms of communication so that you will be sensitive to the sorts of purposes and situations for which they will be useful.

The acquisition of this understanding will not be easy, for surprisingly little research on nonverbal communication has been done. We have no knowledge comparable to that which we have for verbal communication. In discussing nonverbal communication, therefore, we will largely be raising questions for you to consider and, at the same time, attempting to present to you the little that is known about this aspect of communication.

Nonverbal functions

Though any nonverbal stimulus may be used for a variety of purposes, you should generally have a primary purpose in mind for each and develop it in such a way that it will best serve that purpose. Among the many purposes that a nonverbal stimulus might serve are the following:

1 *To catch and hold the attention of your audience.* Here, the usual quality of the stimulus and its contrast with the environment is important. The eye patch on the man in the Hathaway shirt ads is a good example of a nonverbal stimulus used to gain and hold attention.

2 *To orient the listener or reader to your mood or intent.* Here, nonverbal stimuli function the way feedback does to orient a speaker to his listeners. Thus your posture, actions, and tones of voice suggest to listeners and viewers whether your verbal message arises from such bases as mirth, fear, surprise, anger, or approval.

3 *To evoke a favorable impression of credibility and personality.* Your facial expression, vocal quality, gesture, dress, and other actions affect the audience's perceptions of your credibility and whether you think your topic is important. Keep in mind that relatively simple nonverbal cues can sharply alter the audience's perceptions of you or the ideas about which you are talking.

4 *To emphasize meaning.* A great deal of evidence shows that the use of visualization increases retention of information and, in many cases, increases the probability of audience acceptance. For example, when agricultural extension workers wanted to persuade farmers in this country and abroad to adopt hybrid seed corn, they planted a field of hybrid corn beside a field of regular corn. As the corn in the two fields grew, the "message" was obvious to everyone and, hence, quite persuasive. Nonverbal stimuli can help an audience learn to recognize an object (e.g., to recognize a tufted titmouse from its appearance or sound), to make needed associations (e.g., to associate the picture of a bird with the Spanish word for bird), and to reconstruct an object (e.g., to be able to draw a tufted titmouse or imitate its sound).

5 *To suggest an intangible idea.* Biologists, for example, have used models to illustrate the idea of inherited traits. Advertisers have attempted to suggest the taste of a cigarette (whether successfully or not, we do not know) with the photograph of an attractive girl on the seacoast with wind blowing in her hair.

The qualities of a good nonverbal message are analogous to the qualities of a good verbal message: clarity, simplicity, a bit of redundancy, and appropriate adaptation to the audience. If you plan the nonverbal aspects of your message with clear purposes in mind, and you understand your audience and the communication situation, you should have no problems. It will also help if you keep your nonverbal messages as simple as possible, stripped of nonessentials. Never try to say too much with a single visual aid; avoid clutter; and definitely keep the amount of verbal material on a visual prop to a minimum. In addition, keep the size of the intended audience in mind or, more specifically, the maximum distance of any audience member from your visual prop. Adjust the size and loudness of your nonverbal stimuli to audience distance. The best sort of redundancy, to ensure comprehension and retention, is that which results from the same or similar things being "said" through different modes of communication. The attention of the audience will probably be held better and they will retain more of the material if an idea is communicated both verbally and visually, rather than simply being repeated in the verbal mode.

Above all, in planning your nonverbal stimuli, use your imagination. Take a cue from the designer who thinks less of *symbols* and more of the *symbolic value of things*. If one were attempting to communicate the essence of the modern age, and especially the intangible notion of man's control over the universe, such a designer would probably select the push button as the most relevant symbol. It can start a vehicle toward the moon or turn on a vacuum cleaner.

The meanings of meaning

One of the most important concepts for you in understanding both language and nonverbal symbol systems is the concept of *meaning*. Most of us have an oversimplified notion of what meaning is, and because of this, we often fail as communicators. For example, when we have some question about the possible meanings of a word, we are confident that we can find the answer in a dictionary. We do not realize that dictionaries provide only a small portion of the meanings in our language and fail to reflect accurately the wide range of meanings for many terms within various groups in our population.

Often, people's absolute faith in dictionaries is probably due to a belief that symbols, especially words, have "basic" or "real" or "universal" meanings. We think that it is useful to think of symbols as flypaper, something to which meanings get stuck. Consider, for example, the meanings which have become "stuck" to the cross, which is merely two perpendicular sticks. The fact that the cross does not have the same meanings for all men helps to call our attention to the fact that the locus of the "sticking" is not at the point of the object, but within the mind of the individual person. Thus, to utilize verbal or nonverbal symbols effectively, you must understand your audience.

How often do you assume that a symbol must be clear to others because its meaning is perfectly clear to you? It might be interesting for some of your assumptions to be put to the test, as they often are for other communicators. One author, for example, who has suggested the need for an international symbol for "fragile," tells the story of a crate of glassware being unloaded from a ship in India. On top of the crate was a symbol often used to indicate that the contents of a box are fragile—a broken wineglass. The Indian dock worker saw the symbol and thought it very strange. He could not understand why anyone would want to buy a box of broken glass. He shrugged, picked up the crate, and threw it onto the back of the truck.[4]

[4] Dick Shea, "Toward a Universal Non-language," *New York Times Magazine*, Nov. 22, 1964, p. 66.

A writer of dictionaries, like a compiler of the "meanings" of visual symbols, is primarily a historian; his job is to tell us the various
ways a word has been used in the past. He does not attempt to tell
us what each word "really" means (as many users of dictionaries
assume) or what it "ought" to mean. Thus, a dictionary is a useful
guide; it is not an infallible rulebook. New situations create new
meanings. As S. I. Hayakawa has noted, looking under a "hood"
500 years ago we should ordinarily have found a monk; today, we
find an automobile engine.[5]

There are many meanings of meaning, or types of meaning, all of
them relevant to an understanding of the processes of communication. The first and most generally recognized type of meaning is
denotation. It is for this type of meaning that dictionaries are most
useful (though not infallible). Denotation is like pointing to the
referent, or thing named. It is like a label. If it is not obvious to
you that denotation is not synonymous with meaning, consider the
terms "George Washington" and "the first President of the United
States." These have the same referent, but different meaning. If
they had the same meaning, "George Washington was the first President of the United States" would mean the same as "George

[5]S. I. Hayakawa, *Language in Action*, Harcourt, Brace & Co., New York,
1941, p. 58.

Washington was George Washington."[6] This example shows not only that meaning is not identical with the denoted object but also that we can denote the same object with more than one sign of a different meaning. For example, the man lounging on your sofa can be denoted by the words "Joe," "him," "my friend," "that guy," etc. Conversely, since meaning is not identical with the denoted reality, different objects can be denoted by the same sign, e.g., the "foot" of a mountain or the "foot" of a table.[7]

The second and somewhat less generally recognized type of meaning is *connotation*. This is the type of meaning Hayakawa was talking about when he noted that some words snarl and other words purr. It is largely connotation which causes us to respond differently to the words "sweat" and "perspiration," even though they have the same denotation. In short, connotation refers to the attitudes, feelings, emotions, and values which we associate with a symbol. Connotative meanings develop, in large part, from the prior experiences an individual has had with a term, whether those experiences were pleasant or unpleasant, or whether the context in which the term was usually encountered was positive or negative. These factors which affect the connotative meaning of a term quite often vary systematically among individuals so that there is much more heterogeneity in the connotative meanings that people have for many terms than in the denotative meanings that they have for the same terms. Some scholars divide connotative meaning into *expressive* and *evocative* meaning. By expressive they mean those utterances which are the emotional responses of a speaker or a writer to some stimulus. By evocative they mean those utterances which are designed to evoke an emotional response from the hearer or reader. In trying to understand communication and to improve your ability to communicate, this may be a useful distinction.

[6]Example suggested by G. A. Miller, "Some Preliminaries to Psycholinguistics," in R. C. Oldfield and J. C. Marshall (eds.), *Language*, Penguin Books, Baltimore, 1968, p. 204.

[7]This distinction between meaning and the part of reality denoted has been discussed extensively by Laszlo Antal. See especially his *Questions of Meaning*, P. Mouton & Co., The Hague, 1963, pp. 30–31, in which the last two examples were suggested.

A third important kind of meaning is *structural* meaning. This is the meaning which is dependent upon the ways in which words are used in relation to each other. The pattern in which the words are used or encountered communicates a particular meaning. To demonstrate the influence of structure, cast some sounds which have no denotative or connotative meaning in the usual sense into a sentencelike structure. You will discover that the statement evokes certain meanings in those who hear it. For example, "The pflugit has pligims."

A fourth important type of meaning is the *contextual* meaning. We seldom use words in isolation. In communication, their meaning is affected not only by the structure of which they are a part but also by the words that surround them—in phrases, sentences, paragraphs, and even at times in longer units of discourse. This fact is recognized, consciously or subconsciously, when a public figure complains of being quoted "out of context." There is the realization that taking a word or phrase or sentence out of the total communication context in which it was uttered changes the meaning which it evokes in the mind of the listener. There are two quite different types of factors which affect contextual meaning, one linguistic and the other nonlinguistic. Among the linguistic factors which affect the meaning of a term, as we noted before, are the other words with which it is surrounded. Among the nonlinguistic factors are the situation in which the term is used and the facial expressions and gestures which one uses when he says the word. Some terms are ambiguous until we are given a context. The word "nut" is an example. It would have a different meaning in the context of a speech about plumbing and a speech about strange people, just as it would have a different meaning if the speaker held up a hard, dry seed or if he pointed to you as he said the word. Context is important for other kinds of words because their noncontextual meaning is relative. For example, the word "hot" when applied to the weather denotes quite a different temperature than when applied to soup or molten steel. The context adds precision to the term.

As a communicator, you must try to learn the various ways in which individuals acquire different meanings for symbols. Perhaps even more important, you must try to learn which meanings they have and have not acquired. Many examples can be cited (in addition to that of the shipper of glassware) of assumptions which communicators make about the meanings people have for stimuli, assumptions which, upon investigation, turn out not to be valid. Beliefs about film and television transitions are a prime illustration. Film and television directors and textbook writers tell us of the distinct meaning of each type of transitional device, that "a slow fade has the psychological effect of a descending curtain in the theater, saying 'This is the end,' " that the combination of a fadeout and fade-in may be used "to denote a lapse of time when two successive scenes take place in the same set," etc. Yet, there is research showing not only that these transitional devices do *not* have a common meaning for members of the audience; they do not even have a common meaning for filmmakers. Many of us have similar beliefs about the meaning which is evoked in audiences by various musical devices, certain vocal qualities, certain movements of the body, or certain graphic devices. To what extent are these beliefs justified? Under what conditions are they so? For what types of audiences? Under what conditions are they not so? The truth of the matter is, we do not know. These are basic communication questions which you must attempt to answer through observation and study.

Changes in meaning

Whatever type of meaning we consider, it is extremely important to recognize that meanings are dynamic and that they are changing more rapidly today than ever before. The senior editor of the *Random House Dictionary of the English Language* estimates that of the roughly 450,000 "usable" English words that we have today, William Shakespeare would have comprehended only about 250,000. If he were alive today, he would be a semiliterate. This lexicographer also estimates that a third of this turnover in language has occurred in the last fifty years alone.[8] In short, meaning, like communication itself, is a process. No single theory of linguistic change is adequate to explain the changes that we see going on. We know only that change moves in many directions and for many reasons. Though most meanings change slowly—or communication would be rendered virtually impossible —they do change. If all the parties to an act of communication are aware of this fact and are sensitive to the sorts of changes which are occurring, there can be a greater sharing of meaning and, hence, more effective communication.

One of the clear indications of the way in which the meaning of symbols is constantly changing is the changing verbal taboos and the related fact that verbal taboos vary among groups in our population. Words related to physiological and sexual matters in our culture appear to encounter the most taboos. These are changing but, among most groups, words referring to the act of sexual intercourse, for example, are still taboo. However, words referring to most parts of the body are more easily accepted today than they were not too many years ago when people would say "limb" rather than "leg." It is important for you to be aware of the taboos of the individuals or groups with whom you communicate, and of your own taboos. As a receiver, do not let your taboos interfere with your reliable reception of messages. As a speaker or writer, do not violate the taboos of your audience unless you are aware of what you are doing and want the effect that such violation tends to bring. Be aware that, for many individuals with whom you communicate, taboo terms can drown out the rest of your message.

"Good" English

Our reference groups, the groups or individuals to whom we look for norms or with whom we compare ourselves, have a great

---

[8] Alvin Toffler, *Future Shock*, Bantam Books, New York, 1971, p. 169.

influence on our linguistic habits. You should be aware of these influences on yourself and on those with whom you communicate. You should be aware of the fact that your concept of "proper" English and the concept that others have of "proper" English is probably the result of reference-group influence. You should be aware of the fact that there is no absolute criterion of "correctness," just as there is no absolute criterion of the "beauty" or "aesthetic merit" of language. Our attitudes on these matters are conditioned by our culture and vary widely among groups. Robert Hall lists eight types of norms, each of which would lead to a different concept of "correctness."

1 The literary norm in which the usage of the "best" authors serves as a model.

2 The historical norm in which the criterion is the usage of an earlier time.

3 Popular speech, set up more or less in opposition to literary usage or to the language of the upper classes. One manifestation is the deliberate use of forms such as "ain't" or "he don't" to show one's independence.

4 The norm of efficiency in which that language which serves its function with the least ambiguity and expenditure of effort is the model.

5 The norm that may be set by an authority, from a "schoolmarm" to a dictionary.

6 The presumed "logic" inherent in the grammatical structure of some particular language sometimes sets the norm. However, no language perfectly follows any logic. In Sapir's terms, "all grammars leak."

7 Geographical norms or regional standards. You will find different norms of correctness in different parts of the United States, and even in different parts of some cities.

8 Although the myth of an aesthetic absolute is dying,

the linguistic norm of some groups is still influenced by
the idea of beauty or aesthetics.[9]

Adapting symbols to your audience

For optimum communication, the choices of symbols which you
make must be affected by those with whom you are communicating. We are not concerned here with symbols in the abstract; we
are concerned rather with the optimum use of symbols for communicative purposes. Our criterion of language use, for example, cannot be some abstract notion of "correctness"; it must be rather the
situational notion of "appropriateness." There are situations in
which it is appropriate to say "yeah," and there are situations in
which it is not. There are situations in which it is appropriate to
use "head" to refer to a dope addict, and there are situations in
which it is not. Fred Williams and Barbara Wood, who have studied
the linguistic habits of children from economically depressed areas,
describe what they label "home talk" and "school talk." They
note that these children clearly distinguish between what is appropriate talk for school and what is appropriate talk within the neighborhood gang.[10] At one time, educators, employing the traditional
absolute standard of "correctness," would have labeled the "home
talk" as inferior. As we have become more conscious of the pri-
macy of the communicative function of language, however, we
have realized the untenability of that position. "School talk" not
only would be less effective than "home talk" with one's fellow
gang members, it could also result in a punch in the nose or even
getting thrown out of the gang, just as "home talk" in the school
could result in a trip to the principal's office and possibly being
thrown out of school. Though these are extreme examples, they

[9]Robert A. Hall, *An Essay on Language*, Chilton Books, Philadelphia, 1968,
pp. 39-43.

[10]Frederick Williams and Barbara Sundene Wood, "Negro Children's Speech:
Some Social Class Differences in Word Predictability," *Language and Speech*,
13:141–150, 1970.

have their counterparts in all the communicative situations in which we become involved. Accepting this position clearly does not mean that you accept the position that "anything goes"; quite the contrary. It does not mean that you *need* to follow *no* rules; it simply means that you must find your rules in the audience, rather than in the traditional grammar book or dictionary alone. "Correctness," in other words, should be defined in terms of acceptability and what is understood by your particular audience rather than in terms of some arbitrary canons of good usage.

This does not mean that you need never be concerned with what we have traditionally considered to be good grammar, for there will almost certainly be times when you want to communicate with others for whom rulebook grammar is the norm, and they will expect other educated people whom they respect to adhere to it.

With nonverbal communication also you will be able to understand and predict the responses which your stimuli will evoke and will be able to create more effective nonverbal messages if you first try to understand the audience more thoroughly. The prior knowledge, attitudes, and experiences of the receiver will have a tendency to shape the meaning of nonverbal stimuli to which he is exposed (just as they tend to shape the meaning of the verbal stimuli). In planning any sort of nonverbal message, or the nonverbal part of a message, you must consider whether the intended receiver has learned your meanings for the stimuli or whether, in the course of the communication encounter, you can ensure his learning them. Has he learned to associate bar graphs or pie charts with such concepts as the cost of living or the disposition of the tax dollar? If not, can you provide cues in the context which will help him to understand such associations? You might take a cue here from the Russian film theorist Pudovkin and from more recent communication scholars in this country, who demonstrated the way in which the meaning which the audience "sees" in a facial expression can be altered by the visual stimuli which precede it. In one series of experiments, these scholars used a basic motion picture scene showing a man approaching and turning to look at something. This was followed by a close-up of his face which, when viewed alone, appeared relatively emotionless. However, when shots of a baby, an attractive girl, an accident, and a man on a burning tankcar were alternately edited into the film, adjacent to the close-up of the man's face, members of the audience reported seeing different emotions being expressed on the man's face, emotions which were consistent with the context.

The implication of these findings for you as a communicator should be clear; you must be conscious of the need for an audience member to organize his environment in a way that makes sense to him. In doing so, he may give meaning to elements of your message that you did not intend and, so, misperceive your intent. Sometimes, these elements are so minor that you might not even think of their existence or, if you do, might not realize that they will be noticed by an audience. In any message, there are many elements which are irrelevant to the sender's purpose, except insofar as they are needed to carry the basic elements. As an obvious example, if a communicator's goal is to help a viewer understand what a sphere is, the color of the sphere is probably irrelevant to the communicator, but it must be some color in order to carry the spherical quality. When a speaker is involved in a discussion of campus regulations, his posture, the clothing that he wears, the fact that he does or does not have a beard may be irrelevant. Yet they may affect the perceived meaning of the verbal message. One of your problems as a communicator is knowing how to minimize irrelevant or distracting cues, how best to help the receiver realize what is most important and relevant, and what is least important and relevant. There are many examples of communication failing because the audience attended to an irrelevant aspect of the message or gave unintended meaning to it.

Major nonverbal stimuli

The nonverbal stimuli with which you, as a communicator, must be most concerned are those which any speaker creates, whether consciously or not, and whether he tries to control them or not.

These are the stimuli created by his person as an instrument of communication.

1 Facial expression

2 Eye contact

3 Posture

4 Gesture

5 Other movements of the body

6 Clothing

7 Vocalization

8 Inflection

9 Rate

All of these elements "say" something to an audience. Some of the things they say are obvious and predictable; others are not. Clearly, if you speak very rapidly, in a monotone, with a minimum of bodily movement, and an expressionless face, most members of the audience will infer that you are not very interested in what you are talking about. If the audience is generally well dressed and you are unkempt, they will probably infer that you do not care what they think about you and that you do not think much of them; hence, your credibility will be reduced. On the other hand, if you are interviewing or speaking with a group of poor persons in a ghetto, "dressing up" or dressing very fashionably can also reduce your credibility. In many cases, perhaps in most, the meanings which these nonverbal cues evoke from an audience have nothing to do with the intent or state of the person being observed. For example, he may avoid eye contact with the audience because he is nervous, but the audience is very likely to infer that he is "shifty-eyed" and, hence, not to be trusted. Interestingly, many studies of audience perceptions of the emotions being communicated by facial and vocal expressions show a fair degree of reliability among the perceivers. However, very often, even though there is high reliability among receivers in their judgments, the emotion that they perceive is not the one felt by the person being observed. In other words, the meaning evoked fairly consistently from the audience is not necessarily the "true" meaning, the meaning intended by the source. From these findings and those from some of the cross-cultural studies, it is clear that we learn to respond to the cues of facial and vocal expression. Hence, it should be possible to improve our skill at both sending and accurately perceiving such cues. It also seems clear from the cross-cultural studies that there are differences among cultures in their nonverbal as well as in their verbal languages.

Certain ways of expressing a specific emotion as appropriate for a situation are learned in the process of living in a culture. The learning operates not only for the person expressing the emotion but also for the individual who must judge the emotional expression. It is by such learning of larger contexts that the happy Chinese girl is seen as "happy" by her fellow villagers and as "shy" or "bland" by Westerners.[11]

Thus, if you are to use your voice and face and body for optimum communication—for communicating what you want to communicate—it is essential that you become sensitive to the particular kinds of persons with whom you will be communicating and attempt to adjust your behaviors to them.

Effects of symbol variation

Research on communication gives abundant evidence that some language variables can affect the comprehension and retention of information. The variables which are found most consistently to be important are complexity or unfamiliarity of the words in the message and length of sentences. Some researchers have used these

[11] Renato Tagiuri, "Person Perception," in Gardner Lindzey and Elliot Aronsen (eds.), *The Handbook of Social Psychology*, 2d ed., Addison-Wesley Reading, Mass., 1969, vol. III, p. 403.

basic findings in further research in which they developed formulas for determining the "readability" or "listenability" of messages. Rudolph Flesch, for example, has developed various formulas for "reading ease." The most useful is probably the one which considers the average number of syllables per 100 words and the average sentence length in words.[12] This index and variations of it have been found to correlate to a high degree with comprehensibility of both spoken and written materials.

Some people find this reduction of style to formulas abhorrent. We are not advocating that you test everything you want to say with one of these formulas before you say it. We are not even advocating that you necessarily ever formally test a message with one of them. We are advocating that you be aware of the effect of language complexity and sentence length on comprehension. Though the use of unfamiliar or complex words and long and complex sentences may impress some listeners, they reduce the amount which these listeners will understand and retain from your message.

In attempting to determine the simplicity or complexity of visual materials or other nonverbal stimuli, we have no research evidence which is as useful as that which we have for verbal messages. We have little reliable data on the factors which make one visual aid, for example, simpler or more complex than another, or which make one gesture more communicative than another, or which contribute to the association value of a nonverbal symbol. Hence, we are not able to predict the effects on comprehension and retention of different nonverbal messages as precisely as we can predict them for verbal messages.

When we turn from comprehension and retention to persuasion, there are few useful generalizations that we can make about the effects of either verbal or nonverbal complexity. It is not even certain, for example, that the clarity of a message affects its persuasiveness. It does seem certain, though, that the language which you use will affect your audience's perceptions both of you and of your message. Using language which is very much at variance with

[12] Rudolf Flesch, "A New Readability Yardstick," *Journal of Applied Psychology*, 32:221–233, 1948.

the norms and expectations of your audience will have a very different effect than using language which is consistent with those norms and expectations. It may be an effect that you want; you may want to shock the audience or cause them to think that you are quite different than they are. In general, though, if you vary much from the norms and expectations of your audience you will hinder, rather than aid, effective communication.

PROJECTS AND PROBLEMS

1 Present a speech in class in which you explore further one of the ideas on language presented in this chapter. Use ample illustrations in your talk. The references cited at the end of this chapter should help you in the preparation of this presentation. Possible subjects for your presentation:

    a One's thinking is as wide as his vocabulary.
    b The word is not the thing.
    c Two-valued orientation. (See especially S. I. Hayakawa, *Language in Thought and Action,* for ideas on this topic.)
    d Slang of college students.
    e Changes in language in recent years.
    f Criteria for "good English" and the justification for those criteria.

2 Some communications scholars have asserted that meanings are in people, not in words. Do you agree or disagree? Why?

3 Observe and describe a sample of the language used by some of the students in your college in informal conversation. How do you suppose this language differs from the language of the same students when they are giving an oral report in a college class?

4 Read one of the following sections from these works which are listed in the bibliography for this section and report to the class as indicated following each reference below:

Clifton Fadiman, "On the Utility of U-Talk," in Kottler and Light, *The World of Words,* pp. 179–187. What is Fadiman's point? Do you agree or disagree? Why?

Wendell Johnson, "The World of Words," in *People in Quandaries,* pp. 112–142. Discuss Johnson's ideas on verbal levels of abstracting.

———, "Practical Devices and Techniques," in *People in Quandaries,* pp. 203–239. Discuss the practicability of Johnson's ideas for today's communicator.

George Orwell, "The Principles of Newspeak," in Kottler and Light, pp. 347–356. What is Newspeak? Is it a good thing? Why?

F. A. Philbrick, "Bias Words," in Anderson and Stageberg, *Introductory Readings in Language,* pp. 176–184. Discuss biased words, using examples other than those in the paper by Philbrick.

I. A. Richards, "The Command of Metaphor," in Anderson and Stageberg, pp. 228–240. Discuss the use of metaphor in informative or persuasive discourse.

Harrison E. Salisbury, "The Gang," in Kottler and Light, pp. 168–179. Same as for Sandburg paper.

Carl Sandburg, "Kid Talk—Folk Talk," in Kottler and Light, pp. 23–29. What inferences do you draw from this paper about "good" English? Are Sandburg's descriptions dated?

Thomas Wolfe, "The Language That I Seek," in Kottler and Light, pp. 47–53. For someone concerned with communicating about important issues—to inform or persuade—rather than to write novels to entertain, what useful ideas can be gleaned from Wolfe?

5 Observe two people in conversation. Describe as accurately and completely as you can the nonverbal communication occurring during their interaction. Among other things, indicate what you can infer about their attitudes toward each other from these nonverbal cues.

6 Have two members of the class converse for a few minutes in the front of the room. Each of the other members of the class should write in as great detail as possible his description of the nonverbal communication that took place. Then, in class discussion, compare results. Note especially variations in perceptiveness and in interpretation of what was observed.

7 Carry on a "conversation" for three or four minutes with another member of the class using only nonverbal communication. Afterward, evaluate your success or lack of success and the reasons for it. What kinds of things did you find most difficult to communicate by nonverbal means? What kinds of things did you find to be relatively easy to communicate without words?

REFERENCES

Anderson, Wallace L., and Norman C. Stageberg (eds.), *Introductory Readings on Language*, rev. ed. New York: Holt, Rinehart and Winston, 1966.

Benjamin, Robert L., *Semantics and Language Analysis*. Indianapolis: Bobbs-Merrill, 1970.

Birdwhistell, Ray L., *Kinesics and Context: Essays on Body Motion Communication*. Philadelphia: University of Pennsylvania Press, 1970.

Brown, Roger, *Words and Things*. Glencoe, Ill.: Free Press, 1958.

Condon, John C., Jr., *Semantics and Communication*. New York: Macmillan, 1966.

Davitz, Joel E., *The Communication of Emotional Meaning*. New York: McGraw-Hill, 1964.

———, *The Language of Emotion*. New York: Academic Press, 1968.

Dean, Leonard F., and Kenneth G. Wilson (eds.), *Essays on Language and Usage*, 2d ed. New York: Oxford University Press, 1963.

DeCecco, John P. (ed.), *The Psychology of Language, Thought, and Instruction: Readings*. New York: Holt, Rinehart and Winston, 1967.

Duncan, Hugh D., *Symbols in Society*. New York: Oxford University Press, 1968.

Hall, Edward T., *The Silent Language*. Garden City, N.Y.: Doubleday, 1959.

———, *The Hidden Dimension*. Garden City, N.Y.: Doubleday, 1969.

Harrison, Randall, "Nonverbal Communication: Explorations into Time, Space, Action, and Object," in *Dimensions in Communication: Readings*, ed. James H. Campbell and Hal W. Hepler. Belmont, Calif.: Wadsworth, 1970, pp. 256-271.

Jacobovits, Leon A., and Murray S. Miron (eds.), *Readings in the Psychology of Language*. Englewood Cliffs, N.J.: Prentice-Hall, 1967.

Johnson, Wendell, *People in Quandaries.* New York: Harper & Brothers, 1946.

Kottler, Barnet, and Martin Light (eds.), *The World of Words: A Language Reader.* Boston: Houghton-Mifflin, 1969.

Ore, Oystein, *Graphs and Their Uses.* New York: Random House, 1963.

Partridge, Eric, *The Gentle Art of Lexicography.* New York: Macmillan, 1963.

Pei, Mario, *The Many Hues of English.* New York: Knopf, 1967.

Ruesch, Jurgen, and Weldon Kees, *Non-verbal Communication.* Berkeley, Calif.: University of California Press, 1956.

Salomon, Louis B., *Semantics and Common Sense.* New York: Holt, Rinehart and Winston, 1966.

Sledd, James, and Wilma R. Ebbitt (eds.), *Dictionaries and That Dictionary.* Fairlawn, N.J.: Scott, Foresman, 1962. A collection of papers on dictionaries as history versus dictionaries as law and the controversy which followed the publication of Merriam-Webster's *Third New International Dictionary.*

your
SENSORY
cHANNELs of
cOMMUNICATION

7

The channels of communication can be looked at in two quite different, though equally important and related, ways. They can be conceived of as the various human senses (sight, hearing, touch, taste, and smell) or as the various media of communication (face-to-face, print, film, radio, and television). In this chapter, we will examine communication channels in terms of the senses. In the next chapter, we will examine them in terms of the various media of communication.

Within each of these category systems, sensory and media, a sophisticated communicator must differentiate among subcategories within a particular channel. For example, as indicated earlier, you must understand the differences in the possible uses and effects of various kinds of messages designed to be perceived through the sense of sight. There are probably critical differences in the ways that gestures, facial expressions, dress, photographs, colored light, and charts affect audiences.

It is fruitful to think of the five senses as five major pathways through which your message can get "inside" the members of your intended audience. For any stimulus to affect an audience member, he must first sense it through one or more of these pathways—through hearing it, seeing it, touching it, tasting it, or smelling it.

127

It is probable that, in most instances, your message will be most effective if you utilize more than one of these channels—not only because one channel may reinforce the other or because different aspects of the message are better suited to different channels, but also because it enables you to *control* these channels and keep out distractions, or what communications theorists call "noise." For example, when you are speaking, the members of your audience will be seeing something. Whether that something distracts from or reinforces your aural message is probably dependent upon whether you create something relevant for them to see. This may be a set of gestures and facial expressions which can help to evoke some of the responses that you seek, or it may be a set of pictures or graphs or even a demonstration. In other words, the more you control the total communication environment, assuming that you do it intelligently, the greater the chances that you will be able to achieve the purposes for which you are speaking.

Channels, purposes, and content

Since we usually depend upon one primary channel for any particular message, many communicators and communication scholars have asked which channel is superior to the others for communication. Analysis of the studies that have been done shows clearly that this is not a meaningful question. More meaningful, because it may be answerable, is the question of which particular channel is superior to the others *for a particular audience, under particular conditions,* and *for a particular purpose.* Thus, before deciding on a channel, you ought to have clearly in mind the audience which you hope to reach, the sorts of communication skills and habits the audience members have, what each receiver is to do with the data he receives, and the situation in which the communication is to occur. Of these considerations, the most important is what the receiver is to do with the information that he receives. Clearly, for some goals, a number of channels or media are interchangeable; one will be as effective as another. (Thus, it should have been no

surprise that when studies were done comparing the retention by
college students of lecture material they (1) heard from a "live"
teacher, (2) heard from a teacher on television, and (3) read from
a text, differences were negligible.) On the other hand, for other
sorts of things which you might hope your message will do for
your audience, there are sound theoretical reasons and some evidence indicating that different channels will not be equally effective. For example, if your goal is to have receivers recognize some
part of your message when they encounter it again, the optimum
channel for the message is that in which they will encounter it in
the future. For example, if you want receivers to be able to recognize something when they *hear* it in the future, you probably
ought to use an audio mode for the original message. On the
other hand, if you want them to recognize it when they *see* it,
you probably ought to use the visual mode for the original message. In other words, the more closely a communication situation
approximates the situation in which learned responses are to be
made, the more successful the communication will be.[1]

Usually, of course, as a communicator in your business or family
or organization, you will not be concerned solely with a single message but, rather, with a set of messages—a campaign or a continual
series of communication encounters to keep the organization running and to help the individuals and the groups to achieve their
and your goals. Whether at any given moment you are considering
such a series or a single message, you ought to think through the
probable relationships between your purposes and the available
channels.

Multichannel messages

In a large proportion of the communication in which we engage,
we use more than one sensory channel. This is obviously so in a
film or a television program, or when a speaker uses visual aids.

---

[1]See S. S. Stevens (ed.), *Handbook of Experimental Psychology,* John Wiley
& Sons, New York, 1951, pp. 663–666, 676.

However, even in an ordinary speech, discussion, or conversation, we employ both speech and visual cues, for we gesture and display some sort of facial expression while we talk and listen. In planning such multiple-channel communication, or in trying to understand the situations in which it goes on, it is important to distinguish at least four types of multiple-channel messages:

1 Those in which the content in one channel is basically unrelated to that in the other channels.

2 Those in which the content in the two channels are related, though not the same.

3 Those in which essentially the same content is presented via both channels.

4 Those in which contradictory content is presented via the two channels.

In general, when essentially the same information is presented simultaneously to two senses (vision and audition have been tested most), the evidence is clear that receivers tend to retain more than when it is presented to only one sense. This seems to be especially true where there is interference with the message.[2]

It also appears that when *related* content is presented to two senses, receivers tend to retain more than they do from information presented to a single sense. However, the evidence is less clear here than it is for more purely redundant information to two senses.

If one carefully examines the studies on multiple-channel learning, the most reasonable explanation for the usual superiority of utilizing multiple senses is that using more than one provides additional cues or stimuli to which the receiver can learn responses.

However, these additional cues are useful only if they are present in the situation where the learning is to be used. In cases where they are not—where the cues can be received through only one sense—the original message is just as effective, perhaps even more effective, if it is presented solely in that one sensory channel.

[2] E.g., see Hower J. Hsia, "Output, Error, Equivocation, and Recalled Information in Auditory, Visual, and Audiovisual Information Processing with Constraint and Noise," *The Journal of Communication*, 18:325–345, 1968.

The cues to the second or third sensory channel are irrelevant. As one would expect, when unrelated information is presented simultaneously to two senses, comprehension and retention are reduced. The loss increases with the increasing difficulty of the messages, and when the messages to the two senses are of unequal difficulty the less difficult messages suffer most.[3] In general, it appears that brief auditory stimuli are more "attention demanding" than brief visual stimuli. However, you must always consider the particular demands of the situation in which communication is to take place. A housewife listening to the radio while cleaning house probably attends to what she hears less than someone alone in his car listening. Similarly, if someone is alone in his car, he probably attends more to what is on the radio than someone driving with others in the car.

Though we utilize the senses of touch, taste, and smell in much of our communication, our primary sensory channels for purposive communication are the aural and visual ones. In other sections of this book, we discuss in detail various ways in which you can communicate verbally through these two senses. In Chapter 6 we talked about communicating with your body—through posture, gesture, facial expression, and eye contact. In the remainder of this chapter, we will consider some of the nonverbal aspects of aural communication—specifically, the effective use of your voice and articulatory mechanism.

Importance of vocal control

The chief purpose of voice study is to help you achieve professional competence in its use. By competence we do not mean necessarily "golden tones" or the sepulchral voice of the opera announcer on the radio. We mean, rather, adequate *flexibility* and control for your purposes. For some purposes—those of the teacher, preacher,

[3]A more detailed analysis of multiple-channel communication can be found in a paper by Frank R. Hartman, "Single and Multiple Channel Communication: A Review of Research and a Proposed Model," *Audio-Visual Communication Review*, 9:235–262, 1961.

broadcaster, actor, personnel worker, airport traffic-control operator, salesman, etc.—a great deal of flexibility and control is essential Of course, there are people who get by sometimes with almost any kind of voice, but you should not be satisfied with "getting by." The time you do not get by may be the most important time in your life.

Inferring meaning from voice

Besides its function in communicating words, your voice also serves several supplementary communicative functions. Others infer many things from it: your emotional state at the moment, your attitude and purpose in speaking, and some characteristics of your personality. Are you lazy, careless, insensitive? Rightly or wrongly, people will infer an answer to this question from your voice. We even have research which shows that some people infer whether you are fat or thin, what your occupation is, and whether you have leadership ability from your voice.[4]

The quality, loudness, pitch, and time patterns of the voice serve as cues to your attitudes, moods, and personality, as well as your linguistic meaning.[5] Skillful use of the voice is also positively

[4]See, for example, the series of studies by P. J. Fay and W. C. Middleton, including: "Judgment of Occupation from the Voice as Transmitted over a Public Address System and over a Radio," *Journal of Applied Psychology*, 23:586-601, 1939; "Judgment of Kretschmerian Body Types from the Voice as Transmitted over a Public Address System," *Journal of Social Psychology*, 12:151-162, 1940; "Judgment of Emotional Balance from the Transmitted Voice," *Character and Personality*, 10:109-113, 1941-1942; "Judgment of Introversion from the Transcribed Voice," *Quarterly Journal of Speech*, 28:226-228, 1942; "Judgment of Leadership from the Transmitted Voice," *Journal of Social Psychology*, 17:99-102, 1943; "Judgment of Confidence from Voice," *Journal of General Psychology*, 30:93-95, 1944.

[5]See Delwin Dusenbury and Franklin H. Knower, "Studies in the Symbolism of Voice and Action," *Quarterly Journal of Speech*, 24:424-436, 1938, and 25:67-75, 1939; Franklin H. Knower, "Analysis of Some Experimental Variations of Simulated Expressions of the Emotions," *Journal of Social Psychology*, 14:369-372, 1941

correlated with ratings of general effectiveness in speech.[6] Obviously, voice control will not assure your being an effective communicator, but lack of control will almost certainly limit your effectiveness.

Causes of vocal ineffectiveness

Many speakers have weak, indistinct voices. Others artificially declaim or "orate." Many are unable to project and seem to ignore their audience. Some are breathy, speak too fast, or have a monotonous delivery. A few have organic difficulties, such as cleft palate, poor teeth, and vocal paralysis. No attempt is made in this book to analyze or discuss treatment for organic defects, but many of them are remediable. If you find that you need to correct a defect of this type, you should consult a speech pathologist for guidance.

Some speech deficiencies are caused by nervousness, irritability, and lack of confidence. Inadequate preparation also causes poor voice control, uncertainty, and lack of confidence. Quite apart, then, from organic handicaps, most speech students need to give serious attention to controlling voice production both in conversation and in more formal speaking.

Improving your voice
and voice control

At least four steps are involved in voice improvement: (1) a clear understanding of breathing, phonation, and resonance, and the related attributes of loudness, rate, pitch, and quality; (2) a clear understanding of your own vocal skills and limitations; (3) systematic practice in voice improvement; (4) systematic evaluation of your progress.

[6]Franklin H. Knower, "The Use of Behavioral and Tonal Symbols as Tests of Speaking Achievement," *Journal of Applied Psychology*, 29:229–235, 1945.

An important factor in voice improvement is the ability to hear your own voice. This sounds simple, but it is not. This learning can best begin by listening to the voices of others and learning to distinguish among slight variations in loudness, rate, pitch, and quality. Then you must learn to make these discriminations in your own voice.

Listening carefully to recordings of effective speakers is a good way of becoming acquainted with desirable vocal characteristics. Recording your own speech will be helpful in comparing your habitual voice with these standards. Learn the sensations involved in producing standard tones. A competent critic who can listen, advise, and point out differences will be a great help in guiding you to the development of new voice standards.

When you have clearly distinguished between familiar vocal habits and those you must work to develop, the next step is systematic and persistent practice. Practice at first on material planned to make the new forms of expression easy. Drill materials are commonly of this type. (See, for example, the projects at the end of this chapter.) As soon as possible, you should practice with material and in situations in which the new habits are expected to function. You cannot expect the speech laboratory voice drills alone to be sufficient to fix the new habits in daily speech.

Practice in oral reading and in rehearsing extemporaneous speeches is helpful in voice improvement. Just keep in mind that the purpose of developing control of your voice is not display, but rather the facilitation of the communication of ideas through the ability to state and shade these ideas accurately.

Cultivate proper breathing Adequate use of the power mechanism is the first requirement in developing a good voice.

Proper breathing in speech depends upon three factors. First, the lungs must retain enough air to make it unnecessary to pause within a phrase to breathe. Second, the muscles which regulate expiration must be sufficiently controlled to exert strong and steady pressure upon the breath stream. And third, this pressure must be exerted without causing undue tension in other muscles involved in voice production, particularly in the muscles of the larynx. The development of good breathing habits for speech is a process of modifying natural and accidentally acquired habits so as to achieve the necessary supply of controlled air pressure with the least exertion and tension.

Cultivate proper phonation The second process of voice production is phonation. When the vocal folds of your larynx (vocal bands) are brought closely together and set in vibration by the force of the breath stream, a vocal tone is initiated. The pitch and some other characteristics of your tone are the result of the nature and operation of the vocal folds and other muscles of the larynx. Whispered speech and unvoiced or voiceless sounds are produced without the vibration of the vocal folds. The fundamental pitch of the voice is determined by the rate of vibration of the vocal folds as a whole. The overtones are produced by the segmented vibration of the folds, and the rate at which the folds vibrate is dependent upon their length, thickness, and tension. The quality of your voice is influenced by the capacity of the folds to set up vibrations at the frequency which can best be reinforced by your vocal resonators (air chambers in the head and throat).

Cultivate a pleasing and responsive voice quality Voice quality is determined primarily by resonance or lack of resonance. The main vocal resonators are the pharynx, the mouth, and the nasal cavities. Hanley and Thurman have described the problems which result in the major undesirable vocal qualities:

Nasal quality is characterized by strong modification of the vocal cord tone by resonance from the nasal cavities during the production of sounds normally essentially nonnasal.

Breathy quality results when the vocal cords are not brought closely enough together during the production of tone, and air rushing through the glottis produces friction heard as a whisperlike noise in addition to the vocal cord tone.

Thin quality is essentially lacking in resonance. It is flat and colorless, and it gives the impression of "smallness."

Strident quality sounds hard and piercing; it is apparently caused by strain and tenseness in the resonators during voice production.

Harsh quality is unpleasant and rough; it is caused, apparently, by strain and great effort in the larynx.

Hoarse quality is characterized by a rasping, grating, sometimes husky sound as is often heard in persons with laryngitis. It may also be a result of misuse, such as too much shouting at a sports event.[7]

Improvement in voice quality requires analysis of personal problems and practice in the new pattern of resonance until it becomes habitual. Work to sharpen your ear for the changes in quality of voice. Free your neck, throat, and mouth muscles of interfering tensions.

Articulate properly Articulation, the fourth of the physiological processes of voice, will be discussed in detail later in this chapter.

Cultivate control of loudness The voice should be sufficiently loud to be heard easily. Listeners who must strain to hear are likely to stop listening. Forceful ideas uttered in an indifferent manner lose some of their vigor. A speaker who cannot suit the vigor of his voice to the vigor of his ideas seems insincere. *Variation* in vocal intensity is necessary to emphasize and subordinate ideas, to stress certain syllables for acceptable pronunciation, and to make speech interesting. Listeners tire easily of uniform loudness. So it is not surprising that the quality that distinguishes effective from ineffective speakers is not the ability to be loud, but rather the ability to control and adapt one's loudness to the situation and to one's intended meaning.

You need not shout to achieve force in speaking. But your voice

[7]Theodore D. Hanley and Wayne L. Thurman, *Developing Vocal Skills,* Holt, Rinehart and Winston, New York, 1962, p. 166.

must be firm, vigorous, and well controlled. You must learn consciously to control your loudness in order to adapt to the situation in which you are speaking. No one, for example, likes to converse with someone who shouts at him as though he is giving an oration in the school auditorium. Obviously, you will need more force to be heard by a large group of listeners than by a small group. Speaking outdoors or in the presence of competing noises and other distractions requires more force than speaking indoors and in places where there are no distractions.

A vigorous voice is dependent upon breath control and, often, upon simply opening one's mouth more. Loudness can also be increased by raising the pitch of the voice. Experiment with modification of vocal intensity by variation of pitch, oral activity, breath pressure. Find the best pattern of resonance for giving your tone body and volume. A cramped throat and mouth, with muscles tensed, may make the voice more piercing, but ordinarily not more pleasant or vigorous. Avoid letting your voice trail off at the end of a sentence. Practice intensity control in exercises and everyday speaking activities until it becomes a habit.

Control your speech rate Your speech should be fluent but neither too hesitant nor too gushy. Say your words slowly enough to be understood and fast enough to sustain the audience's interest. In speaking, this is ordinarily between 130 and 150 words per minute, and in oral reading between 150 and 175 words per minute. The discussion of light subjects and the presentation of simple narrative material and exciting ideas can be carried on at a faster rate than the presentation of complicated instructional material in unfamiliar subject-matter areas. When a number of listeners are included in the discussion (other things being equal), the rate should be slower than when there are only one or two persons. Situations involving distraction require a slower rate than situations which are free from distraction.

Rate variation is an effective way of suggesting the nature of the thought being expressed and the relative emphasis to be given to it. The timing of the punch line, for example, is very important.

Practice to determine your most effective rate in speaking and oral reading. Your speaking rate should vary with the relative importance of the ideas, and it should never be so fast that your phrasing or emphasis suffers. If you are dependent on such excess vocalizations as "er" and "ah," have a friend listen to your speech and signal you whenever you use one of these sounds. This will be distracting at first, but it will help to break your dependence on this habit.

Develop satisfactory pitch control The pitch of your voice is an important signal of your intentions. It communicates to the listener as much as rate and loudness do, and it should suggest the mood of what you want to say.

The best pitch level for your normal speech is determined by the structure of your larynx, or voice box, and by your resonators. It is probably the pitch which you have developed by habit. If you believe that your habitual pitch level is *not* your optimum one, do not try to change it without the advice and guidance of an expert. In general, your pitch should be high enough to permit lowering and low enough to permit raising for contrast. Inflectional slides, steps, and patterns are useful in communication. Remember, however, that regular pitch changes that disregard meaning and produce singsong effects are confusing and distracting.

In order to develop effective control over pitch, you should learn to hear pitch patterns. Become aware of pitch in ordinary communication and practice exercises such as those suggested at the end of this chapter.

The importance of articulation and pronunciation

Articulation and pronunciation both concern the formation of the sounds of spoken language. Articulation refers to the systematic modification of vocal tones to form the vowel and consonant sounds used in speech. A sound is misarticulated when it is formed in a way that is not acceptable to the auditors. Pronunciation, like articulation, refers to the acceptable utterance of language sounds— specifically, to the production of the sounds contained in individual words without substitutions, additions, omissions, inversions, or misplaced accents. Since certain differences in procedure are appropriate for the study and improvement of articulation and pronunciation, we will discuss one of them at a time.

The most important criterion of satisfactory articulation is that *sound must be so articulated that speech is intelligible.* Even though your pitch, rate, loudness, and quality may be well controlled, your speech may be impossible to understand if you run words and syllables together; if you mangle your medial or final consonants; if you fail to distinguish between similar but different sounds, as in "tin" and "ten," "fife" and "five," "wet" and "whet," "fussy" and "fuzzy."

A second criterion of satisfactory articulation is *social acceptability.* By this we do not mean acceptability by "high society"; we mean, rather, acceptability by whomever you are speaking with. There is no authority in our country to prescribe the exact manner in which sounds are to be made. A degree of exactness acceptable to some persons is considered crude and unpleasant or a sign of phoniness by others. Some standards which would not be questioned in lively, informal speech would be inappropriate for some formal occasions. In other words, your standard must be determined in large part by the *expectations of your audience in the particular situation* in which you are talking. You should achieve the skill and the control of your articulation so that you can meet the demands of any situation and any audience.

Methods of improving articulation

Study the organs of articulation Persons who acquire a clear understanding of the function of the organs of articulation find that it helps make sense out of the principles of articulation and accelerates the process of improvement. These organs are the jaw, lips, teeth, tongue, hard palate, soft palate, and breathing mechanisms. In a sense, the ear also serves as an organ of articulation. Unless we hear clearly the sounds we make, we tend to articulate poorly. Our purpose here is not to study the structure and function of the articulatory organs in detail.[8] An explanation of the organic basis of articulation, however, will help us understand the classification of the sounds of English speech.

Study the sounds of English speech The purpose of the study of articulation is not to obtain perfect uniformity among all persons; sounds exist in families called *phonemes*. You should simply learn to make each sound in such a way that it is clearly understood and acceptable as a member of the phoneme to which it belongs.

Most people associate sounds with the letters of the alphabet. It is more helpful to think of sounds as the units of articulated speech. The sounds of "hurt," for example, are h-r-t rather than "aich-you-are-tee." Scholars of language sounds have developed a set of phonetic symbols in which each sound family, or phoneme, has one symbol. If you plan to become a professional in the field of communication, you should learn these symbols. The diacritical marks used in the dictionary are an attempt to provide symbols for sounds by using marks over the regular letters of the alphabet. For the purposes of most students, diacritical marks will be sufficient.

Distinguish among vowels, diphthongs, and consonants These are the three main types of speech sounds. *Vowels* consist of relatively unmodified voice (that is, voice in which there is little interference with the outgoing air), whereas *consonants* consist of voice modified by the same type of friction or stoppage which, in part, produces the sound. One or more of the organs of articulation modify or interfere with the free exhalation of air to produce consonants. *Diphthongs* are combinations of vowel sounds produced as one sound. The principal diphthongs are the *u* of "use," the *o* of "hole," the *ou* of "ouch," the *a* of "days," the *i* of "lights," the *e*

[8] If you wish to study articulatory processes in detail, you will find some of the works cited at the end of this chapter helpful.

of "feet," and the *oi* of "oil." Although some of these are considered single sounds, careful study will reveal them to be combinations of sounds.

All consonants may be classified as either voiced or voiceless.
Voiced consonants are accompanied by a vibration of the vocal
cords (bands or folds). Many consonants are matched or paired.
The muscular adjustments that produce the voiced and voiceless
"twins" are alike except that the cords are vibrated to produce the
voiced sound. Examples are *g* and *k*, *d* and *t*, *b* and *p*, and *v* and *f*.
Nasal consonants are resonated cheifly through the nasal passages:
m, *n*, and *ng*. The stop plosives, as the term implies, are formed by
blocking the air stream and then releasing the sounds explosively.
Voiced stop plosives are *b*, *d*, and *g*. Voiceless stop plosives are *p*,
t, and *k*.

Identify the sounds with which you have difficulty Test yourself
systematically to determine these sounds. Without a systematic
test, you are not likely to be aware of your shortcomings. When
people tell you to slow down or to talk louder, they may merely
mean that you should articulate more clearly. Make a systematic
analysis of your articulatory habits in order to discover and correct
your personal variations.

Methods of improving pronunciation

**Use the pronunciation which will be understood by and acceptable
to your audience** Though we often speak of the three major dialects within the United States—Standard American, Eastern, and
Southern—there are many subdialects within each of these. The
extent to which these *subdialects* should be considered *substandard* is a major issue among linguists and other educators today.
Many linguists stress that there can be no one "correct" pronunciation, that language is dynamic, and that we must consider the
community or part of the community in which communication is
occurring. We believe these things to be true, but urge you not to

use these facts as an excuse for careless speech. You must learn to *control* your pronunciation, just as you learn to control all other aspects of your communicative behavior. This means that you must be able to meet the pronunciation standards of the well-educated persons of the region in which you expect to spend your life, as well as the most acceptable standards of the well-educated persons of your particular community or neighborhood. Good pronunciation is that pronunciation which will be clearly understood by those with whom you speak and which will not call attention to itself.

Foreign accents and dialects present a problem closely associated with regionalism in articulation and pronunciation. Some foreign languages do not employ all the sounds of English. Other languages contain sounds which differ considerably from analogous English sounds. It is these sounds which cause the most difficulty in learning a new language. Differences in the inflectional patterns and intonations of language also cause difficulty. Although it is no disgrace for your speech to reveal the country of your origin, dialectal characteristics are a source of distraction and confusion in communication. The use of dialect is especially to be deplored when the speaker trades upon it as a sort of affectation in speech to which he attaches false cultural values.

Reproduce speech sounds accurately   There are five common classes of pronunciation errors: substitution, addition, omission, inversion, and misplaced accent. Although it is not always possible to place a mispronounced word in one of these classes exclusively, the classification serves a practical purpose in understanding and improving pronunciation. Some examples of each class are listed below:

Substitutions

agin for *again*
fer for *for*
bak for *bag*
wuz for *was*

Additions

ca (l) m for *calm*
fore (h) ead for *forehead*
rem (i) nent for *remnant*
pang (g) for *pang*
across (t) for *across*

Omissions

col for *cold*
reconize for *recognize*
dimond for *diamond*
eights for *eights*
battry for *battery*

Inversions

calvery for *cavalry*
interduce for *introduce*
pervide for *provide*

Misplaced accent

adúlt for *adult*
résearch for *reseárch*
superflúous for *supérfluous*
impotent for *impotent*
futilé for *futile*

What are the causes of these pronunciation errors? Words are mispronounced for a number of reasons. One is spelling. Words are not always pronounced as their spelling suggests; moreover, spelling provides no clue to accent. Some errors are caused by failure to note changes of pronunciation for words serving different linguistic functions. Words are sometimes mispronounced because they are confused with similar words. Other words are mispronounced because of misarticulation of sounds contained in them.

Probably most mispronunciations occur because the words were first heard mispronounced or because the first pronunciation was a bad guess which initiated the habit of mispronouncing. It is better to make a good guess at a new word than to mumble it, for mumbling always produces mispronunciation. But there is no substitute for the habit of checking pronunciations in a good up-to-date American dictionary. Moreover, pronunciations, like other language forms, change with time. If most well-educated people "mispronounce" a word in a certain way, this pronunciation is almost certain to be accepted in a short time. The dictionaries attempt to follow rather than dictate acceptable pronunciation.

Let the requirements of the speaking situation govern your pronunciation When you are speaking in a large auditorium or when you are competing with noises, you must pronounce your words carefully to ensure the listener's comprehension.

Obtain a good dictionary and check your pronunciation constantly As we noted in Chapter 6, though, the dictionary is not infallible, for it is based on past usage, and language and our pronunciations of language are constantly changing. Also, and perhaps even more important, dictionaries generally fail to take into account the many dialects within any language and, hence, the different pronunciations which are acceptable—and, at times, even expected—within each group. For all these reasons, use a dictionary as a guide, not as a bible.

The skills in voice production, articulation, and pronunciation that you acquire by drill or in isolated projects must be exercised in the pattern of speech activity as a whole if they are to be of much value to you. Only perpetual attention to their development in the normal social uses of speech over a long period of time will produce lasting results. If you develop vocal skills and skillful pronunciation and articulation in isolated situations, however, you should with effort be able to transfer these skills to your everyday speech.

Improving voice, articulation, and pronunciation through reading aloud

One of the best means of learning to control your voice production, articulation, and pronunciation is through oral reading. Not only can it give you the opportunity to practice with a great variety of materials while concentrating upon these skills, it is also valuable for itself alone. You will find many occasions during your lifetime when you need to read aloud. We all read a bit of something we wish to share with a member of our family or friends. Much formal speaking and discussion calls for something to be read, as in teaching or religious services. Resolutions, motions, and the minutes of meetings are often read aloud.

Oral reading can also be an end in itself, an attempt to enjoy yourself through reading aloud and listening to literature. The purpose of most art is to give pleasure, and for most literature, whether poetry, short stories, or drama, the pleasure can be enhanced through oral interpretation. For many kinds of oral reading, one of your important jobs will be to make the material you are interpreting so vivid for an audience that their experience approximates the experience depicted in the work. This will necessitate not only your thorough understanding of the work that you are interpreting but also the control of your voice and articulatory mechanism necessary for communicating that understanding. A wide repertoire of vocal expressions makes effective oral interpretation possible, just as familiarity with a wide range of superior works of literature and rhetoric increases your repertoire of stylistic devices and treatments of various kinds of ideas.

To gain these benefits from your practice of reading aloud, some knowledge of the principles of such reading should be helpful.

Study the meaning of the material you are to read You must have a sound understanding of its intellectual and emotional content and its imaginative ways of dealing with this content.

In studying a work which you plan to read to an audience, consider *its purpose* (what it is trying to achieve), *its method* (how it is trying to achieve it), and *your purpose* in using it. There are many cues in a work which can help you to discover its purpose. The title of a work is clearly your first cue, though obviously not an infallible one when considered alone. In many works, you can find the theme stated quite clearly in a phrase or sentence or paragraph near the beginning. Think about the symbolism used by the author. Has he used objects or characters or actions to represent something else—some larger group of objects, characters, or actions or perhaps some abstract idea? Is the entire work a symbol, as each Aesop fable is? In these fables, as in a work such as Hemingway's *Old Man and the Sea*, the symbolism is quite obvious if you think about the matter at all. In many literary works, it is much less obvious, and you must be sensitive and imaginative in order to appreciate fully its significance. A fourth means of getting at the purpose of a work is to consider *its attitude*. Normally we think only of people having attitudes, but a piece of literature or rhetoric does also, and we discover those attitudes in the same way we discover them in people. We see how the work describes the object, the kinds of language used, and the other objects with which this one is compared and contrasted.

In addition to discovering the purpose or purposes of a work you are to read, obviously you must also understand the words and the ways in which they are put together. Study each sentence to find the methods of phrasing which make the meaning clear. Phrasing within the sentence is often, but not always, revealed by punctuation. Consider the differences in meaning of the two ways of punctuating or phrasing the following sentence:

The Captain said the mate was drunk today.
"The captain," said the mate, "was drunk today."

Develop empathy for the material and your audience   "Empathy" is probably one of the most abused terms in the English language; it has been used to indicate a wide variety of phenomena. Yet, almost all of the phenomena for which the term has been used are relevant to oral interpretation. You must have some understanding and sympathy, in the broad sense of that term, for the author of the work being interpreted and for the characters within the work, if any. You must understand both the author's point of view and the point of view of the audience for whom you must interpret that author. Though you will probably not go so far as some actors do in "feeling the emotions" of the author or the characters in his work, you must be able to put yourself into their shoes to some extent in order to adequately communicate their attitudes and emotions. Closely related to this is the need which you will often have to mimic, either overtly or covertly, the actions of characters within the works you interpret. Covert mimicry will help you to interpret the work. At times, a bit of overt mimicry will help you to communicate that interpretation more effectively to your audience. In every case, though, you must remain in *control* of your instrument of communication, your body and your voice. You should never become "lost" in the work you are interpreting or you risk a complete breakdown of communication between you and the audience. In other words, do not become like those actors of the "mumble school" of acting who claim to truly feel the role, but whom the audience cannot understand. Oral interpretation, like any other form of speech, should be a communicative act, not solely a personal experience for you as the interpreter.

Read ideas, not words   If you learned to read by words, rather than by ideas, with careful and distinct—pronunciation—of—each—word, you may now have difficulty communicating ideas from the printed page. Familiarity with meaning, as described above, concentration upon the meaning while reading, and practice should help you to overcome this problem.

Be aware of the differences between silent and oral reading   In silent reading, you often skim a paragraph or page to get the meaning of the section as a whole. This is important for many purposes, but the habit of doing this may impair your reading aloud for quite different purposes. It will impair good oral reading if it causes you to race, run words together, and mumble. Since the listener does not have the benefit of punctuation marks, you must use techniques of phrasing and inflection to take their place. Rapid and monotonous oral reading generally fails completely to convey intended meanings.

Develop maximum voice control In no other form of oral communication is control of the voice more important than it is in oral reading. Everything that we said about the voice earlier in this chapter should be considered as you work to improve your ability to interpret literature or other material to audiences. Voice quality, pitch, loudness, rate can all help you to help your audience get the full impact of what you are reading.

Phrase or group words to make the meaning clear One of your most effective means of communicating certain meanings when interpreting another's work is silence: doing nothing, pausing. These pauses must be controlled by the variety of meanings which the word has for you and by your sensed need to give the audience additional cues to these meanings, or to give them an opportunity to assimilate an idea, or to give them a sense of anticipation or suspense.

Pauses help you both to communicate meaning and to maintain adequate control of your breathing for vocalization. Though the pause is the major means of phrasing, varying the rate, pitch, quality, and loudness of different phrases also helps to differentiate them and to make their meaning clear. Overphrasing, or the mechanical breaking up of sentences into minor units, is undesirable. It confuses rather than clarifies meaning. For most speakers, however, underphrasing is more of a problem than overphrasing.

Acquire skill in emphasizing and subordinating ideas In spite of the fact that the ideas in any reading passage vary in importance, one of the common weaknesses or faults of oral reading is monotony. Monotony does not result only from a lack of variation; rhythmical variations in voice which produce a singsong pattern may be just as monotonous as a lack of variation. In addition, arbitrary variations for the sake of arousing attention can be confusing. The variations that you use must be developed from the meaning of the material. Use vocal emphasis to make transitions clear. Indicate a climax by using minor vocal variations in the introduction and more radical variations near the point of greatest emphasis.

Read loudly enough to be heard easily   The level of intensity of a bedtime story is not adequate for group reading. There is no communication if the audience cannot hear. Note that some sounds in the English language are difficult to hear unless you use sufficient force to project them clearly and sharply. Such unvoiced sounds as *f, t, p,* and initial *th* are especially difficult.

Adjust to the materials and situation   Do not become so engrossed in your materials that you act them out. Respond with facial expression and bodily action to ideas, but avoid distracting mannerisms. It is possible to read emotionally toned materials in a manner which reveals the mood without immersing yourself in the emotion. However, you must *respond* to the mood if you are to be convincing.

Adjust your oral reading to the listeners   The ultimate objective of oral reading is to affect your listeners, not to exhibit your talent. Keep the social purpose of your reading in mind, and develop the techniques which will achieve it. Think of your work as projection to *listeners* rather than merely reading *from a manuscript.*

PROJECTS AND PROBLEMS

1   Present a brief example in class of each of the four types of multiple-channel messages described in this chapter. They may be either examples that you find or examples that you make up.

2   Examine any textbook on educational psychology or the latest edition of *The Encyclopedia of Educational Research.* What do you find there that is relevant to understanding how to use the different sensory channels of communication?

3 Turn to one of the speeches in the Appendix or in a recent issue of *Vital Speeches* and select a two- or three-minute portion to read aloud to the class. Your instructor and other members of the class will evaluate your reading, concentrating chiefly on your interpretation of the speech, your vocal control and use, and your articulation and pronunciation. They will offer suggestions to you for improvement.

4 Pronounce the word "well" to indicate the following meanings:

I never would have thought it possible!
What do you want? I am very busy.
That's a small matter.
Now, let me think a minute.
So you thought you could get away with it!
I am very pleased to see you.

What do you infer from this exercise about the vocal variations which are most useful in shaping meaning?

5 Read the question "What are you doing?" as it would be expressed by the following characters: a burly policeman; an old man or woman; a half-frightened child; an uneducated, shiftless tramp; a fond young husband or wife.
    Do you find the same sort of vocal variations important for this exercise as were important for project 4?

6 Bring to class a poem or piece of emotional prose of your own choosing; demonstrate the use of pitch variation in communicating the meaning of the passage. Listen to the reading of others to develop an awareness of pitch changes.

7 Practice the voice, articulation, and pronunciation exercises in the Hahn et al. and the Ogilvie and Rees books cited in the bibliography at the end of this chapter, or exercises in similar books.

8 Practice the following exercises on sound combinations and prepare to do them individually when called upon.
    a Peter Prangle, the prickly, prangly pear picker, picked three pecks of prickly, prangly pears from the prickly, prangly pear trees on the pleasant prairies.
    b Big black bugs brought buckets of black bear's blood.
    c Pillercatter, tappekiller, kitterpaller, patterkiller, caterpillar.

d A big black bug bit a big black bear.

e Better buy the bigger rubber baby buggy bumpers.

f A tutor who tooted the flute
Tried to tutor two tooters to toot.
Said the two to the tutor, "Is it harder to toot, or
To tutor two tooters to toot?"

g Betty Botta bought a bit of butter.
"But," said she, "This butter is bitter.
If I put it in my batter
It will make my batter bitter;
But a bit of better butter
Will make my bitter batter better."
So she bought a bit of butter.
Better than the bitter butter
And it made her bitter batter better.
So 'twas better Betty Botta
Bought a bit of better butter.

h Thomas a Tattamus took two T's,
To tie two pups to two tall trees,
To frighten the terrible Thomas a Tattamus!
Now do tell me how many T's that is.

i He was a three-toed tree toad, but a two-toed toad was she.
The three-toed tree toad tried to climb the two-toed tree
toad's tree.

j How much wood would a woodchuck chuck if a woodchuck
could chuck wood?

k Sister Susie went to sea to see the sea you see.
So the sea she saw you see was a saucy sea.
The sea she saw was a saucy sea.
A sort of saucy sea saw she.

l Seven shell-shocked soldiers sawing six slick, slender, slippery,
silver saplings.

m A skunk sat on a stump. The stump said the skunk stunk,
and the skunk said the stump stunk.

n A biscuit, a box of biscuits, a box of mixed biscuits, and a
biscuit mixed.

o Theophilas Thistle the successful thistle sifter in sifting a
sieve full of unsifted thistles sifted three thousand thistles
through the thick of his thumb. See that thou, oh thou unsuccessful thistle sifter, sift not three thousand thistles
through the thick of thy thumb.

p Amidst the mists and coldest frosts
He thrusts his fists against the posts
And still insists he sees the ghosts.

q Let the little lean camel lead the lame lamb to the lake.

r Nine nimble noblemen nibbling nonpareils.

REFERENCES

Bacon, Wallace, *The Art of Interpretation.* New York: Holt, Rinehart and Winston, 1966.

Bronstein, Arthur J., *The Pronunciation of American English.* New York: Appleton-Century-Crofts, 1960.

———, and Beatrice F. Jacoby, *Your Speech and Voice.* New York: Random House, 1967, Chaps. 1 to 5, 15 to 18.

Brooks, Keith, Eugene Bahn, and L. LaMont Okey, *The Communicative Art of Oral Interpretation.* Boston: Allyn and Bacon, 1967.

Eisenson, Jon, *The Improvement of Voice and Diction,* 2d ed. New York: Macmillan, 1965.

Hahn, Elise, Charles W. Lomas, Donald Hargis, and Daniel Vandraegen, *Basic Voice Training for Speech,* 2d ed. New York: McGraw-Hill, 1957.

Hanley, Theodore D., and Wayne L. Thurman, *Developing Vocal Skills.* New York: Holt, Rinehart and Winston, 1962.

Heinberg, Paul J., *Voice Training for Speaking and Reading Aloud.* New York: Ronald Press, 1964.

Mattingly, Althea Smith, *Interpretation: Writer-Reader-Audience,* 2d ed. Belmont, Calif.: Wadsworth, 1970.

Ogilvie, Mardel, and Norma S. Rees, *Communication Skills: Voice and Pronunciation.* New York: McGraw-Hill, 1969.

Van Riper, Charles, and Dorothy Edna Smith, *An Introduction to General American Phonetics,* 2d ed. New York: Harper & Row, 1962.

your
media
channels of
communication

8

We have come a long way since the days when information and man moved at the same rate. In early times, the range for immediate communication was the range of the human voice and ear or the range of the human eye; the speed of information flow across a greater range was limited by the ability of man to run. Man has increased his speeds greatly in recent years, with the assistance of the horse, the combustion engine, and now the jet, and will undoubtedly increase them even more; it has been predicted that he will someday move at 30 to 40 percent of the speed of light. However, the movement of information has been equal to the speed of light for a number of years since the advent of broadcasting. The result is that today one can literally talk to millions of people simultaneously. Because of this and the fact that such a large percentage of the attention of most people is focused upon the media, one scholar of human behavior has asserted that one cannot even be heard today if his message is not transmitted by the media—if it is not given the "amplification" of the mass media. For some purposes, such as trying to get a political candidate elected or trying to market a product on a nationwide basis, this is undoubtedly true. On the other hand, for other purposes, such as teaching a class or influencing the operation of a club or normal-sized business establishment, it is clearly not true. In this chapter we will suggest some of the factors that should influence your choice of media of communication and which will help you to understand and use them more intelligently.

In the previous chapter, we noted the dangers of overgeneralizing about the uses or effects of different kinds of messages simply because they are received through one sensory channel. Similarly, within any one of the gross categories of media, you must discriminate among carriers. There are important differences within the print medium, for example, between communicating via the mimeographed throwaways used by some groups on college campuses, or through the student newspaper, *Playboy* magazine, *Harper's*, *The New York Times*, or *The Village Voice*. Each is most useful for some purposes with some audiences. Do not assume that, because all of these are print media, all the same generalizations about communication can be applied to each.

Channels and impact

Most studies which have tested the difference in effects on attitude change among messages communicated by different media have failed to find any significant difference.[1] However, there is some evidence that attitudes toward a speaker can be affected by the medium of communication through which one is exposed to him. For example, in one study done some years ago of three potential presidential candidates who appeared on the "Meet the Press" television program, it was found that college students who saw the television program with Senator Robert Taft became less favorable toward him, but those who read the transcript of the program instead of seeing it became more favorable toward him. The attitudes of those who simply heard the sound track remained unchanged. For Governor Thomas Dewey, the findings were

---

[1] See, for example, Don Richardson, "Shift-of-Opinion and Retention of Material as a Function of Reading and/or Hearing," *The Southern Speech Journal*, 32:41–48, 1966.

reversed. Those who saw his television appearance became more favorable; those who read the transcript became less favorable; and again, those who heard the sound track remained essentially the same. On the other hand, attitudes toward Senator Richard Russell became more favorable whatever the medium of communication through which the students were exposed to him.[2]

When one turns from differences among the effects of single messages which are sensed in different ways to differences among the effects of the mass media in general, the problem changes in both quantitative and qualitative ways. Not only are some of the differences magnified, but some completely different questions arise about the effects and, hence, optimum uses of the various media.

Some variations in effect and, hence, optimum uses, are related to the differences in the situations in which a member of the audience is ordinarily exposed to the medium. One seldom gives undivided attention to the radio; he listens while driving, while working around the house, while studying or reading, etc. One tends to view television with one or more other members of the family and, again, while intermittently talking or reading or doing other things. Reading, of course, is generally the most individual and independent sort of media consumption.

Another difference among the media is in the timing of exposure. If you examine your media habits, you will discover that there are generally particular parts of the day when you read the newspaper, listen to the radio, view television, attend a motion picture, or read books. With radio or television especially, one can predict the kinds of people in the audience fairly well by the time of day that a broadcast occurs.

There are also differences in the attitude of receivers toward each medium of communication and in their expectations of it. The major difference in effect here, though, is probably between one of the mass media and face-to-face communication. The simple fact that one's message is carried by a mass medium increases its

[2]Samuel L. Becker, "The Impact of the Mass Media on Society," in Raymond V. Wiman and Wesley C. Meierhenry (eds.), *Educational Media: Theory into Practice*, Charles E. Merrill, Columbus, Ohio, 1969, pp. 34-35.

credibility. Two communications scholars, Paul Lazarsfeld and Robert Merton, have termed this the "status-conferral function" of the mass media.[3] The fact that one is on television or on radio or is writing for the daily newspaper gives him and his message a status which they would not have if, instead, he simply knocked on a receiver's door and gave him the same message.

Channels and message structure

The last of what we believe to be the major differences among media is the way in which each medium structures messages and, at times, affects content. We will return to this point in a moment.

It is unlikely that you will ever give a formal speech on radio or television or publish an essay in a commercial newspaper or magazine. It is *not* unlikely that you will want to use the media to communicate messages to one or more publics. However, unless you become President of the United States, or hold another high office, or become a broadcast commentator or newspaper columnist, your message will need to take forms other than the formal speech or essay to get into the media. You may want to buy or, if yours is other than a commercial purpose, talk the management into giving you space for a newspaper advertisement or time for a twenty- to thirty-second radio or television spot. You may try to get your message into a newscast or onto the pages of the newspaper as a news story. Some British politicians, for example, have become quite skillful at developing two or three extremely short sections in their speeches which make their major points and stand out as interesting and isolatable segments, and which can therefore be easily spotted and picked out by a newsman for quotation on radio or television or for recording or filming for newscasts. These politicians develop such sections carefully so that they will be short enough to fit as items on such newscasts. Other political candidates

[3]Paul F. Lazarsfeld and Robert K. Merton, "Mass Communication, Popular Taste and Organized Social Action," in Wilbur Schramm (ed.), *Mass Communications*, University of Illinois Press, Urbana, Ill., 1960, pp. 497–499.

in Britain, as in this and other countries, ensure use of the newspaper and broadcasting stations for the amplification of their messages by the distribution of press releases or complete copies of their speeches to reporters. This is generally done long before the speech is given so that the reporters can write their stories and have them ready to go to press immediately after the speech is delivered. You can use these same techniques for any messages that you want widely circulated, whether you are campaigning against air pollution, raising funds for a rehabilitation center, or starting a movement for more student participation in politics.

Planning the media presentation

If you are to gain access to the media in these ways, you must understand the needs and practices of the particular station, newspaper, magazine in which you want your message placed. You must know deadlines for particular newscasts or editions, kinds of materials they are likely to use, and the form in which they are likely to use it. Establishing good working relationships with program directors of stations and with newsmen can increase the probability of your message being disseminated via the mass media, and their help can ensure its publication in the best way. Those who work in the media know its requirements and its audiences. They will help to keep you aware that most members of the radio or television audience did not tune in just to get your message, nor did many readers buy a paper in order to read your story. People come into the mass media audience for a great variety of reasons, the most usual of which is to be entertained. They are generally not committed to the same aims as you; they will not view or listen or read your message just because you think it is important. They are ready to turn away from you the moment they are bored or believe that your message is irrelevant to their interests. It is your job, with the help of the professionals who work in the media, to be certain that your message is not boring to, or perceived as irrelevant by, this audience

The media audience

You can probably see this point most clearly if you think about making a speech favoring the organization of a voter registration rally at a student political meeting and making the same speech on the local radio or television station. In the former situation, most of the audience members will probably be there because they want to hear the kind of thing you are speaking about. The audience will be relatively homogeneous and, because they are in close proximity as they listen to you, the reaction of one will tend to affect others; there will be a crowd effect. Very often they will know beforehand the kind of thing that you will say, and they will tend to be interested already and to agree with you. If they do not agree with you or if they are not interested, they most likely will not come. When you speak on radio or television, on the other hand, whether you are giving a fifteen-minute speech or a twenty-second speech or commercial, a very large proportion of your audience will listen only because they happen to be listening to the program that precedes yours and have left their receivers tuned to the same station. Thus, you have an audience with less initial interest in you or what you have to say and, if they are interested, they have a higher probability of being in disagreement with you when you start speaking. Equally important, your television or radio audience is not gathered in a group to listen to you; each member of your audience is listening alone or with one or two other members of his family. This is the reason we believe it to be misleading to speak or think of a "mass audience." Instead of an audience of thousands or millions of people, it is more accurate and useful to think of thousands or millions of audiences, each made up generally of one, two, or three persons. The third important difference between the audience for your broadcast speech and the audience at your political rally is that the people in the latter group are doing little else generally but concentrating upon what you are doing and saying; it is unusual for them to be engaged in other activities while listening to you. The broadcasting audience members, on the other hand, are almost always doing other things while listening to you.

These differences may seem to you to make the face-to-face rally situation much more attractive. The idea of coming into someone's home and trying to give a speech to two or three members of the family while they are reading the newspaper, talking to each other, doing homework, and wandering in and out of the room may not seem very fruitful. However, there is a growing body of research evidence that indicates that what appear to be disadvantages of mass media communication at first glance may truly be advantages. If you are trying to persuade, the least susceptible people tend to be those who are already interested in what you are advocating and, therefore, those who have already made up their minds. Research shows clearly a close correlation between lack of interest and neutrality and between neutrality and susceptibility to persuasion.[4] And your chances of reaching those who are low in interest, neutral, and hence susceptible to persuasion are highest through the mass media, especially broadcasting. There is also a growing body of evidence which indicates that even the distractions which characterize the listening and viewing situation for broadcasting may be an advantage for the persuader. Some distractions from the persuasive message appear to prevent silent counterarguing by the listener and, thus, cause him to lose one of his important defenses against persuasion.

The major disadvantage of radio and television is that it is difficult to catch and hold any of the attention of the audience members. As far as most members of your audience are concerned, radio and television are *entertainment* media. You are competing with rock groups, plays, and comedians for their attention. There is a much greater need to interest the audience immediately, before they walk into another room or before they switch to another station or turn you off psychologically. As with any audience which is uninterested or not in agreement with you at the

4See, for example, Leon Festinger and Nathan Maccoby, "On Resistance to Persuasive Communications," *Journal of Abnormal and Social Psychology,* 68:359–366, 1964; Philip Zimbardo, et al., "Modifying the Impact of Persuasive Communication with External Distraction," *Journal of Personality and Social Psychology,* 16:669–680, 1970.

beginning, you must immediately establish need. You must immediately give them a good reason for listening to you—either because you are interesting or because you have something to say which will help them or, ideally, both.

In speaking on radio or television, keep in mind that you are sitting in someone's car with him or in his family room. You must adjust your manner of speaking to these types of situations. The style you would use at Convention Hall in Chicago, or at a political rally, or even in front of a class is not appropriate when you are invited into someone's family room or when you are sitting beside him in his automobile. These situations, whether you are there in person or have been "invited" via the electronic media, demand a conversational style; don't speak *at* your audience, converse *with* them.

Though you cannot see your radio or television audience, and so do not get some of the cues from them which help your audience adaptation in a face-to-face situation, audience adaptation in radio or television speaking is far from impossible. Obviously, you can make certain predictions about the nature of the audience from the subject matter, the format, and the method of presentation of the program. You can predict the nature of the audience even more precisely if you take into account the time of day, the program which is on the station preceding your program, and the programs which are on other stations during your program. Media audiences are fluid, but they change in predictable ways. Knowing these ways will help you to pinpoint the nature of your audience quite accurately, so that you can adapt.

Radio versus television

The obvious difference between radio and television communication is the importance of the visual dimensions of your message in the latter. A !ess obvious difference for the listener, but most obvious for the speaker, is the amount and kind of distraction which confronts the speaker. When speaking on the radio, you will probably feel relatively isolated. Quite often, you will be alone in the studio in which you are speaking, isolated even from the engineer in his glassed-in booth. Since even he will not appear to be listening to you sometimes, you will often get the uncomfortable feeling that you are isolated from the world and speaking only to yourself. When speaking on television, on the other hand, you will often be performing in the midst of what appears to be complete chaos. The cameramen will be pushing their cameras about while you are speaking, the floor manager may be standing between the cameras giving you signals, someone else may be swinging a microphone boom over your head, and other people may be wandering around the studio out of sight of the cameras but well within your range of vision. The lights will be uncomfortably bright and warm. Looking into the terrifying depths of the television camera lens will make remembering what you wanted to say almost impossible. You may decide at that point that it is a completely impossible situation in which to try to speak. If you stick with it, though, you will be amazed at how quickly you can become accustomed to the situation and virtually oblivious of the chaos, so that you can just talk intimately and informally with those people who have invited you into their homes.

Delivery

Though the technical problems of radio and television speaking are simple, they can interfere with good communication if you are not aware of them. When speaking on either radio or television, your voice level will be tested beforehand and microphone "levels" set so that you can maintain an easy conversational tone and yet be clearly heard. Once these levels are set, you should not increase or decrease your loudness too abruptly during your speech without warning the engineer or you will blast your audience off their seats or fade out so that they cannot hear you. If it is important to be louder in one section, move slightly back from the microphone; if it is important to speak more softly in a section, move slightly closer to the microphone. Otherwise, try to maintain the same distance from the microphone throughout your speech. In addition, because microphones are sensitive, they pick up many sounds which are not heard in the usual speaking situation. One of the most irritating and distracting to audiences is the sound of scripts rattling or pages turning. Therefore, if you use a manuscript, be extremely careful that you turn pages silently.

It will usually be necessary in radio to work from a script, but in writing the script keep in mind at all times that it is to be delivered orally. It must sound extemporaneous and it must be easily understood. Use short and simple rather than long and complex sentences. Personalize your style. Don't talk about "listeners" or "people"; talk about "us" and "you."

In television, if you are to be seen while you are speaking, it is best not to have a manuscript or even notes in your hand. If needed, your notes or script should be on large cue cards or on teleprompters which are placed near the camera lens at which you will need to look. In radio, even with a manuscript, you can and should sound as though you are extemporizing. In a face-to-face public speaking situation, audiences generally accept the fact that speakers use note cards or manuscripts. In television, audiences do not seem to accept these aids except when used by newscasters. They have become accustomed to the illusion that television speakers of all other sorts simply look them in the eye and talk. If you do otherwise, you risk the audience concluding that you do not know what you are talking about.

Timing

Because time generally is so critical in radio or television, you will need to plan the timing of your speech for one of these media much more carefully than you do for other situations. Often, it is a good idea to have a "cushion"—material near the end which can be added or deleted to help you finish on time without losing the impact of your closing because of unplanned cuts or additions or without your needing to slow down or speed up your speaking rate to an unnatural level. In radio, there will usually be a studio clock which you can watch and to which you can adjust your presentation. In television, the floor manager or one of the cameramen will probably give you signals. Check beforehand on the kinds of signals which he will give you and at what points in time they will be given.

Very often, of course, your speech will be prerecorded on audio or videotape. In such cases, timing is less of a problem because if your speech does not run the right length the first time, you can record it again or edit the tape.

The visual dimension

Television, of course, is a visual medium. This does not mean simply that the audience is able to see as well as hear you. It also means that you must *plan* the visual portion of your presentation as carefully as you plan the oral portion. The visual portion includes your appearance, what you do, and what you show.

Unlike the usual situation in which you speak to a relatively large group of people at a meeting or in a classroom, audiences are able to scrutinize closely every facet of your appearance, the slightest expression of your face, the smallest gesture. This is why those who work in television refer to it as an "intimate" medium. Because of the searching nature of the television close-up, which can cast your face into people's living rooms not only in "living color" but also larger than life-size, you must be sure that your grooming, dress, gestures, and facial expression contribute to, or at least do not detract from, your speech.

Unless you are an extremely skilled actor, do not try to be anything but yourself. Then, if you are confident of your material, believe in what you are saying, and care about the audience, these attributes should come through in your facial expressions, in your voice, and in your gestures.

As for any other type of speech, dress in a way that is appropriate to the situation. In a sense, proper clothing is like good scenery in a play; it should not call attention to itself. You know you have dressed appropriately, just as you know you have the right sort of scenery, if no one can describe it afterward—if it was so right for the situation that no one thought of paying special attention to it. For television, of course, you must avoid certain kinds of things, especially shiny jewelry and black and white clothing. For most purposes, it is best to wear various shades of gray, or colors which will appear as various shades of gray on monochromatic (black and white) receivers. You will generally want to use relatively bright colors for visuals and for clothing, since a large proportion of viewers now have color receivers, but the colors must be such that they provide some contrast when seen in monochrome. Otherwise, you will appear to be wearing just one gray blob. It is a good idea to check what you plan to wear with a director at the television station. Similarly, you should check the colors to be used in the visuals that you will show.

When you plan a radio or television speech, although it is important to understand the medium as fully as possible and to utilize the particular aspects of each medium for optimum impact, never forget that the most important and interesting programs on either medium are those in which there are interesting people talking in interesting ways about important subjects. Never forget either that, although one must clearly adapt to the medium, speaking on radio or on television or in a face-to-face situation is like Gertrude Stein's rose; good speech is good speech is good speech. To make a good speech on one of the media, it is first necessary to be able to make a good speech.

The media as sources of information

Up to this point, we have been talking about the media largely in terms of your using them to distribute your messages through time and space. For the sorts of communication which you will probably be using most of the time, the media will be even more important to you in quite a different way. Not only must you think of them as means of reaching audiences, you must understand them as fully as possible as sources of information for you and because those with whom you communicate have gotten, are getting, and will continue to get information from the media which affect their responses to your messages. Therefore, you must be aware of the effects of the media on information diffusion and on the "shape" of the information diffused.

Until relatively recent years, virtually the sole source of information that one had about events beyond the scope of one's immediate experiences was interpersonal communication. For the small core of elites, there was also the book—primarily the novel. Today, most adults obtain most of their information from the popular press, the film, and the electronic media. The result is that the information available to all men varies less; there is greater commonality in their picture of the world to which they respond. Former Republican National Chairman Leonard Hall recognized this fact in his story about the state of Maine, traditionally a Republican state. People were born Republicans, so they went to the polls and voted Republican. Then suddenly, they voted for some Democrats. Hall says that he asked an elderly Maine resident about what had happened. "Well," was the response, "we can't do anything with this television. Our children were brought up to think that Democrats had horns. Now they see them on television and realize some of them don't have horns a-tall."

This is not to say that this picture of the world in the heads of man is now an accurate one, that the media transmit events without distortion. There is bias in the selection of events to be covered and distortion of those events which are selected. Most readers, listeners, and viewers never question the cliché that the media cover the events they do because these events are news. "All the News That's Fit to Print" reads the masthead of the *New York Times*. Audience members fail to realize that such assertions are tautological, for the events covered are "news" solely *because* they are printed in newspapers or broadcast on radio or television. Thus, because the media equate news with conflict or, at times, with entertainment, people tend to get a lopsided image of reality. We usually learn of the interaction among nations only when they are in conflict, of relationships among the races when there is trouble, and of student-faculty-administration actions on college campuses when these groups are in disagreement.

The public gets a distorted picture of reality not only because of the selectivity of the media in covering events but also because the requirements of each medium result in a "shaping" of each event that is covered. Rarely is a newspaper story organized in an accurate time sequence. Newspaper stories tend, rather, to be organized like a pyramid, with the most spectacular part of the story first and the details on which the story is based last, where many readers never see them. In broadcasting, every event, no matter what its nature, must be constantly interesting so that the attention of the audience will be held. The result, to cite a trivial example, is that there never has been a dull baseball game on radio. A content analysis of presidential campaign telecasts in 1960 and 1964 demonstrated the way in which not only the medium of television but also the program format within this medium affects the content of messages.[5] When candidates appeared on interview programs, they were "far more apt to justify their positions on reasoned grounds and also more inclined to critically assess their stands vis à vis the opposition." On the other hand, in their straight speeches, they tended more to "concentrate instead on attacking rival policy positions and give little attention to the business of defending their views against opposing criticism." They also tended to depend on unsupported assertions more in rallies than in interviews.

Not only do the media and the program formats used "shape" the messages which they transmit, they are sometimes responsible for changing the event itself. Radio and television, for example, are credited with changing our national political conventions because the parties wanted to make them more continually interesting to

[5] C. David Mortensen, "The Influence of Role Structure on Message Content in Political Telecast Campaigns," *Central States Speech Journal*, 19:279–285, 1968.

the broadcast audience and to eliminate anything that might show the parties in a poor light. The mass media are responsible for the development of the presidential press conference, and as each new medium of communication has spread across the country, the conference has been adjusted to fit its demands. Election campaigns are now planned largely with the opportunities afforded by the mass media in mind.

As a communicator, it is essential that you study the media and the ways in which they are used by those with whom you communicate if you are to be successful in working in the contemporary context.

PROJECTS AND PROBLEMS

1 Read "Media Managers, Critics, and Audiences," by Gilbert Seldes, in the White and Averson book noted in the bibliography at the end of this chapter. Consider the following dichotomies which Seldes sets up on page 41:

Demand precedes supply—Supply creates demand.

The public gets what it wants—Audiences take what is offered.

"Ratings" prove popularity—"Ratings" indicate preference between simultaneous offerings.

The audience is always right—The Managers concept of the audience is often wrong.

Have class discussions on these dichotomies. Try to come to a decision in each case on which position most accurately describes mass communication in America.

2 Consider and report to the class on your sources of information and ideas. For what kinds of information do you turn to television? Radio? Newspapers? Magazines? Other people? What differences do you usually find among these various sources when they deal with the same general topic?

3 It has been claimed by some scholars that the world pictured by our entertainment media—radio, television, film, the novel—must be taken into consideration if we are to understand the effect of one of our speeches or the way in which any of our discourse functions. In a speech to the class, indicate whether you agree or disagree and present a persuasive case for your position. You may find relevant material in the Warshow book noted in the bibliography at the end of this chapter.

4 Read "Contemporary Functions of the Mass Media" by Jack Lyle, on pages 187–216 of the government report "Mass Media and Violence," noted in this chapter's bibliography. Discuss the implications of the ideas in this paper for someone like you who is interested in improving communications.

5 Watch one of the President's speeches or news conferences on television. Report to the class on your assessment of his skill at using the medium and the ways in which you believe his presentation on television differs from the presentation that he would make in a conventional platform speech.

6 If your school has a videotape recorder which your class can use, record a brief persuasive presentation which would be suitable for broadcast on your local or regional television station. After listening to it, write a detailed critique in which you assess the strengths and weaknesses of the presentation for television. Or, using an audiotape recorder, do the same for a radio broadcast.

7 Rewrite three minutes of copy from your local newspaper, adapting it to an aural radio style. Read it to the class to see whether you have achieved the sort of conversational style desirable for radio. Report to the class on the kinds of changes which you found to be necessary to change your stories from newspaper to radio or oral style.

8 Read some of Edward R. Murrow's broadcasts in *In Search of Light*, edited by Edward Bliss, Jr. Report to the class on the ways in which Murrow made his broadcasts sound conversational, even intimate. What in the broadcasts seems to account for the strong personal feelings which many listeners developed for Murrow?

REFERENCES

Bliss, Edward, Jr., *In Search of Light: The Broadcasts of Edward R. Murrow, 1938–1961.* New York: Knopf, 1967.

Carpenter, Edmund, and Marshall McLuhan (eds.), *Explorations in Communications.* Boston: Beacon Press, 1960.

Chester, Edward W., *Radio, Television, and American Politics.* New York: Sheed & Ward, 1969.

Greenberg, Bradley S., and Edwin S. Parkers (eds.), *The Kennedy Assassination and the American Public.* Stanford, Calif.: Stanford University Press, 1965.

Head, Sydney W., *Broadcasting in America,* 2d ed. Boston: Houghton Mifflin, 1972.

Hilliard, Robert L. (ed.), *Radio Broadcasting: An Introduction to the Sound Medium.* New York: Hastings House, 1967.

Klapper, Joseph T., *The Effects of Mass Communication.* New York: Free Press, 1960.

Lange, David L., Robert K. Baker, and Sandra J. Ball, "Mass Media and Violence," in *Report to the National Commission on the Causes and Prevention of Violence,* vol. XI. Washington: Government Printing Office, 1969.

Summers, Robert F., and Harrison B. Summers, *Broadcasting and the Public.* Belmont, Calif.: Wadsworth, 1966.

Warshow, Robert, *The Immediate Experience.* New York: Atheneum, 1970.

White, David Manning, and Richard Averson (eds.), *Sight, Sound, and Society.* Boston: Beacon Press, 1968.

discussional
COMMUNICATION

9

As you well know, most college students regularly discuss the problems, trivial or major, that touch their experiences and immediate interests. Discussion is the art of cooperative group talking. Little resembling the silent generation of twenty years ago, today's students react with vigor to such issues as college grading systems, student ratings of teachers and "firing" of incompetent ones, justification of student demonstrations, virtues and vices of the reigning political party in Washington, the American commitment to the defense of Western Europe, international controls of atomic power, the United Nations, the military draft, and the best route to peace. In classrooms, corridors, student unions, and wherever one finds the ebb and flow of people, the talk goes on.

Discussion also plays an important role in business and industry. John Kenneth Galbraith, for example, has pointed out that "decision in the modern business enterprise is the product not of individuals but of groups.... This is how men act successfully on matters where no single one, however exalted or intelligent, has more than a fraction of the necessary knowledge. It is what makes modern business possible, and in other contexts it is what makes modern government possible."[1] At each corporate level, discussion is used for planning and for dealing with a ceaseless series of operational problems. Discussions are also important at sales promotion meetings, national and regional conferences, and conventions of trade associations with industrywide problems.

Participants in community chest and other fund-raising drives meet to discuss the direction and methods of their campaigns. "Great Books" groups, other adult study clubs, community forums, interracial councils, labor union conferences, the League of Women Voters, and the Young Republican and Young Democratic Clubs constantly utilize discussion in their deliberations, as do the members of the innumerable organizations of all types that typify America.

In education, both at elementary and at higher levels, discussion is an important part of the learning processes. Elementary school children give and take in their "sharing" sessions as well as in much of their other classroom work. More and more sophistication of the oral "sharing" process is exhibited as older educational groups deal with economic, social, literary, and other subjects, even in graduate seminars. These discussions generally follow some form of reflective intercourse.

Radio and television too have been agencies for establishing and extending the popularity of discussion through panels, dialogues, round tables, and audience-participation programs. "Face the Nation," "Directions," "Meet the Press," "Issues and Answers," "The Advocates," and other programs have stimulated listening millions to carry out their own off-the-air discussions.

What is discussion?

Discussion is not mere talking. Conversation serves a useful purpose in promoting good fellowship and exchange of ideas and attitudes, but it does not systematically focus on specific ideas or necessarily attempt to resolve differences or solve a problem. Discussion, moreover, is not debate. The debater or arguer, even

[1] John Kenneth Galbraith, *The New Industrial State,* Houghton Mifflin, Boston, 1967, p. 65.

before he faces his audience, has already analyzed the subject, framed his arguments, and presumably made up his mind. He sets out to influence others to accept his propositions. Discussion, furthermore, is not persuasion in the usual sense of that term. The highly skilled persuader, especially one who manipulates modern advertising media, bypasses the arguments or the bases for the positions of an audience and attempts to substitute other standards of reference, that is, other drives or motives.

Discussion directly faces problems and attempts to resolve them through a mutual and rational exchange of information and ideas. It is an attempt to bring out all the arguments and all the possible bases for each position so that the best decision can be arrived at.

Discussion, then, has the following distinctive characteristics: (1) Its purpose is to analyze and attempt to resolve a problem. (2) Its method is primarily that of group interaction. (3) It evokes reflective thinking rather than emotional reactions. (4) It is deliberative rather than advocative. (5) It is usually oral communication.

1 *Discussion aims to analyze and resolve a problem.* This problem may be one of fact or of policy. The concern may be with any perplexing situation, whether immediate need for better information or for a long-range pattern of action.

2 *Discussion is a group activity.* Discussion requires the association of several minds in thinking and acting. The assumption here is that group judgments are generally superior to those of one individual because these judgments are evaluated and refined by the composite judgments of those involved. The personality of each individual is thus emphasized, rather than submerged, as individual judgments are inspected and diagnosed objectively. This assumption about group judgments has been verified by experimental studies that suggest that groups of individuals discussing tend to accomplish more creative thinking than individuals who are isolated in their creative experience.[2]

We believe that the probability of wise decisions by a group is

[2]See Bernard Bass, "Group Effectiveness," in *Small Group Communication: A Reader,* William C. Brown, Dubuque, Iowa, 1970, pp. 7–18.

increased if there is maximum interaction within the group. As a
member of a group, therefore, you should participate actively and
react to each of the other members just as each of them should react to everyone. If you were to chart the communicative exchanges
of a group which is working well, you would find that you had
drawn lines between all members of the group, rather than merely
between each member and the chairman.

In other words, if we had three round tables with six discussants
in each and were to find that our chart of the interactions looked
like those on the accompanying diagram, we would predict that the
best decisions were made by the group on the bottom. The participants on the left largely ignore the chairman and the other discussants. Each pair goes its own way; genuine discussion is absent.

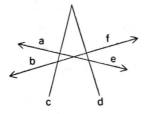

Wrong communication
chairman

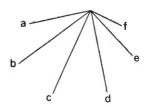

Wrong communication
chairman

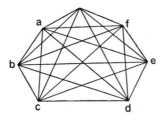

Better communication
chairman

What is happening on the right is more nearly discussion—but centers on the chairman and largely ignores the other contributors. Below them, better communication is taking place in that each member integrates fully with the utterances of each other member. The chairman is not ignored, but the group is not too dependent on him.

3 *Fruitful discussion evokes reflective thinking in contrast to emotional responses.* The atmosphere of a good discussion encourages intellectual activity; it rules out disorganized and aimless talk. The purposeful reflective thinker distinguishes assumptions from facts, studies contexts and backgrounds, notes causes and effects, tests authorities and testimony, generalizes in view of the facts, and checks his own tendency and that of others to mistake assertions for proof and to substitute biases and prejudices for well-reasoned conclusions. Reflective thinking is characterized by a disciplined attitude and an orderly testing of evidence and argument.

4 *Fruitful discussion inquires rather than advocates.* The discussant, somewhat like the scientist, is typically an inquirer. Note below how discussion temporarily ends as advocacy takes over.

We are not here condemning debate; we only want to point out that its purpose and method are different from those of discussion. Once the group arrives at a point where discussion is no longer fruitful, debate may take over in the attempt to secure parliamentary action. Once the debating conclusions are arrived at, discussion may once again ensue. Below are listed the major steps in a problem-solving discussion. Discussion may end during any one of these and debate ensue. The steps which are most likely to be points of disagreement, conflict, and therefore debate, are indicated by asterisks.

  a Explanation of terms*
  b Goals in analyzing and solving problems*
  c Analysis of the "felt difficulty," or problem, including description of the disturbing phenomena, their causes, and results*
  d Statement of hypotheses or probable solutions to be listed*

   e Weighing of solution *A*
   f   Weighing of solution *B*
   g Weighing of solution *C*
   h Validation of the preferred solution (*A* or *B* or *C*)
   i   Determination of a program to implement the solution
      preferred

5 *Discussion is oral communication.* Discussion is socialization
of thinking accomplished by oral communication. Although oral
communication is cheaper and more expedient than written communication, it is often less carefully thought out. Its advantages
are nevertheless obvious for occasions where decisions must be
made quickly. Even more important is the opportunity it gives the
participants to test ideas, get immediate feedback, adjust, try revised ideas, etc., until one's ideas are honed to a sharp and effective
point—or lead to a group decision.

Rationale of discussion

According to Gordon Wiseman and Larry Barker, research in discussion has provided "at least five general conclusions that appear
to be reliable":

1 Attitudes toward social problems do change because of
discussion.

2 People tend to become closer on an interpersonal level
because of discussion.

3 As a result of discussion people tend to develop more
sound and acceptable ideas.

4 The greatest influence in discussion is exerted by the
person with the greatest competency and ability.

5 The make-up of the group is very important in its success. One member can enhance a group far beyond his

numerical weight. The more objective the individual
members of the group are, the better the group will be.[3]

Discussion and psychological adjustment

Discussion, because it represents socialized thinking and speaking,
fosters teamwork and group solidarity. The egocentric talker soon
abandons his dominant tendencies, or he retires to more congenial
regions. When he remains, he learns more about his own personality and finds new sources of satisfaction. As he discusses, he tends
to share more in the mental explorations of the group and in their
ultimate satisfactions. He learns to be more sensitive to other people and their responses to him. In mental hospitals and in other
psychiatric and psychological milieus, discussion has been widely
used for the treatment of a variety of mental or personality disorders. Certain kinds of interactions of the individual with others
who have similar problems have been found to have important
therapeutic value.

Therapy discussion differs from the traditional type in that "the
reinforcement of identity through interaction . . . induces personal
change, whereas in other types . . . interaction influences group consensus. The identity of the member in a therapy group is presumably so severely threatened that he needs help to discover himself."[4]

Discussion in the service of democracy

Discussion, because it provides a climate for self-realization through
self-directed mental activity and because it motivates its participants to grow in social consciousness, becomes an ally of

[3]Gordon Wiseman and Larry Barker, *Speech—Interpersonal Communication*,
Chandler Publishing Co., San Francisco, 1967, p. 193.

[4]Gerald Phillips, *Communication and the Small Group*, Bobbs-Merrill,
Indianapolis, Ind., 1966, p. 57.

democracy. The functioning of our representative republican government depends on popular participation and many kinds of group decisions. Constitutional safeguards to ensure freedom of assembly, speech and writing, the protection of minorities, and legal dissent—all these factors combine to make possible effective talk and discussion and, hence, make our American democracy work. The assumption underlying our form of government is that we as citizens are sufficiently well informed and intelligent to work out our political program together and to apply sound group judgment to the solution of our affairs.

The programs of democracy and discussion are the same. You who investigate and apply the techniques of discussion are engaged in the furtherance of democracy. Probably the chief contribution of discussion is its enforcement of this technique characteristic of the American character. If in this or any country the deliberative processes of discussion, debate, and the orderly resolution of common issues are rejected, there is little hope for a later restitution of free thought, free speech, and social progress. Those who would substitute terror, intimidation, and violence for free and open discussion must be made aware of the long-range consequences of these methods of resolving conflicts. No humane and democratic society can long exist if its methods of resolving problems are not humane and democratic. Important among these methods are those proposed in this chapter—honest and intelligent deliberation, discussion, and debate.

Small-group and public discussion

As we suggested above, many forms and varieties of discussion are practiced. These range all the way from the casual or incidental exchange by two people to the large gatherings of organized groups. Within these variations in group size and formality, the format and purposes may range from enlightenment (information) to problem-solving, policy decision, and action. The motives and sponsorship thus may be industrial, political, economic, or educational. Many formats and practices which are labeled discussion are discussion in name only and turn out to be a series of public speeches, debates, or conventionalized persuasive occasions.

We summarize here representative types of discussion in which you may now, or in your later career, participate.

The small group

1 *Conversation.* Two or more people may spontaneously engage in exchange of information and opinions concerning a problem. Usually the talk soon moves on to other ideas or problems, though it may later affect the behavior of some of the participants.

2 *Round-table or informal discussion.* A discussion in which perhaps five to ten people participate in a casual atmosphere, without a contributing audience, can be called a round table. Although there may be a chairman, he does not function formally. The participants should understand discussion techniques and the purpose of the specific discussion. Usually the aim is learning and expression of opinion.

3 *Committee discussion.* The purpose of committee discussions is to prepare a report to the larger organization. The discussion is conducted like a round-table discussion, but because of its purpose, it is under greater control by the chairman. He sees that the agenda is closely followed, that a secretary records the proceedings, and that the report itself is completed and accepted by the members of the committee. At times he calls for a group vote in order to determine group wishes. Committee discussions usually have specific purposes. Somewhat related is the public hearing, in which a congressional or other committee holds public meetings to gather information on some problem of public policy.

4 *Problem-solving or case-oriented discussion.* This is the kind of discussion most often found in a good business or research organization in which a relatively small group of people with different kinds of expertise or ways of looking at a problem pool their ideas in an attempt to solve a particular problem. The problem

may be how to make an automobile safer or how to sell more automobiles, to determine the major sources of a river's pollution, or ways to persuade more citizens to contribute to the United Fund drive. This kind of discussion group often meets periodically over a rather long period of time.

5 *Panel discussion.* A panel is made up of a chairman and a small group. An audience, not too large, is present and should be seated near the speakers. All present should be able to hear each member of the panel. After the discussion, the auditors should present brief questions and comments. At the end, the chairman summarizes. The success of the occasion will depend partly on the extent to which the audience participates in group thinking. At least half the total time should be given to remarks from the floor. Each of these contributions, however, and the reply by a member of the panel, should be brief.

6 *Colloquy.* This procedure may be limited to a discussion between two communicators. Informal conversation prevails, but with well-organized analysis and synthesis. The audience participates. An alternative pattern is to have an audience panel supplemented by experts who serve as resource agents to contribute needed facts and ideas.

7 *Symposium.* The symposium consists of three or four speakers, each of whom is assigned a phase of the problem to be discussed and usually given a specified amount of time in which to deliver a prepared speech. Each speaker must adjust his prepared remarks to the preceding contributors. The purpose of the individual contributors is chiefly to provide information and an analysis of the issues. At the conclusion of this standardized part of the program, the chairman and discussion leader will direct the meeting so that the audience dominates the thinking and discussion.

The large group

1 *Public forums and large-group participation.* The panel and the symposium are conducted with small audiences, preferably not more than 100 people. The public forum may have an audience of as many as 2,000 to 3,000. This occasion is discussion in name only. The speaker must be an energetic and experienced public speaker, who lectures for perhaps thirty minutes, creates an atmosphere of open inquiry, and then invites (although the chairman may offer the actual invitation) audience comments on the issues on which he has lectured. The speaker must create an atmosphere of discussion. If he is a rabid protagonist for a cause or if he propagandizes, the discussion will probably not be very fruitful.

2 *Radio and television discussion.* Discussions over the air are not distinct in form or content from the types of discussion we have described; they may take the form of the round-table discussion, the symposium, or the panel. Even the forum can be televised to show the audience in action. However, broadcasting techniques impose limitations that modify the spirit of the discussion. Time allotments, the selection (on some programs) of audience participants, and preliminary rehearsals tend to remove the element of spontaneity. The radio-television programs such as "Meet the Press," "Face the Nation," and "Issues and Answers" are usually cross-examination challenges and replies that seldom reflect the method or spirit of true discussion, even though often labeled as such.

Agenda for discussion procedure

Topics for discussion should be of interest and concern to all participants. Since the object of discussion is to reach a group decision or to further group thinking, the topic should concern a problem about which the participants must eventually reach a decision. Note the following principles in selecting subjects:

1 *Select a controversial question.* Be sure that there are at least two defensible points of view connected with the problem. Subjects on which no real difference of opinion exists are expository and hardly make for interesting or fruitful discussions. Avoid also those topics about which everyone long ago made up his mind.

2 *Select a question either of fact or of policy.* If we argue a question of an event or situation, we aim to establish in our minds the truth or falsity of the alleged fact. Otherwise, our inquiry may be an attempt to develop a program for solving a given problem.

3 *The question should be capable of solution.* "Should the Student Senate of my college allocate $2,000 to the debate team?" cannot be settled strictly on the basis of concrete evidence, but a decision can be arrived at. For these kinds of questions we must simply recognize that judgments must be made. Narrowing a question often makes group decisions easier to arrive at. "Should the grading system at my college be modified?" may well be changed to the more specific "Should the grading system at my college be limited to 'pass' and 'fail' grades?"

4 *Select a problem that the group can help solve.* Subjects that result in agreed-upon solutions or in action create greater interest for the discussants, and hence a greater willingness to participate in future discussions.

5 *Limit the question.* Many discussions are futile because the issue is too broad or is vaguely stated. The time factor may limit the choice of a problem. Narrower subjects require more specific information, but they produce better results in discussion.

6 *Always state the issue as an impartial question.* The question form is symbolic of the discussion process and sharpens the direction of the thinking.

7 *Phrase the issue clearly.* Vague or ambiguous terms are likely to occur in the phrasing of issues unless an effort at clarity is constantly exercised. Note the vagueness or ambiguity of the italicized words in the following: "Should all *general education courses* in American colleges be abandoned"; "Should the Iowa legislature pass a law requiring the Board of Regents of the public universities to *discipline* any student or employee who engages in a *campus disturbance*?" Sometimes the terms even beg the question: "Can we honestly say that smoking cigarettes is harmful to the lungs?" Even carefully worded questions sometimes present a problem in word meaning. Many discussions have failed because the terms, seemingly sensible, led to widely different interpretations.

Outlining the discussion

The following skeleton outline for a discussion illustrates how a pattern of organization can be applied to a problem of policy.

The question is:...
  I. What explanations are needed?
     A. What is meant by...?
     B. What is meant by...?
     C. What is meant by...?
 II. Does this question constitute a major economic, social, or political problem that calls for solution?
     A. What are the chief facts or events that created the problem?
        1. What are the alleged economic causes?
        2. What are the alleged political causes?
        3. What are the alleged social causes?
     B. What are the chief causes of these disturbing facts or events?
        1. What are the alleged economic causes?
        2. What are the alleged political causes?
        3. What are the alleged social causes?
     C. What are the alleged economic, political, and social results of the problem?
III. What are the proposed solutions?
     A. What is solution A?
     B. What is solution B?
     C. What is solution C?
 IV. Are the suggested solutions for dealing with this problem satisfactory?
     A. What are the alleged advantages and disadvantages of solution A?
        1. What are the alleged advantages?
        2. What are the alleged disadvantages?
     B. What are the alleged advantages and disadvantages of solution B?
        1. What are the alleged advantages?
        2. What are the alleged disadvantages?

    C. What are the alleged advantages and disadvantages
       of solution *C*?
       1. What are the alleged advantages?
       2. What are the alleged disadvantages?
 V. In view of the discussion above, what solution is on
    the whole preferable?
    A. What are the advantages of this solution that in-
       dicate its superiority over others?
    B. Does the operation of this preferred solution jus-
       tify its selection on grounds of practicability?
VI. What program for putting the proposed solution into
    operation should be set up?

An individual outline is no doubt of much value to the participant, even though he should modify it much in the discussion itself. A guide for the panel, drawn up in advance, is also advanta-
geous if those involved are free to modify, ignore, or otherwise
depart from rigid methods which inhibit group thinking and decision making.

Leadership in discussion

Discussion develops from the participation on an equal footing of
the individuals who make up the group. Because discussion often
requires administration, many groups choose or appoint a leader.
Sometimes a leader or leaders emerge during the course of the discussion. At other times, in a leaderless group, each member carries
out some of the leadership functions. The functions of the
chairman-leader are to guarantee genuine discussion and to prevent
any discussant from impeding the free flow of ideas. Actually,
every discussant should be qualified to act as moderator.
   What special qualifications should a moderator have? He should
(1) know the subject to be discussed, (2) be familiar with general
discussion techniques and the special techniques required for this
meeting, (3) know the audience if there is one and understand how
small and large audiences behave, (4) have the personal qualities

which induce trust and respect, (5) be able to extemporize freely, (6) know the discussants and see that a group outline, if it can be helpful, is in their hands before the meeting, (7) create a favorable climate for the discussion, (8) properly introduce the subject, (9) help develop the discussion pattern, (10) use frequent summaries and transitions, and (11) draw out nontalkers and control overly aggressive discussants.

Rank-and-file participants

As a participant in most discussions you should:

1 *Share in the selection and tentative wording of the subject.* Use your influence to limit the subject and to reword the issue when necessary.

2 *Prepare thoroughly.* Patronize the library; collect and digest several books and many articles on your topic. Take diligent notes that may be read by others, for no substitute has yet been found for the orderly recording on paper of the gist of your systematic reading.

3 *Prepare an individual outline and, if your group so proposes, a group outline.* At any early point in your study, crystallize your findings and thinking in the form of an individual outline that conforms to the structure and details illustrated in this chapter. This skeleton pattern should be supplemented by a group outline, the product of the panel rather than of a single spokesman.

4 *In the discussion itself, cultivate open-mindedness, tolerance, group sensitivity, and cooperation.* Only in an atmosphere of open-mindedness, free from prejudice and dogmatism, will discussion be profitable. Analyze your own attitude as you enter into a situation and abstain unless you have adopted a mood favorable to genuine discussion.

5 *Contribute relevant evidence.* Insist on mustering a sufficient number of pertinent facts to illustrate the point fully and to justify the individual and group generalizations. Check your facts constantly with those of your colleagues. Cite sources adequately but without boring details. Don't flounder among your notes.

6 *At every stage, use the principles and methods of sound argument.* Question arguments and ideas that seem to you fallacious, but do so with calmness and tact and with counterevidence. Help to expose propaganda. As the discussion evolves, modify your original stand if you have honestly changed.

7 *Contribute to the organization of the discussional thinking.* Like the leader, you will become a sponsor of the logical pattern outlined in this chapter. You, too, will insist upon definitions, statements of goals, tracing causes and effects, and testing panaceas and specific programs— exposing their weaknesses and validating their foundations. You will encourage and help other participants to make their optimum contribution to the discussion. Your summaries, introductory statements, and citations of facts will be an index of your cooperativeness.

8 *Adjust your oral style to that of the group.* You may know other members of the group well enough to use first names. How much you incorporate broken sentences, personal pronouns, and interruptions will depend on the occasion.

9 *Make your delivery appropriate to the occasion.* Round-table contributors often assume that their discourse is strictly private and that it may be excused from vocal excellence. On the contrary, you should have good voice quality, sufficient loudness, a lively sense of communication, and clear articulation and enunciation; these are the major determinants of desirable delivery. As you move from a private round table to a more public situation—panel, symposium, or larger forum—the demands will be greater. But you will continue to exercise the basic qualities of proper communication before this larger audience.

10 *Be a good listener.* Just as fluent speaking is required, so is genuine listening. Listening does not mean silence; it means active cooperation. You are engaged in a dialogue —rather, a succession of dialogues—as each member of the group speaks and speaks again. Though you are inaudible, you are constantly feeding back. You should be able to summarize the discussion at any moment.

11 *Ask sensible questions.* Intelligent listening is accompanied by intelligent questioning. Questioning takes place both in the constant give-and-take of a closed discussion session and in the questions from the floor by a panel or forum audience. Your interrogations in any case should be short and simply framed. You may call for further information, repetition of a statement, inference from certain data, or additional citation of expert testimony. You may invite a speaker to summarize the state of the controversy; or you may ask specifically, "What should be done about this problem?"

Evaluation of discussion performance

How is discussion to be evaluated? What tests do you apply to yourself? How do you judge your skill in analysis, evidence, logic, language, interpersonal relations with the group, and oral communication? How do you measure your general effectiveness? Having a sound knowledge of the problem under discussion, understanding your role as an inquirer after truth and as a cooperative thinker with your colleagues, being able to handle facts skillfully, to reason soundly, and to adjust your delivery and speaking personality to discussion rather than to strong persuasion or debate will make you a satisfactory participant or leader in almost any discussion.

The following evaluation scales are suggested as rough guides for you, for outside critics, and for each member as he rates himself, his colleagues, and the group.

	Low				High	Comments
Knowledge of subjects						
Group relationship						
Evidence and reasoning						
Development of the discussion pattern						
Participation by all						
Delivery and personality factors						
Further comments						

PROJECTS AND PROBLEMS

1 Have a class discussion in which you attempt to reach consensus on what the class assignment should be which would be most useful in helping members of the class learn the material in this chapter.

2 Do the assignment agreed upon in project 1.

3 Assign a topic to the entire class and have each of six or seven groups prepare an outline. After each group has worked out its outline, have the class confer as a unit and synthesize the outlines. Use the resulting group outline for a classroom discussion.

4 Read "Confrontation as a Pattern of Persuasion in University Settings" by Herbert W. Simons. It is on pages 316 to 325 of *A Reader in Speech Communication* edited by James W. Gibson (McGraw-Hill, New York, 1971). What relationship, if any, do you see between the kind of communication with which Simons is concerned and the kind of communication discussed in this chapter? What inferences do you draw, therefore, about discussion and confrontation?

5 Read one or more of the papers in Chapter 2 of Cathcart and Samovar's *Small Group Communication: A Reader,* cited in the references at the end of this chapter. What new ideas or further development of the ideas in this chapter can you get from this reading about the processes of discussion? Report this new information to the class.

6 Divide the class into groups of four to six persons and have each group plan and carry out a discussion in class on a question of policy. Afterward, the discussion should be criticized first by the members of the discussion group and then by the rest of the class. The critiques should be the kinds which will help the discussion participants to be more effective in their future participation in discussions.

7 Attend a discussion on your campus. It may be a public forum, a meeting of the student senate, a dormitory council, or any other group to which you have access. Observe the discussion carefully and prepare a 200- to 400-word analysis of the way

in which it operated, including an assessment of the kinds and quality of leadership which existed.

8 You have been chosen to organize and prepare a community group for a single discussion on a timely topic. Explain the steps and procedures you would follow. Be as specific as possible.

REFERENCES

Baird, A. Craig, *Discussion: Principles and Types.* New York: McGraw-Hill, 1943.

Barnlund, Dean C. (ed.), *Interpersonal Communication: Survey and Studies.* Boston: Houghton Mifflin, 1968.

Bormann, Ernest G., *Discussion and Group Methods: Theory and Practice.* New York: Harper & Row, 1969.

Cartwright, Dorwin, and Alvin Zander, *Group Dynamics—Research and Theory.* New York: Harper & Row, 1970.

Cathcart, Robert S., and Larry A. Samovar (eds.), *Small Group Communication: A Reader.* Dubuque, Iowa: William C. Brown, 1970.

Crowell, Laura, *Discussion: Method of Democracy.* Chicago: Scott, Foresman, 1963.

Gulley, Halbert E., *Discussion: Conference and Group Process,* 2d ed. New York: Holt, Rinehart and Winston, 1968.

Huseman, Richard C., Cal M. Logue, and Dwight Freshley, *Readings in Interpersonal and Organizational Communication.* Boston: Holbrook Press, 1969.

Phillips, Gerald M., and Eugene C. Erickson, *Interpersonal Dynamics in the Small Group.* New York: Random House, 1970.

Potter, David, and Martin P. Anderson, *Discussion.* Belmont, Calif.: Wadsworth, 1966.

Wagner, Russell, and Carroll Arnold, *Handbook of Group Discussion.* Boston: Houghton Mifflin, 1965.

information
communication

10

We live in an age which places a high value on information. Education is seen as a way of disseminating that information, as well as a way of advancing knowledge. Underdeveloped countries recognize a basic problem in their lack of information. The mass media are hailed as the way of extending the spread of information among peoples and of keeping us up to date in a swiftly changing world. More people throughout the world travel now than ever before. The basic rationale of travel is that it is educational. The changing world offers more alternatives to man. We know that important decisions about our lives must be weighed carefully. They should not be made by snap judgments. To make decisions one needs to know about choices and their consequences. This calls for information.

"Information" is such a common word that you may feel you know all you need to know about it. Perhaps you do. But if information is so important in our lives, then perhaps one ought to understand the subject in some depth. It is not a simple matter. And it is often misunderstood and misinterpreted. There are various ways of conceptualizing information. Some have limited application, and some are more general. For example, Shannon and Weaver, in *The Mathematical Theory of Communication*, say,

"The word *information* in this theory is used in a special sense that must not be confused with its ordinary usage."[1] Yet modern information-science engineers dealing with problems of library storage and retrieval employ the word "information" in its ordinary usage.

What is information?

Is information a commodity? Some persons refer to it as such because it is something that men exchange or can be given. Cherry points out, however, that it is a different kind of commodity than men ordinarily exchange.[2] How is it different? It is different because the person who gives it doesn't have less of it after he has given some away. In fact the process of giving seems at times to increase the amount, or at least the clearness, of information in the mind of the communicator. Perhaps it shouldn't be thought of as a commodity at all. But it does have other similarities to such commodities as apples, salt, or coffee. Information can be stored, go unnoticed until it is needed, and then, if one's memory serves him well, is retrieved. Available information is to some extent a process, or skill, in adapting to situations. It is also helpful to think of information as a resource, something to be used as needed. If one doesn't have it when needed, it may make more difficult the solution to life's many problems.

Information may be considered a psychological achievement of man. Through the stimulation of his sense organs, and covert electrochemical responses, he becomes aware of the world about him and his organismic responses. His interpretation of the qualities of this awareness is information. A whole system of these response capabilities was once called "mind." It is today more

[1]C. E. Shannon and W. Weaver, *The Mathematical Theory of Communication*, University of Illinois Press, Urbana, 1949, p. 99.

[2]Colin Cherry, *On Human Communication*, MIT Press, Cambridge, Mass., 1957, p. 36.

frequently called "cognitive behavior."[3] This cognitive behavior includes not only man's sensory awareness but also his memory of at least some of his past experiences, his perceptions, his use of symbol systems which have been conditioned as associations with experience, and his free capacity to imagine sources of stimulation not present in time or place. Those response patterns serving immediate needs are called *consummatory*. Other patterns or the same patterns of response at other times are merely *instrumental*. Instrumental responses include those stored in memory to be used as needed. Thus information is man's mental structuring of his world, a source of what he knows, and the material with which he thinks.

Information may be interpreted as having a certain quality of news about it.[4] The receiving of a message about something one already knows is not considered information. If one doesn't understand what he hears or sees, it can be considered information in only a limited sense. Only when the stimulus adds something new to current awareness can a message be considered informative.

Information may be thought of as existing at various degrees of depth. Surface levels of information are referred to by Bloom as knowledge, whereas he considers a deeper insight into a subject as comprehension.[5] This deeper level of understanding is sometimes referred to as *wisdom*. Although the wise are usually knowledgeable, a man may know much about some subject and not act wisely about it. Knowledge in depth seldom exists without some organization. To organize one must analyze. And analysis is a process of breaking the subject down into categories. Knowledge also involves associations and synthesis. The cognitive process of synthesis seeks to answer the question "What is related to what?"[6]

[3]*Ibid*, p. 256.

[4]*Ibid*, p. 14.

[5]Benjamin S. Bloom (ed.), *Taxonomy of Educational Objectives*, vol. 1, *Cognitive Domain*, Longmans, Green, New York, 1956.

[6]George Gerbner, Ole E. Holsti, Klaus Krippendorff, William J. Paisley, and Philip J. Stone (eds.), *The Analysis of Communication Content*, John Wiley & Sons, New York, 1969, p. 130.

both within the subject and between any subject and those to which it is related. We shall have more to say about analysis and synthesis in thinking later in this chapter. Since knowledge is developed and relative, one seldom will know everything that can be known about any subject.

Several efforts have been made to identify different levels of knowledge.[7] Experts in educational testing have identified such levels as recognition, recall, and application. Free *recall* is thought to indicate more knowledge than simple *recognition*. The ability to apply knowledge calls for more information than simple recall.

All information one accumulates into knowledge is learned. That which we do by instinct and become aware of is often called *knowledge*. We say we know how to walk. Yet the average person knows very little about his walking. He just does it. This is probably similar to what happens in much animal behavior which may at times seem to be a knowledge response. Subconsciously conditioned response behavior has many forms in man. To refer to it as knowing ignores the fact that knowledge is largely an awareness phenomenon. Conditioned behavior can occur without awareness.

Learning, like information, can be carried on at various levels. Perhaps the simplest level is a first-order experience, although experience also is a learning procedure at all levels of knowledge. An old saw tells us that "experience is the best teacher." Learning through experience is also referred to as "learning the hard way." Although some experience is necessary to provide a foundation for much learning, studies have shown that it is also an expensive and sometimes self-defeating way. In opposition to experience as a way of learning, there is learning through listening, observing, and reading. These are called *vicarious learning*. Most of higher education has depended primarily on vicarious learning. Vicarious learning is largely learning through some form of communication.

The first level of communicative learning and the second level in the total scale we may refer to as the *nominal level*. It is the level identified by Bloom as the level of knowledge. We have all had the

[7] Jack A. Adams, *Human Memory*, McGraw-Hill, New York, 1967, chaps. 1 and 10.

experience of having to learn the vocabulary of a new field of
study. For example, you may have taken a first course in botany.
You had to learn not only many new names but also to what plants
they applied. A stroll across campus or through the park enabled
you to identify by name much of the plant life you may not even
have noticed before. Yet, with all this new vocabulary and your A
grade in the course, you realize that you still do not know much
about botany. But categories of botanical concepts and their
names are a beginning.

A third level of learning which takes you deeper into a subject is
description.[8] Scientific description calls for the use of standardized procedures of analysis and measurement. Your observation
may or may not have been instrumented in some way. If it was,
this may have helped you sense certain features you could not experience without it. In description we are primarily concerned
with what is described. It is then essentially analytical. Other
types of description call attention to various features which create
an impression.

The next level, *explanation*, is one in which both analysis and synthesis are used.[9] One can explain by going into a subject to a
deeper level or by relating an unknown feature of a subject to a
known feature of something else. *Exposition* is always a process of
relating the unknown to the known. It tells not only what is, but
why it is as it is. Thus exposition tends to be more concerned with
dynamics than is description.

Evaluation, as a fifth level, cannot be well developed without the
achievement of identification, description, and explanation.[10] Like
explanation, it involves both analysis and synthesis. It also involves
the relationship of the subject to audience-accepted value systems. The word "critical" is often attached to learned evaluations

[8] K. B. Madsen, "The Language of Science," *Theory and Decision*, vol. 1, no.
2, labels this level of the use of language in science as the "data level."

[9] Madsen refers to this level of the use of language in science as the "hypothetical level." *Ibid.*, p. 148.

[10] Madsen writes of this level of the use of language in science as the "meta-
language level." *Ibid.*, p. 148.

to distinguish them from the emotional, whimsical, or capricious evaluations of those unwilling or unable to pursue a discussion of a subject at this level.

A level of *creative message development* may be called a sixth level of information. Although in a certain way any message development is creative, the most creative approach to a subject is apt to come from one who is something of an expert in his field.

What information is not

We have been considering some characteristics of information in order to understand what it is. It also helps in trying to understand the subject to consider what may sometimes pass for information but cannot be considered worthy of a place in that category. Man has not only a mind but also a system of feelings. He has needs, wants, hopes, fears, anxieties. These can influence the way the mind perceives its world. They are sometimes called biases, prejudices, wishful thinking, or rationalization. Standards and goals are not in themselves objectionable. They become so only when they are unsupported in fact and reality. It is what one is biased about that creates the problem. Biased perception also can develop out of the unquestioned acceptance of tradition, myth, and superstition. Although most of what we know should and does feel right, feelings are not good directors of the mind. Because one has long known or believed something doesn't make it right. Misinformation should not be confused with information. Information based on knowledge can be defended as one of the most important factors in the belief or attitude system.

It is also questionable to identify superficial, trivial, or incidental features of a subject as information. The search for and dissemination of information should be concerned with that which is relevant, salient, and important. A paucity of information is closer on the scale to ignorance than to knowledge. Oversimplification is not only inadequate but also misinformative and misleading. Metaphor, simile, and analogy may help to identify one thing in terms of another, but if they lead the learner to assume that because two things are alike in one respect they are also alike in all other respects, they are misinforming.

Persons who wish to be precise in their knowing and thinking take a great interest in language and other symbol systems.[11] This is why scientists lay stress on the use of mathematics and statistics. Here various types of scales from the nominal to the ratio scale and computational procedures are selected on the basis of features of the data. Mark Twain once said that there is as much difference between the right word and the almost right word as between day and night.

What we know about something is also influenced by the way it is thought about. The first matter of importance here is to provide an orientation, a setting, a transition from what others may be thinking to what you know they should think. Your approach to your topic should provide a bridge from where they are to where you want them to go. Your ideas should be organized for unity, sequence, and coherence. The categories should obey the law of Ockham's razor, free from unnecessary cluttering. Inferences should be tested for the presence of major fallacies. Your information should be perceived by your listeners as reflecting good judgment. Above all, you should avoid the unnecessarily abrasive comment or inference. Even your most rigorously derived data and logically sound inferences may not be understood if expressed in an irritating manner.

Tests for the reliability of knowledge

Scholars are constantly concerned with the reliability of their information. They often couch their interpretations and conclusions in qualified terms. They know that their conclusions may be influenced by the methods by which their data are derived. They use

---

[11] May Brodbeck, *Readings in the Philosophy of Social Science,* Macmillan, New York, 1968, p. 5.

extensive checks to test the manifest nature of their facts. One simple method of checking is to replicate a study. Another is to carry it out by different methods. Replicated findings which confirm each other are better than a single study. Replicated studies done by two capable but independent researchers are better than replication by the same person. The same findings from two different but appropriate methods are more credible than a study done by one method. The working of instruments, logical inferences, and statistical analyses can be checked for situation control, functional operation, accuracy of inferences, and computations.

Checking is done to test for consistency. Other factors being what they are, consistency enhances but does not guarantee the probability of accuracy. There is a credibility factor in information as well as in persuasion. Statements from one dedicated to truth, open-minded, objective, one who has been tested and found right many times and who has no vested interest are more to be trusted as right than statements from one without these virtues. He may not be more right than another, but the chances are in his favor. The expert is more apt to be right than the novice. He knows more about the information. He has a reputation to build or uphold. He can't afford to make bad mistakes. Although even the expert makes mistakes, the probabilities again are against it.

The accuracy of information can sometimes be tested by pragmatic tests. Does it work? Is it feasible? Of course, even a theory that works may work in spite of the theory and for some other reason. But we are protected here too by the probabilities of such coincidences. Truth seldom yields up its best self in a hurry. Study and learning tasks take time and patience. They accomplish most when carried out in a deliberate and painstaking manner.

When we concern ourselves with informative communication, we do not imply that information is limited to those situations in which it is an end in and of itself. Information and the cognitive processes involved are also useful in discussion and in persuasion where the goal or purpose is to change attitudes. The point is that information is a concept of convenience in its own right. It need have no other goal than to enlighten the mind. This is its instrumentality. Types of human response behavior are so complex and variable that we cannot assume they all influence and are influenced by people in the same way. The psychology of man is best understood when we concern ourselves with the variable specific types of human behavior.

When we use the sentence construction "Information communication is. . . ." we do not intend to imply that there is only one way to conceive of this process. General semanticists have long warned us of the ambiguity and confusion arising from the "is of identity" construction.[12] Wherever we say "Informative communication is. . . ." our intent is to suggest that this is a convenient, realistic, and, we hope, helpful way of thinking about and understanding this type of communication behavior.

Educational psychologist Robert Gagne's summary of the functions of communication in instruction may help you to remember the major things that you must do in any informative or instructional speech:

Controlling attention

Informing the learner of required performance

Recalling previously learned capabilities [reminding the audience of what they already know that is relevant]

Guidance of learning [suggesting, through statements or questions, the kinds of things the audience ought to be thinking about while they listen, so that they do not get sidetracked]

Presenting the stimulus [or information]

Providing feedback [or reinforcement]

Promoting transfer of learning[13]

[12] S. I. Hayakawa, *Language in Action,* Harcourt Brace, New York, 1941, p. 88.

[13] Robert M. Gagne, "Learning and Communication," in Raymond V. Wiman and Wesley C. Meierhenry (eds.), *Educational Media: Theory into Practice,* Charles E. Merrill, Columbus, Ohio, 1969, p. 110.

Types and forms of
informative speaking

An informative purpose in speaking can be achieved through various forms of speech. Even a persuasive speech may also be informative. A distinction between the informative speech and the persuasive speech is that the informative speech seeks no other objective than the development of the understanding. Its goal is primarily cognitive. It is sometimes said to be "descriptive" rather than prescriptive. Informative speaking is certainly not limited to public speaking. It can occur in conversation, discussion, interviews, and other forms. The following discussion of forms and principles is designed to show how one may inform by proceeding in different ways. The way in which the speaker proceeds will depend upon such factors in the situation as the particular goals he has in mind, how much the audience already knows, and how much time he has to develop the subject.

Historical narrative, orientation

One's understanding of a subject is influenced by the degree to which he has had relevant knowledge and experience and by his ability to associate these meanings with a topic under discussion. A speaker can do much to help a listener make the proper chains of associations by the way the topic is presented. Any situation has certain cue stimuli in it. A perceptive listener becomes aware of these cues. When a history of the situation is presented, additional cues are revealed. They add to and reinforce original cues to enable the listener to maximize his meaningful associations. The more clearly one can relate new stimuli to meaningful associations, the better the communication and the understanding it seeks.

To be ignorant of history is often to be void or weak in perspective. In the discussion of most subjects which are relative, to lack perspective is to create a barrier to understanding. Historical data

that can be applied to any present situation are orientational.
The doctor's case history provides a good example. The case history is also widely used in counseling. The quality of the case
history is critical in such cases, as is the quality of all history, if
it deserves the label. This type of information must be carefully
selected and evaluated. Use original sources where possible. Consult sources which test the authenticity of significant points.
Sources should be identified and revealed. Gaps in data also may
be significant. Fill them in when possible. Mistakes in the interpretation of a communication are often due to a failure in orientation and perspective.

Definition, analysis

Informative communication must be developed on the basis of
establishing a common ground. The degree to which that common ground is perceived often depends on *definition.* Therefore,
what your words mean to you is important to your listener. For
example, communication theory has many words that mean different things to different people. Consider such words as
"source," "message," "code," "delivery," "process," "behavior,"
and "media." A common definitional procedure is to define by
using a synonym. Although the concepts for which the words
stand may be similar in some respect, they can be different in
other respects. Unless differences as well as similarities are
stressed, the metaphor, simile, or analogy may be more confusing than informative. Definition by example, although useful at
times, also may be misleading. What one person notices in a case
may not be seen by another.
    A logical form for definition tends to avoid the kinds of weak-
nesses we have been discussing. It tells us to identify the object
or concept defined in the general class of things to which it belongs and then differentiate it from other objects or concepts in
the same class. The scientist employs the principle of the logical
definition in his concept of the genus and species.

In general, the problems of definition are related to the procedures for analysis. Analysis can be thought of as determining the various categories in a system. The categories are the subsystem types which can be identified as different. A strictly logical classification is governed by a set of rules for the categories. Categories should be:

1 Based on a single principle

2 Free from overlapping

3 Exhaustive

4 Meaningful in terms of distinctions

One could not say, for example, that 50 percent of a class are Republicans, and the other 50 percent are of German origin. Politics and nationality of origin are different principles. In this case, politics and nationality are overlapping categories. The identification of a miscellaneous category means that we have not exhausted the possibilities. If we were to add another category, such as "They do or do not eat Mother's Oats for breakfast," it might be considered a meaningless category in comparison with such categories as politics and country of origin.

Another type of analysis commonly used in the organization of message ideas is called *topical analysis*. It is used particularly in the discussion of human qualities for which we may not have strictly logical categories. To say that our government has legislative, executive, and judicial functions is helpful in understanding it. It may not be rigidly logical since some of these functions overlap, but it gives us a convenient plan for talking about government. We use topical classifications, then, when we need a set of categories into which broad subjects such as government are to be broken down, but for which we are unable to devise a strictly logical analysis.

These procedures help with such aspects of a message system as identification, discriminating specificity, and organization. They are essentially nominal and analytical. They tell us "what is" about our subject. Exposition by example is close to a process of definition by example. Cases—concrete and hypothetical—general illustration, and analogy are various forms of the example used in informative communication.

Description, operationalism

Description is essentially a detailed definition arrived at through an analysis into parts and the application of standardized concepts to those parts. To describe a 1972-model car, for example, one can apply such concepts as design, power, economy, and safety features. Design would include such changes as length, height, and shape. Power can be described in terms of horsepower measurements and the load the car will pull. Economy can be discussed in such terms as equipment, guarantees, cost, and mileage. Safety features would include visibility for the driver, brakes, body, and bumper construction. *Operationalism* provides a step-by-step procedure in reporting how something is done. It is in effect a kind of dynamic description.

Descriptions can be realistic or impressionistic. The realistic description usually is carried out in terms of verifiable events and quantities. An impressionistic description may resort instead to a report on how one feels about these events and quantities. Such descriptions are most common in the discussion of works of art and in value-laden principles or events. Description may involve synthesis as well as analysis, in that some descriptions are best understood through comparisons and contrasts. It also provides a kind of definition and analysis in depth. It then may tell us not only "what is" but also "what is important."

Explanation, causal relationships

Exposition as explanation is carried out in different ways. A common form is to explain one thing in terms of something else that is similar. Another is to explain in terms of a deeper or a more penetrating and verifiable analysis. To explain is essentially to show cause, or to show why what happened occurred as it did rather than in some other way. Man's curiosity, his desire to find more fundamental levels of analysis, has taken us deeper and deeper into various specialized and professional areas of knowledge. The problem always is to find the most reliable and meaningful level of knowing why things are as they are and, when they are not to man's liking, what he can do about his thinking to bring it closer to reality. There are a number of fallacies in causal thinking. To test his causal explanation man needs to apply rigid tests of causal inferences. See Chapter 11 for a further discussion of causal inference.

Evaluation, critical interpretation

To communicate an evaluation of some concept, process, event, or object on the objective basis of the extent to which it measures up to selected appropriate standards is considered essentially informative. As we said earlier, a critical criterion of objectivity is that it is descriptive rather than prescriptive. The intellectual understanding of value systems is cognitive rather than affective behavior. The more universal the value systems used by the critic, the less apt is his evaluation to degenerate into advocacy. Since critical evaluation is an important aspect of education, since its goal is to educate the intellect and to stand always for high ideals, the critic is obligated to seek and maintain high standards in his communication.

To insist that the critic must maintain high standards in his art is not to dictate to him a particular basis for criticism. We need ask only that his criticism conform to appropriate aspects of such activity. First, he should give evidence that he understands the nature of criticism. He must know its structure, its functions, and its procedures. Second, he must show his knowledge of the subject of his criticism. The art critic should know a great deal about art, the music critic about music. Without such knowledge the critic lacks a normative basis for comparison. The third task for the critic is the selection of an appropriate set of values which are applied to the subject criticized. Finally, he must so relate the value system to the subject criticized that revealing and instructive conclusions are drawn. The critic who can achieve such a standard for criticism will not be whimsical or capricious. He will be the educator rather than the advocate. He will be in a broad sense descriptive rather than prescriptive.

Creative information

The deepest level of knowledge is the level at which information is significantly creative. Of course, one may accidentally stumble on a new idea, but there is not much probability of this happening. That a person creates what is for himself a new idea doesn't mean that it is creative. It may be self-generated information, but if others have had it, tested it, and rejected it, then it cannot be considered creative. The most significant new idea in any field is one which is labeled a "breakthrough." A breakthrough is not planned or ordered. It is not the normal, small, bit-by-bit improvement on old ideas. It is a significant development in knowledge or conception which may revolutionize an aspect of knowledge, life, or culture. Although substantive creativity is sought by many, it is achieved by few.

Combinations of methods in informative speaking

The several types of informative communication may be used as single methods, or, more likely, they will be used in various combinations. They are not inherently inconsistent. The selection of method will be influenced by your own knowledge of your subject, by the persons to whom you speak, and by the length of your speech. See the chapters and sections on speaker attitudes, language, inference, and nonverbal symbol systems.

PROJECTS AND PROBLEMS

1 Prepare a five-minute informative speech based on at least two of the readings in the bibliography at the end of this chapter. Narrow the subject sufficiently so that it can be adequately covered in five minutes.

2 Choose a popular song or poem which you believe has a relevant message for today. Develop a speech around the theme of the song or poem and, within the speech, include an oral interpretation of it.

3 Develop a visual which you might use in presenting an informative speech on some subject. Demonstrate to the class the way in which this visual can help you achieve your informative purpose.

4 Teach the members of the class how to carry out some specific set of operations or activities. It might be the set of procedures for giving artificial respiration, fly casting, or hybridizing a plant.

5 Give a three- to four-minute speech in which you describe a scene, object, or event so vividly that those who hear you will almost believe that they have experienced the event or seen the object or scene. Select a scene, object, or event which lends itself to an interesting and colorful description.

6 Prepare and present to the class an account of the historical background of a contemporary issue, event, or institution. It might be free speech, modern law, school desegregation, the labor movement, the National Farmers Organization, or the modern university. The historical account should be designed to explain how the issue, event, or institution came to be what it is today.

7 Present a four-minute speech in which you analyze and explain an issue through classification and division. You may want to explain a new idea by categorizing it or relating it to an older, familiar idea. Or you may take an idea and break it down into parts so that you can explain one part at a time. Thus, for example, you might want to explain the women's liberation movement in terms of each of the major goals of the movement: equal pay for equal work, day care centers, abortion on demand, etc. (We recognize, of course, that not all members of the movement are concerned with the same set of goals.)

8 Present a four-minute speech in which you explain an idea through the use of illustrations, examples, or analogies.

9 Prepare and present a three- to five-minute speech in which you trace the causes of some event or phenomenon. For example, you may want to talk about the causes of mental retardation (with this topic, you would also need to divide the general phenomenon into the various types of retardation), the causes of water pollution, of drug abuse, or voter apathy.

10 For this assignment use the speaking exercises above or a three-to-four-minute informative talk of any sort to the class. During the first one and a half minutes of your talk the class will be very attentive, clearly indicating when they are following you and when they are not. All of their feedback should be the sort which will help you as a speaker and make your task more pleasant. For the remainder of your speech, the class will give you negative feedback. They will ignore you or, if any members pay attention to you, they will indicate their boredom and disagreement in other silent ways.

After all students in the class have had a chance to speak and to experience the effects on themselves of these two forms of feedback, discuss these effects with the entire class and see what conclusions you can draw.

11 Briefly describe and evaluate for the class a play, concert, book, painting or entire art show, film, or television program that you have recently experienced. In your presentation, attempt to follow the suggestions about evaluation made in this chapter.

12 Discuss the informative communication ability of teachers in your college. If possible, select some specific teachers with whom most of the members of the class are familiar and see whether you can agree on which of them do the best job of informative communication and which do the worst. Analyze what they do and try to discover as many as possible of the characteristics which make for effectiveness and ineffectiveness.

REFERENCES

Bloom, Benjamin S. (ed.), *Taxonomy of Educational Objectives,* vol. I, "Cognitive Domain." New York: Longmans, Green, 1956.

Bruner, Jerome, *Toward a Theory of Instruction.* Cambridge, Mass.: Harvard University Press, 1966.

Chisholm, Roderick M., *Theory of Knowledge.* Englewood Cliffs, N.J.: Prentice-Hall, 1966.

Connolly, James, *Effective Technical Presentations.* St. Paul, Minn.: 3M Business Press, 1968.

Fogel, Lawrence J., *Human Information Processing.* Englewood Cliffs, N.J.: Prentice-Hall, 1967.

Gagne, Robert, *The Conditions of Learning.* New York: Holt, Rinehart and Winston, 1965.

Howell, William S., and Ernest G. Bormann, *Presentational Speaking for Business and the Professions.* New York: Harper & Row, 1971.

Kibler, Robert J., Larry L. Barker, and David T. Melis, *Behavioral Objectives and Instruction.* Boston: Allyn & Bacon, 1970.

Krathwohl, David R., Benjamin S. Bloom, and Bertram B. Masia, *Taxonomy of Educational Objectives,* vol. II, "Affective Domain." New York: Longmans, Green, 1964.

MacDougall, Curtis D., *Interpretative Reporting,* 6th ed. New York: Macmillan, 1972.

Meetham, Roger, *Information Retrieval.* Garden City, N.Y.: Doubleday, 1970.

Olbricht, Thomas H., *Informative Speech.* Glenville, Ill.: Scott, Foresman, 1968.

Payne, Stanley L., *The Art of Asking Questions.* Princeton, N.J.: Princeton University Press, 1951.

Powell, Len S., *Communication and Learning.* London: Pelman, 1969.

Richardson, Stephen, B. S. Dohrenwend, and David Klein, *Interviewing.* New York: Basic Books, 1965.

Rogers, Everett M., *The Diffusion of Innovation.* New York: The Free Press, 1962.

Schroder, Harold M., et al. *Human Information Processing: Individuals and Groups Functioning in Complex Social Situations.* New York: Holt, Rinehart & Winston, 1967.

Singer, T. E. R., *Information and Communication.* New York: Reinhold, 1958.

Skinner, B. F., *The Technology of Teaching.* New York: Appleton-Century-Crofts, 1968.

Travers, Robert M. W., *Man's Information System: A Primer for Media Specialists and Educational Technologists.* Scranton, Pa.: Chandler, 1970.

Wilcox, Roger P., *Oral Reporting in Business and Industry.* Englewood Cliffs, N.J.: Prentice-Hall, 1967.

Wittich, Walter A., and Charles F. Schuller, *Audiovisual Materials: Their Nature and Use.* New York: Harper & Row, 1967.

PERSUASION: COGNITIVE ASPECTS

11

Persuasion, and attempts to persuade, go on endlessly. In class-rooms, among friends, in the mass media, we all join in controver-sial challenges and replies on subjects of all sorts, both trivial and important. We debate whether our basketball team is as good as it was the year before or which political candidate we should support. A widespread argument during the early 1970s concerned whether the abandonment of South Vietnam by the United States would re-sult in the triumph of communism; whether the federal government should share tax returns with the fifty states; whether eighteen-year olds should be given all legal rights of adults since they have been given the vote.

Because persuasion is so pervasive and so important, it has been widely studied for centuries. We believe that these studies have given us some useful perspectives for understanding the varied phe-nomena which we label persuasive communication or which are involved in such phenomena.

What is persuasion? According to the *Century Dictionary and Encyclopedia Lexicon,* it is "the act of influencing or winning over the mind or will to some conclusion, determination, or course of action by argument or the presentation of suitable reasons, and not by the exercise of authority, force, or fear." This definition suggests that, in our study of persuasion, we consider especially what constitutes "suitable reasons" and what factors affect people's conclusions or courses of action.

In general, the studies of persuasion which have been made have centered on one of these two questions, either the question of what constitutes suitable reasons or the question of what factors affect the probability of people's being persuaded. In a sense, the first question has to do with the logical, or cognitive, aspects of persuasion and the second question with the psychological or motivational aspects. Though these are not perfectly independent, we believe that it will help your understanding of persuasion if we treat them separately. This chapter, therefore, will concentrate primarily upon the logical aspects of persuasion. The next chapter will deal with the psychological aspects. You may find it useful to consider this chapter in terms of your role as a receiver in communication processes, and to consider the next chapter in terms of your role as a sender. As a receiver, you must be able to analyze the logic and quality of messages so that you can assess whether there are good reasons for doing what the speaker or writer is advocating. To some extent, even as a creator and sender of messages, you should help your audience make their decisions about actions or attitudes on the basis of the logic and quality of your arguments. That is, in the process of communication itself, you should be helping your audience to become the intelligent, ideal audience.

None of this is to say that, in either your sending or receiving roles, you should not consider psychological appeals—appeals, for example, to your emotions or to the emotions of others. First of all, it is often impossible to separate the rational or logical from the emotional. Secondly, even in those cases or for those aspects of communication where we can separate them, we should note that there can be good reasons for being influenced by psychological motives or emotional appeals; the satisfaction of one's motives or emotions is important for each of us. For example, some persons have criticized advertising that appeals to men and women's desire to be loved rather than to their desire to be clean or to save money. The implication is that it is more rational to want money or

cleanliness than to want love. Even if one agreed with this strange
definition of rationality, we would insist that the need for love is
still a good reason, and that there are often good reasons for being
influenced by one's emotional needs or other motives.

In short, though the division that we have made for these two
chapters is a useful one for analysis and learning, you should recognize that it is arbitrary and that in understanding and practicing
persuasion, you must integrate the material on both logical and
persuasive grounds.

Steps in cognitive persuasion

Effective persuasion in its logical-argumentative development depends upon (1) the persuasive purpose of the speaker, (2) adjustment to and cooperation with the audience at every turn, (3) analysis of the specific problem, as indicated by the speaker and audience orientation, (4) tentative overview of the structural factors in
relation to the hearers, (5) framing tentative propositions in line
with rhetorical goals, (6) evaluation of the facts, data, evidence
(again, as interpreted by audience concepts), (7) evaluation of the
inferences that support or reject the tentative propositions, (8) language composition that attempts to frame the persuasive content,
cognitive and affective, to affect audience comprehension, stimulation, and behavior, and (9) delivery to express effectively the communicative aims.

Decide on your persuasive aim   Consider your specific persuasive
aim and plan each aspect of your communication in terms of that
aim. For example, if your aim is to move people to attend a political speech, you will operate differently than if it is to move them
to vote for a particular candidate or to become a campaign worker
for that candidate. For some purposes, it will be important to provide a great deal of information; for other purposes, little if any
new information is needed. At times, you may have more than one
purpose: for example, to strengthen the commitment of the

already persuaded, to develop commitment in those who are indifferent or neutral, and to convert those who are committed to the other side. Each of these aims presents unique problems.[1]

Secure cohesion with your audience   All communication, including persuasion, is based to some degree upon speaker-audience cohesion or identification. All listeners and observers have their minds set, their prejudices, their individual drives and motives for resisting or accepting suggestions that differ from their usual attitudes and conduct. Your problem is to understand the general and specific attributes of those you would influence and to modify your behaviors so as to facilitate your communication with them. We will have more to say on this matter in Chapter 12.

Select and frame the proposition   Persuasion by argumentative speaking is based upon propositions. A proposition is a problem formally stated: "*Resolved*: That Congress should abolish the draft." The same statement may be put in the form of an impartial question: "Should Congress abolish the draft?" The resolution type of statement is to be preferred unless the speaking situation is extremely informal. Exact statement, however, should be the aim, whatever the sentence type.

Limit the scope of your proposition. If the speaking time is five minutes, weigh your subject carefully and limit your proposition to only one phase. For example: "Draftees are not as conscientious in their military duties as volunteers."

Phrase the proposition in a simple rather than a compound sentence. See that it is free from ambiguous, vague, or question-begging terms. If the problem is proposed for a school or college debate, construct it so as to give the affirmative the burden of proof. Borrowed from courtroom parlance, the term "burden of

[1]Cf. James C. McBurney and Kenneth G. Hance, *Discussion in Human Affairs,* Harper & Row, New York, 1950, chap. 1; Halbert E. Gulley, *Essentials of Discussion and Debate,* Henry Holt, New York, 1955, chap. 1; Maurice Natanson, "Rhetoric and Philosophical Argumentation," *Quarterly Journal of Speech,* 48:24–30, 1962.

proof" simply means that the resolution should advocate a change
from the existing order, or a continuation of the existing order in
the rare cases in which it is clear that the overwhelming sentiment
of the audience is opposed to the status quo. This wording means
that speakers opposed to the proposition normally have a majority
of the audience on their side before the argument starts. Word the
statement, then, so that it proposes a change or a policy counter to
audience opinion.

Propositions are of three kinds. A proposition of fact asserts the
truth or falsity of a given view or idea. It calls for intellectual agreement or belief rather than for action. Some typical propositions of
fact are:

Resolved: That in the United States the standards for
graduation from college have declined during the past
fifty years.

Resolved: That Lee Harvey Oswald did not assassinate
President Kennedy.

A proposition of value is one that argues for or against the quality
of a person, event, situation, or idea, according to which it is thought
of as being more or less desirable, useful, important, worthy. The
aim is to evaluate or appraise rather than merely to inform or call
for action. Note these examples:

Resolved: That the concept of county government in the
United States is undesirable.

Resolved: That a liberal arts education is desirable for all
professional students.

A proposition of policy places the emphasis on action rather than
on acceptable information or evaluation. The differences among
the types of propositions can be illustrated by restating some of
the subjects above. Note how mere assent to the facts is changed
to a call for action in those propositions.

Resolved: That the standards for graduation from colleges
in the United States should be raised.

Resolved: That the public should vote in the November election to consolidate county governments into larger regional units.

Analyze the proposition Analysis is the process of dividing the problem into its main and subordinate divisions. To analyze a proposition, (1) define clearly the terms in the statement and any other terms that become prominent as the argument unfolds, (2) outline the conflicting arguments for and against the resolution, (3) discover and state the issues themselves—the controversial points, the answers to which will make up the pattern of the argument. Issues should be stated as impartial questions. Thus on the subject of universal military training, the chief issues might be: Is the present military-power procurement system adequate? Does universal military training fill the need? Is it more satisfactory than other proposals? Is abolishing it practicable?

In the analysis of a proposition of policy, the central questions usually arise from a cause-and-effect analysis of the problem. Inquire into the alleged causes of the resolution. What will be the alleged results of its establishment or application? These questions involve several apparent subissues: (1) What factors call for a change or for action? (2) Is the proposal practicable? Can the organization or machinery necessary for its success be established? Has it demonstrated its successful operation in other places or areas? Is it to be preferred to other proposed solutions?

These questions, representing stock issues, are familiar to most students of argumentation. These inquiries, we admit, are mechanical. They are to be applied only as a means of helping you to focus on the outstanding lines of investigation. Other pertinent questions can be added to this list, for example, (3) Is the proposal fair to the groups that have a stake in the problem?

To illustrate the process, consider the problem, "Shall we start a new political party in the United States?" Following the pattern above will reveal these issues: (1) Are there important problems that political parties should deal with and attempt to settle? If so, do the major political parties face these problems squarely? (The affirmative answers no, the negative, yes.) (2) Would the creation of a new major political party facilitate the settlement of such important problems? (3) Would the establishment of a new major political party be practicable? Stock issues are thus helpful in the formulation of specific inquiries.

Stock issues are also useful in the analysis of a proposition of fact. Methods of discovering the issues involved in such propositions include analysis of the forms of proof (evidence, authority, causal relations, comparisons, instances); analysis of historical periods; analysis of the parties involved (students, faculty, the college in general); and the classificational method, such as division according to social, political, economic, and moral factors. This method is perhaps the most convenient approach to analysis of propositions of fact.

Organize and outline the proposition   The persuasive speech that stresses argumentation should provide answers, with reasons or evidence to support those answers, to the questions or issues raised in the analysis of the problem. These decisions can enable you to state the points you intend to develop in support of or in denial of the proposition. Note the following issues:

Resolved: That Congress should pass legislation providing for a family allowance. (A family allowance means that all parents with dependent children whose income is below a certain amount should be paid a flat sum each month to supplement the family income.)

I. Does the economic-social condition of many families in the United States call for such a federal program?
   A. Do present programs dealing with unemployment provide sufficiently for family needs?
   B. Do present programs providing for retraining for industrial jobs deal sufficiently with family needs?
   C. Does the lack of adequate family incomes contribute to increased juvenile delinquency, crime, and general lawlessness?
II. Would such a program for providing for each family whose income is below a subsistence level minimize strongly the present economic-social evils?

     A. Would the family's economic status be improved?
     B. Would the problem of raising economic standards of such families be largely solved?
     C. Would this program largely alleviate the problem of raising educational standards?
     D. Would this program lessen the problem of broken homes among this group?
III. Is the proposed program practicable?
     A. Would the ultimate cost (for example, 9 billion dollars the first year) be comparatively little?
     B. Would the added family income be largely spent on necessities rather than on "junk"?
     C. Does the experience of some sixty nations that adopted this program twenty years ago justify it?
     D. Would the funds distributed each month to qualified families be properly administered?
     E. Do economic-social authorities and organizations advocate such a program?

The argumentative speech which presents these issues and contentions should have an introduction, a main body or argument proper, and a conclusion. Although these three divisions are flexible and should not be rigidly adhered to at the risk of boring the audience, this standard pattern is of advantage to both the speaker and the listener.

Usually, the introduction should (1) state the reasons for the discussion and the immediate cause of the controversy (in the case of the resolution above, a revenue bill may recently have been introduced in the House of Representatives); (2) explain briefly the terms (in this case, explain a "family allowance"); (3) state the issues; and (4) enumerate the points or contentions to be established. Again, these suggestions are to be freely departed from to avoid unnecessary rigidity of treatment.

The main body, or argument proper, should be a comprehensive treatment of each contention or proposition. Think of each argument as a speech in itself, with its introduction, main body, and conclusion. If you are arguing a proposition of policy, be sure to discuss (1) the necessity (or lack of necessity) for the proposal,

(2) its benefits (or evils), and (3) its practicality (or impracticality). In arguing a proposition of fact, each phase of your classification will be a heading in your main body.

The purpose of the conclusion is to summarize and enforce your points and to appeal for cooperation or action. You may insert a series of persuasive questions or refer again to the occasion.

The entire procedure above suggests a speech of considerable length. Select and limit the introduction, main body, and conclusion according to time at your disposal.

Your argument should be outlined in an argumentative brief. Drafting your outline will clarify your thinking, test the logical consistency and factual completeness of your ideas, and increase the clarity and persuasiveness with which you present your case. From this outline you may draft speaker's notes to be used as you talk. Do not keep your written outline before you as you talk, for you may be tempted to adhere to it mechanically and slavishly. Outlining is, however, a significant though laborious step between investigation and delivery. Review in Chapter 5 the principles and methods of outlining.

Follow a logical pattern of development   Persuasion by argumentative development means that you will rely primarily on the materials of reason and supporting fact. The set of your talk is that of reflective thinking and avoidance of random emotional utterance. The pattern is that suggested by John Dewey when he outlined the process of reflective thought: (1) the recognition of a felt difficulty, (2) description or diagnosis of the problem, (3) description of the representative hypothesized solutions of the problem, (4) rational elaboration of these suggestions and the testing of each, and (5) further verification leading to the acceptance or rejection of the preferred solution.[2]

The details of this reflective process consist of facts, the inferences from these facts, and the conclusions. Reason and inference

---

[2] John Dewey, *How We Think*, D. C. Heath, Boston, 1933, pp. 71–78, 91–101.

occur when we mentally explore and take a position in relation to the facts and related details. Inference, in a sense, is guessing, but it is also a methodical, cautious, and critical survey of the probabilities and hazards that accompany the conclusion that represents a new stand. We leap the gap from facts to conclusions when we are reasonably convinced that our leap is well justified.

When you infer or reason, you do so in one or more of several well-defined ways. You may view details that have similarities, then generalize concerning the whole array (*inference from specific facts*); you may limit your description and inference to a comparison between specific objects or relationships (*inference from analogy*); you may focus on two or more particular events that seem to have an invisible but definite connection (*inference from causality*); you may view the statements of others who speak with surety and experience on an event or theory (*inference from authority*); you may draw specific conclusions from general statements (*inference by deduction*).

These typical modes of logical techniques, considered in detail below, are the practical substance of your talk. They are not rigid forms to be followed in sequence, but are to be flexibily introduced at the points at which you believe they will be useful. These logical forms are not truly discrete logically or as they operate in human thought, but are usually described separately by logicians and students of communication in order to explain them in detail and suggest ways to apply them.

The logical method is to set up the facts or data; to state and explain the inferences that bridge the gap between these data and conclusions; to defend these inferences by refutation, if necessary, from those who disagree with the reasonings; and finally, to frame the conclusions that summarize the specific proposition presumably accepted by the listeners.

Stephen Toulmin, in his "Layout of Argument," suggests that the initial idea or proposition to be advanced constitutes a "claim." To meet the objections, data are to be furnished. If the listener doesn't accept the claim and data, then the speaker will furnish a "warrant." If the opponent questions the warrant, the speaker

will then supply qualifiers for further support of the claim. Thus
the layout of the specific argument may proceed from the simple
to the complex.[3]

1 *Evidence (facts).* The foundations of all communication are
alleged facts. What are "facts"? This term loosely covers all details of experience which are observed and all other reactions to the
world of reality. The events may be important or insignificant.
Facts are the records of personal testimony, statistics, experiments,
chronicles, authoritative utterances, and ultimatums. The experiences may be the reactions of a population to violent rampages of
nature, such as Hurricane Camille or the Chilean earthquake of
June 1971, or to man-made crises, such as the Soviet missile build-
up in Cuba in 1962 which caused President Kennedy and the
United States to demand that Russia withdraw the missiles or
run the risk of a nuclear war.

A fact, in short, is not the object or event itself, but rather the
object or event *as conceived by the audience.* Such a datum may
be an isolated item or a more general fact comprising an entire discourse in its character as knowledge. It may be later revealed as
completely erroneous, but for the present time and audience it is
"true."

Test your evidence by asking yourself these questions: Are the
facts in my argument stated clearly and concisely? Have I included
enough facts? Do acceptable authorities subscribe to them? Can
the sources of these facts or the authorities cited be specifically
identified? Are these authorities unprejudiced, intellectually honest, competent to testify? Do they have special knowledge? Are
the facts acceptable to the audience? Are the facts reasonable
according to the tests of causation?

2 *Inference from causality.* Much argumentative speaking is
based upon reasoning by causation. We conclude that assumed
facts effect alleged results (cause-to-effect reasoning). Or we focus
our attention on these same results or cases and attempt to describe

[3]Stephen Toulmin, *The Uses of Argument,* Cambridge University Press,
Cambridge, England, 1958, chap. 3, pp. 94 ff.

other factors, cases, or situations that may have produced them (effect-to-cause reasoning). Like analogy, inference attempts to establish relationships between particulars.

Note the following example:

Proposition to be proved: The base of the federal income tax should be readjusted to eliminate provisions that permit some individuals and groups with large incomes to pay little or no taxes.

Inference: There is need for such readjustment, for (cause to effect).

Evidence: Many individuals and groups now escape their fair share of federal taxes.

Subevidence: Many foundations, universities, and churches now use their tax-free status to prosper in business and commerce.

Note that the causal argument here, to be valid, would need to be extensively qualified and questioned, for many audiences would extend the types and illustrations to those who avoided federal taxes (e.g., those well-to-do persons who invest in state and local bonds, real estate operators, "big" farmers, investors in the oil and gas business). Note also that the sources and accuracy of the evidence underlying each type of inference should be checked.

What are the tests of such reasoning? In every case logical causality must come from audience beliefs and attitudes. We may ask four principal questions: (1) Does a genuine connection appear between the antecedent (prior fact, event, situation) and the consequent (subsequent fact, event, situation)? (2) If so, is the alleged cause adequate to produce the alleged effect, or is the alleged effect determined by the alleged cause? (3) Even if an alleged cause is sufficient to determine the character of an allegedly related event or situation, are not intervening factors at work to cancel or minimize the controlling influence of the connection or relationship? (4) Have the alleged facts in this case been properly verified?

3 *Inference from specific instances.* Your logical method here is to reason from specific instances to a general conclusion. This

method is probably more widely resorted to than any other because it encourages quick expansion of observation to cover and include cases not directly seen and experienced. One case of a
student breaking into the president's office on a university campus
may lead to a hasty conclusion that all the students of this university are defiant of law and order. Your problem here is to harmo-
nize with audience beliefs. But those beliefs, if the problem is
important to them, will call for divided opinions and conjectures
and so necessitate proper application of reservations, qualifications,
and negative positions to be investigated and dealt with. Henry G.
Baker, of the University of Cincinnati, in an address on June 4,
1971, cited thirteen examples of "heroic vitalism" to illustrate that
the history of the world is the "history of great men": Alexander,
Caesar, St. Paul, Martin Luther, Louis XIV, Johann Bach, Napoleon
I, Robert E. Lee, Abraham Lincoln, Charles Eliot, Friedrich Krupp,
Henry Ford, Mohandas Gandhi.[4]

How can you check your own thinking and that of others as you
generalize from instances? You should note whether the cases are
sufficient in number. Question whether the cases are representative
or typical. Furthermore, look closely at the sources of your facts,
at yourself as observer and collector, and at official or unofficial
sources in print from which you quote. You will check the character, authority, reliability, and corroborative value of your sources.
In the interest of your audience and of sound logic and communication, you will also test the causal factors involved.

4 Inference from analogy. A third type of inference is from
analogy (inference by comparison). The isolated facts, cases, objects, or relationships among such objects are compared with
similar facts, objects, cases, or relationships about which our information is relatively hazy. From such matching and contrast you
may draw conclusions concerning these relatively unknown situations, facts, objects, or relationships.

Astronauts Neil Armstrong, Edwin Aldrin, and Michael Collins,
preparing for their moon flight in 1969, were hailed as launching a

---

[4] *Vital Speeches of the Day*, 37:586–592, July 15, 1971.

voyage more impressive than that of Columbus discovering America. Prior to the actual event, when the comparison was first made, we knew something about the Columbus discovery, but practically nothing about what might happen on a moon landing. The inferences, however, were that the two events had much in common in terms of preparation, intelligent leadership, and so on, so that the unknown elements of the astronautic flight would in effect duplicate the known items of the 1492 precedent. Although the details of each transaction were entirely different, using comparisons which were dramatic rather than logical made them more impressive.

The worth of your analogies or comparisons will obviously depend on the audience's perception of the similarity. This perception, in turn, is dependent on a number of factors. Do the objects or relationships under comparison actually have a considerable number of items in common? If so, have these items significance or importance with respect to the conclusion we would draw? Do important differences exist? Are the alleged facts on which the comparisons are based fully established and clearly stated? Can the alleged comparison or conclusion, in turn, be verified by argument from generalization, by causal reasoning, by testimony of experts? False analogy should be avoided.

5. *Inference from authority.* Still another method of inference is to cite authorities or expert sources for verification of an idea. The gist of such inference is that "so-and-so is true because Mr. X so states." The reasoning really amounts to the assumption that whatever Mr. X has to say on this subject is sound.

The design of such an inference is as follows:

Proposition: The short-term licenses for radio-television stations should be replaced by long-term (twenty-year) licenses, for

Inference: Competent authorities endorse such policy, for

Evidence: A prominent senator who endorses the policy has competency.

Note that this example has obvious logical weaknesses. The

conclusion should be based not only on authority but also on examples, analogies, and causal connections. Furthermore, in this example the senator is not named. The testimony of supporters of the Federal Communications Commission would represent more valid evidence.

Are the facts (if facts are given) properly reported? Is the source especially qualified on this subject? Is he unbiased? Is the testimony offered contrary to the interests of the authority? In general, is the source accepted by the audience? Does reasoning from causal relation, analogy, generalization, and specific instances confirm this conclusion or assumption?

6 *Inference from general propositions and assumptions.* Effective arguments are based partly on general propositions or statements. This is argument from deduction. You use a general statement to apply to a concrete example or case. You may begin with either the general statement or the case to which it applies. These general statements, whether uttered or not, are assumptions, hypotheses, or principles. Practically every speech relates to or implies such basic concepts that give logical solidity to what is said. Many students of American political and economic policy, for example, assume in their remarks that the American system is one primarily of private enterprise. Under such a principle, if accepted by the listeners, any program of governmental economic activity is to be vigorously questioned. Similarly, assumptions are often taken for granted that America is a nation of racial freedom and equality; that the state and church are to be rigidly separated; that all wealth should be equitably distributed; that the government owes every man a job; that speech should be free; and that honesty is the best policy. Each assumption should be analyzed in detail before you base your argument upon it.

Logicians often frame deductions as syllogisms in which the first proposition is labeled the major premise; the related or more specific propositions, the minor premise; and the connecting propositions, the conclusion.[5]

[5] Walter R. Fisher, "The Uses of Enthymene," *The Speech Teacher*, 13:197–203, September 1964.

The following statement with its three propositions is a typical categorical syllogism:

 I. Major premise: Cigarette smoking produces lung cancer.
 II. Minor premise: Harold Howswer smokes cigarettes.
 III. Conclusion: Harold Howswer has or will have lung cancer.

Such inferences, framed to include three propositions, are of two general types: categorical and conditional. The conditional type, again, is subdivided into the disjunctive and hypothetical forms.
  The categorical syllogism assumes or states an unqualified affirmation, as illustrated above. In the disjunctive syllogism, the assumption states choices or alternatives, thus:

 I. Either we cease smoking or we have lung cancer.
 II. We cease smoking.
 III. We will not have lung cancer.

In the hypothetical type, the major premise or assumption is a condition. To illustrate:

 I. If America puts sufficient money and research into outer space, we will land on the moon several times after 1972.
 II. America will put sufficient money and research into outer-space exploration.
 III. America will land on the moon several times after 1972.

Note the logical testing to be applied to such general propositions:
a Rarely are speeches framed as full-fledged syllogisms. You piece out the major premises to examine your own thinking and that of other speakers.
b These major premises, whether stated or implied, are to be carefully proved rather than assumed.

c All general statements are probabilities rather than certainties. Use "some" or an equivalent qualifying term in the so-called categorical statements. Avoid "all"-ness or other unqualified assertions like those applied above to cigarette smoking. Avoid sweeping statements such as "Americans are democratic." The implication here that all Americans are believers in democracy is obviously invalid. At least some oppose democracy.

d Thorough testing of the premises and conclusions of the hypothetical and disjunctive examples above also reveals obvious statements that need full proof and much revision. Use evidence and arguments from causation, analogy, and generalization from specific cases to verify each proposition.

e All facts need to be verified and all terms definitely explained and defined.

f All of the above are guidelines for thinking and planning; you will seldom use formal syllogisms in your actual speeches.

Sometimes, as in discussional situations, instead of inferences, we use "hypotheses." How does a hypothesis differ from an inference? The hypothesis is a preliminary suggestion at a solution, to be verified by appropriate reasoning and facts. It is a proposition that the scientist may use for assembling his data and for securing a fruitful result of his observation and analysis. For hundreds of years the Ptolemaic theory or hypothesis of planetary motions prevailed, until the more plausible Copernican theory succeeded it. The hypothesis is identical with the tentative conclusion that the student of discussion or debate sets up to prove or disprove.

Removing audience inhibitions and applying refutation All argumentative speaking is both constructive and refutatory. All logical positions and conclusions are comparisons on a continuum from valid to invalid. Refutation is the process of producing arguments and evidence that substantiate your own argument by showing the invalidity of others. If you are the sole speaker, you are to understand such possible undeclared arguments and so remove the inhibitions that an audience may have to your ideas and conclusions. In a question period you may also reply to arguments you have heard.

See also the next chapter for psychological factors in persuasion. Here are a few suggestions for your refutatory methods:

1 Before you begin your argument or your reply to another's, arm yourself on the subject.

2 In your own speech or in your reply to another's, begin with a clear statement of the opposing position. Represent fairly and fully what an alternative position and argument have been—or would be if expressed.

3 Express your refutational position clearly and fairly, without pugnacity or dogmatism.

4 Test a rival argument, whether expressed or not, by examination of its underlying assumptions, its hasty generalizations, its weak analogies, its false causal relations.

Argumentative confrontation

A free type of argumentative give-and-take has become more widespread, especially in colleges and universities, since the late sixties. A group of three, four, or a dozen persons, self-appointed or selected, fill the thirty or sixty minutes. Their speaking is neither debate, discussion, or systematic argument. It is heavily individualistic, with little restraint on ideas, language, or delivery. Little attempt is made to stick to the immediate issue or to arrive at some consensus or majority decision. Utterances are extremely extemporaneous or impromptu. The session is one of brief give-and-take, constant interruptions, occasional simultaneous speaking, and above all, testimony of personal experiences and opinion. The logical atmosphere is often flooded with emotional indictment, especially against nationally known opponents.

On campuses these well-publicized rallies for popular causes have such slogans as "Your forum," "Your soapbox," and "High noon," slogans that indicate occasions for speaking by and for the "common man."

Typical of the radio and television shows of this loosely built

format has been "The Firing Line," under the chairmanship of
William F. Buckley, Jr. The topic for Jan. 23, 1972, for example,
was whether the eighteen-year-old vote would be a success. Eight
or ten outstanding undergraduates from representative colleges and
universities sharply challenged each other. The speaking was highly
personal, almost learned here and there, and as messages "on the
firing line," they no doubt stirred many home listeners to deeper
thought on this issue and more activity concerning these new
voters.

Conducting a debate

To ensure that both sides of an argumentative discourse are given,
a more formal debate may be presented. One or more proponents
on each side speaks. Debating is thus persuasion by argument conducted under strict parliamentary rules, as is done in legislatures
and courtrooms. The rules, in theory at least, ensure equal treatment of both sides of an issue. This is the procedure of democratic
government.

Discussion and debate are complementary. Discussion implies
analysis and objective review of arguments and evidence. Debate
emerges when special arguments at any stage indicate the temporary abandonment of cooperative reflection. Discussion is not to
be dismissed as impracticable; we should use it as much as we can.
Debate, however, is justified under certain conditions. When well-
grounded convictions prevail, democratic action requires that the
various positions be argued with votes and action to follow. But
the minority vote is not trampled on. Debate, properly handled,
contains the elements of good discussion. "The Advocates," a
weekly program produced for educational television in the 1970s,
is an excellent example.

Time limits are sometimes important. Intercollegiate debates, for
example, usually last one hour. During this time, according to the
conventional plan, each of the four speakers speaks twice. Each
speaker makes a constructive speech of ten minutes, and each is

allowed five minutes for rebuttal. In rebuttal the order is usually first negative, first affirmative, second negative, second affirmative.

For classroom debates the number of speakers and time limits may be shortened. Four speakers may each have seven and three minutes. If only two speakers are debating, each may have a total of fifteen, ten, and five minutes. The parliamentary rules guarantee to the two sides equal protection and opportunity. The affirmative opens and closes the debate; the negative speaks first in rebuttal, even though in a two-speaker program, he has just completed his first speech.

The purpose of debating is to arrive at and record a decision. In student debates, undertaken for learning purposes, a critic-judge decides in favor of the team that does the most effective debating. A distinction is thus made between debating in realistic life situations and that by students trying out logical techniques in persuasion.

As a student of communication, you will work under the close supervision of your instructor. With your fellow speakers, select a topic that is of interest to you and word it carefully. Prepare or secure a list of references on your topic and take careful notes on the material you read. Develop your argument with constant reference to the logical techniques outlined above. Draw up a tentative brief and submit it to your instructor or adviser for criticism. Revise this brief repeatedly as your command of your material develops.

In preliminary sessions with your teammates (unless you are the sole speaker for your side), report to one another on your readings, analyze the problem, and frame the issues. Decide upon your team case—the series of propositions that you want the judges and the audiences to accept in your argument. For example, the case for an affirmative proposition of policy might follow closely the stock issue propositions.

First Affirmative
I. The present situation is unsatisfactory.
II. Defects are inherent in the present system. (These two contentions "prove" the contention that the proposition advocated is necessary.)

Second Affirmative
I.   The proposal will remedy these deficiencies.
II. It is a practicable proposal.
III. It is preferable to other remedies.

For the negative, the case might be exactly the reverse:

Case A
First Negative
I.   The present situation is satisfactory.
II. The alleged defects can be corrected without destroying the present policy.

Second Negative
III. The proposal will be detrimental.
IV. The proposal is impracticable.

The negative may vary these cases by some such plan as the following:

Case B
First Negative
I.   The proposal is impracticable.
II. The proposal is detrimental.

Second Negative
III. The proposal is not needed.

Case C
First Negative
I.   The plan is unworkable.
II. The plan is detrimental.

Second Negative
III. A better plan is proposed.

Other choices of case are also open to the negative. The case for a proposition of fact resolves itself into a series of statements that usually reflect (1) causes and results or (2) classification of the arguments or evidence.

Sometimes write your debate speech as a means of achieving effective condensation, clarity, and persuasiveness. But leave your written speech at home. Good debating must be extempore.

The outline above, we agree, is oversimplified and mechanical. We are merely suggesting some orderly way to get at the essential problem and develop it fairly and cooperatively with your colleague.

Judging debate How good or bad is a given debate? What standards shall we apply? One method of judging is to get audience response. If most of the hearers vote for your position either by show of hands or by ballot, you have succeeded. But what should be the basis for judgment beyond merely "I like you" or "I like your argument and delivery"?

The critic-judge and you as listener-observer or member of the audience usually base an evaluation on the following: (1) skill in defining and analyzing the subject (selecting the proper issues), (2) skill in the use of evidence, (3) skill in the use of inference, (4) excellence in organization, (5) skill in audience adaptation, including the use of persuasive techniques (see also next chapter), (6) skill in refutation (to be noted especially in the second or rebuttal speech), (7) effective language, and (8) effective delivery. These items overlap; they do not have equal weight, and not all are to be strongly noted in each given speech. But they do suggest and cover pretty well the field of criticism. Critic-judges use these or similar criteria for their decisions "on the merits of the debate" in learning situations.

To measure a debate in a nonclass situation, opportunities for the audience to vote on the merits of the question itself are often provided. These votes on a shift-of-opinion ballot record audience attitudes on the question before the debate begins and again afterward to note whether any shift of opinion takes place.

PROJECTS AND PROBLEMS

1 Find a speech or editorial that uses examples of authorities as proof. Analyze these uses, considering their validity, contrary examples or authorities, and their probable acceptability or persuasiveness for the intended audience.

2 Select a persuasive speech from any recent issue of *Vital Speeches* or from the Appendix. In a five-minute speech in class, describe the major points in that speech and then present a rebuttal, utilizing the principles described in this chapter.

3 Select a suitable topic and prepare and present to your instructor a brief for a five-minute argumentative speech. After the brief has been refined to your and your instructor's satisfaction, develop the speech itself and present it to the class. In the speech, define terms and state the issues, develop a point or two with accompanying evidence and inference, and conclude with a summary and brief appeal for audience acceptance of your proposition. Again, your speech should demonstrate the major principles discussed in this chapter.

4 Divide the class into groups of four and have each group plan and carry out a debate on a topic of their choice. After selecting a topic, each group must agree on who will debate each side and on the precise wording of the topic as a debate proposition. If time is short, you may have only four presentations in the debate: a first affirmative of five minutes, first negative of five minutes, negative rebuttal of three minutes, and affirmative rebuttal of three minutes. On the other hand, if there is ample time, you may have each debater speak twice, as described in this chapter. Possible topics for a debate are: Birth control information should be available to all high school students; the United States should withdraw all military forces from the European continent; letter grades should be abolished in colleges and the granting of degrees should be determined solely by a comprehensive examination administered at the end of each student's four years in residence; college should be free to all students who wish to attend, as our public secondary schools are now.

5 Discuss in class—either with the entire class meeting together or in groups of four or five—differences in the kinds of evidence which are most relevant for a question of fact, a question of policy, and a question of value. During the discussion test your generalizations by exemplifying them with specific questions of each type.

6 Find as many examples as you can of inference from causality, inference from specific instances, inference from analogy, inference from authority, and inference from general propositions and assumptions. Assess the validity of each of the inferences that you have found. Report to the class on your findings and what you conclude from those findings about common fallacies or weaknesses in such reasoning and how they might be detected.

7 Considering the materials in this chapter and other information and ideas from members of the class, see whether the class can agree upon a definition of a "rational person." An "irrational person."

REFERENCES

Anderson, Richard C., and David P. Ausubel, *Readings in the Psychology of Cognition.* New York: Holt, Rinehart and Winston, 1966.

Bettinghaus, Erwin P., *Message Preparation: The Nature of Proof.* Indianapolis: Bobbs-Merrill, 1966.

Campbell, George, *The Philosophy of Rhetoric,* ed. Lloyd Bitzer. Carbondale, Ill.: Southern Illinois University Press, 1963.

Ehninger, Douglas, and Wayne Brockriede, *Decision by Debate.* New York: Dodd, Mead, 1963.

Mill, John Stuart, *Philosophy of Scientific Method,* ed. Ernest Nagel. New York: Hafner, 1950, pp. 211–233.

Miller, Gerald R., *Speech Communication, A Behavioral Approach.* Indianapolis: Bobbs-Merrill, 1966.

——, and Thomas R. Nilsen (eds), *Perspectives on Argumentation.* Chicago: Scott, Foresman, 1966.

Mills, Glen, *Reason in Controversy,* 2d ed. Boston: Allyn and Bacon, 1968.

Newman, Robert P., and Dale R. Newman, *Evidence.* Boston: Houghton Mifflin, 1969.

Toulmin, S. E., *The Uses of Argument.* Cambridge, England: Cambridge University Press, 1958.

pERSUAsiON
ANd
MOTiVATiON

12

Persuasion is perhaps the most widely studied form of communication activity of our time.[1] While the literature of the subject is extensive, it can also be a source of confusion. The development of multiple theories has not been well integrated, evaluated, or reconciled. While the naïve, and indeed some experts, consider many of the theories competitive and inconsistent, there is some question as to whether this is necessarily true. Persuasion theory, like the larger communications theory of which it is a subclass, is so broad and multifaceted that each scholar who has a primary interest in some specific variable is apt to assume that his area of interest is identical with the larger concept of which it is but a part. Tl ere is no a priori reason to assume that it is more useful to think of theories of persuasion as competitive than to think of

[1] See for example such books as Charles A. Kiesler et al., *Attitude Change*, John Wiley & Sons, New York, 1969; Chester A. Insko (ed.), *Theories of Attitude Change*, Appleton-Century-Crofts, New York, 1969; Anthony G. Greenwald et al. (eds.), *Psychological Foundations of Attitudes*, Academic Press, New York, 1968; Robert P. Abelson et al. (eds.), *Theories of Cognitive Consistency*, Rand McNally, Chicago, 1968; and Ralph L. Rosnow and Edward J. Robinson (eds.), *Experiments in Persuasion*, Academic Press, New York, 1967.

them as supplementary.[2] There may well be many ways of persuading different people, or the same people at different times, or in different situations or contexts.

In comparison with other theories today, our theory, if it must have a name, can well be called a "contingency theory." It is to some extent eclectic. We shall make use of the concepts of a number of theories. If persuaders are to achieve a variety of responses under a variety of conditions, we believe such a theory to be the most realistic approach to our subject. Don't be misled by anyone who insists that he can tell you what persuasion is. Indeed it is many things. Our purpose here is merely to try to tell you how we have come to think of persuasion, in order that you may achieve the best possible understanding of this phenomenon at an introductory level.

Persuasion analyzed

Why be concerned with persuasion: You have an idea that you think would help others, your organization, your country, or even yourself. You believe that others do not understand some matter as well as they should, or that they should modify their beliefs or attitudes or the way they have been doing something, or do more or less of something than they have been doing. You want to persuade them to change. You are in a position where the role you play is to ask others to vote in a certain way, buy something from you or for you, contribute to a cause, or interact with you or others. So you try to persuade them. You provide a persuasive stimulus, a message which you hope will lead in the near future to the response you have in mind. Yet the respondents have a choice to respond as you suggest, to make a different and perhaps a counter-response, or even to delay response. It is the task of persuasion to influence that choice. Since a choice by the perceiver is postulated

---

[2] William J. McGuire, "The Nature of Attitudes and Attitude Change," in Gardner Lindzey and Elliot Aronson (eds.), *The Handbook of Social Psychology*, vol. III, Addison-Wesley, Reading, Mass., 1969, p. 187.

as a necessary condition, it follows that he must be aware of what is going on and of his choices in the matter. Although one may accidentally and subconsciously influence another, we are primarily interested in those patterns of stimulation with awareness and intent. We would also limit the concept of persuasion to those patterns of social interaction which are symbolic.

A good persuasion theory is also good communication theory Therefore much that has been written in earlier chapters of this book is relevant here. Persuasion is concerned with some social change, and people change for many different reasons. New information, a new general understanding, a new way of feeling and believing, new experiences, internal as well as social conflicts, changing motivations and values, new interests, the roles one is called upon to play, learning, reinforcement, and a host of other conditions can function as stimuli or variables producing persuasive effects. Yet in spite of the biological facts of physical change in man at all ages, he tends to change slowly. He ignores many messages he may receive, he rejects some which he considers, he forgets some which might influence his choices if he remembered them. Those that somehow get to him and cause him to change must have some special features. Such features are identified through research as *significant variables* in persuasion. We shall concern ourselves in this chapter with those variables we consider most significant for the beginning student.

We must not oversimplify persuasive processes. Any persuasive impact can be realistically conceived of only as the product of a number of variables. Persuasion is then said to be multidimensional. The situation must be ready or made ready for a persuasive response. Predispositions must be such that the action is appropriate. The message must deal with the effects of these variables. Yet prescriptive theories of persuasion are in low estate. We can by description report certain principles which have been shown to operate in certain circumstances. It is understood that these principles are not advocated as universals. Their operation depends upon contingencies which any practitioner must evaluate and to which he must adjust.

Persuasion involves conditions and types of human behavior at various levels. It includes the development of favorable perceptions for an understanding of the message. It may be rejected even when understood, but there is a better chance for acceptance if it makes sense. Communicators are frequently concerned with attitude development or change. If one doesn't have an attitude for or against the subject of a message, the persuasive message may be designed to develop one. If one already has an attitude, a persuader may seek to change it. Or the persuader may seek to develop resistance to attempts to change the attitude or lack of it at any level. Communication may have as its goal the taking of some action or the cessation from some action already under way.

Techniques of persuasion

Cognitive appeals Since Chapter 11 is devoted to the logic of persuasion, we will not extend that discussion here. There are some psychological aspects of cognition to which we will refer briefly. Advertisers believe that getting attention to a message is an important aspect of its success. An important feature of that attention is that it must present the message in a favorable light. What is attended to must be a message which suggests its intended purpose.

The organization of the message can contribute to its impact. Monroe and Ehninger suggest communicating this relationship to an audience through what they call the "motivated sequence."[3] They include five steps in the sequence: (1) getting attention, (2) showing the need or describing the problem, (3) satisfying the need or presenting the solution, (4) visualizing the results, and (5) requesting action or approval. We believe that you can be most effective at relating audience motives to your persuasive ends during the third and fourth steps. While presenting your solution to the problem, you should indicate the way in which that solution fulfills one or more motives of the audience. In visualizing the results or

[3] Alan H. Monroe and Douglas Ehninger, *Principles of Speech Communication*, 6th ed. Scott, Foresman, Glenview, Ill., 1969, pp. 260–277.

probable results of your solution, you should amplify and make vivid the precise ways in which those motives will be fulfilled. In addition, research indicates that it is probably a good idea to put your strongest arguments in the very early or very late parts of your speech; do not bury them in the middle. In the introduction, if your audience is opposed to your idea, do not remind them of their initial attitude and do not warn them that you are trying to get them to change their attitudes or other behaviors; this tends to result in their erecting psychological defenses against your arguments. Some communication theorists even believe that when an audience is forewarned, they will silently argue with you while you are speaking and not give serious consideration to your ideas. To prevent the erection of this psychological wall, it is probably a good idea to emphasize in your introduction areas of agreement between you and your audience, as well as to emphasize those aspects of your background and ideas which will increase your credibility.

Though your persuasive intent is generally better left unstated in your introduction, it should be explicit in your conclusions. The specific attitude which you believe your audience should have or the specific action which you want them to take should be precisely spelled out, rather than left for them to infer. Not making your conclusions explicit reduces your effectiveness, according to the research findings in this field. A further aspect of cognitive behavior is the widely supported theory of cognitive dissonance. The theory holds that a listener's awareness of some inconsistency of thought, attitudes, or other behavior arouses some incentive to bring these types of behavior into a consistent relationship. This theory is consistent with the concept of the value of the need argument as the first of the stock issues in controversy. If the audience can be shown that a need exists which your message proposes to relieve, then the need for listeners to reduce dissonance through accepting your recommended action may follow.

Motive appeal is an important technique in persuasion which relates your proposal to the motives of your audience. Very often, when we become involved in persuasive communication, the impetus is our personally set goals. However, others will not be moved by what *you* need or want; they will only be moved if they are convinced that it serves *their* needs and wants.

Having said that, we should note that this question of motive appeals is more complex than it might first appear to be. Very often, the motives that lead to one's changing his behaviors may not be obvious; the relationship between the change and the motive fulfillment may be quite indirect.

There are many ways of looking at or classifying the motives or needs which can affect the way people respond to different kinds of communication. Some scholars classify them as *basic or physiological needs, social needs,* and *ego needs*. Others break them down into much finer categories, but we believe that this tripartite system will adequately serve your purposes; these can suggest to you the kinds of motives which shape the behaviors of people and which you can use in persuasion. The only additional motive that we would add is related to one of the theories we discussed in Chapter 2. This is the need for an individual to maintain a certain degree of consistency among the things he knows, his attitudes, and his behaviors. (This press for consistency may be closely related to one's need to defend his ego, but we believe that it is useful for you to think of them separately at this point.)

Our *physiological needs* include the need for sex, self-preservation, and avoidance of hunger. In a civilized society, these basic needs are often manifested in less fundamental ways, such as in the drive to accumulate money. However, observation of advertisements for many products or of the campaign against smoking or drug use shows that the need for sex and for self-preservation is still being used in many persuasive campaigns, and apparently often quite successfully.

Social needs are those associated with the desire that each of us has to belong. This is the need which explains why people are affected by their reference groups, as we discussed in Chapter 2. It also explains some of the effects of source credibility discussed earlier in this chapter. If a listener likes a speaker and wants to be approved by him, this desire will increase the probability of his accepting the suggestions of the speaker. Similarly, if he values membership in or recognition by a group, he is more likely to follow the dictates or norms of that group, to believe and act as he thinks other members of the group believe and act. This "need for social approval" explains much of the difference among people in the ease with which they are persuaded. Some persons with very little need for social approval tend to be more difficult to persuade. They have less need to conform to the group or to other individuals, even though they may admire them.

Our third category of motives is the category of *ego needs* or the need to develop or maintain a positive *self-image*. This category is not independent of the need for social approval, of course, since we develop and maintain our ego or self-image in good part on the basis of the ways in which others respond to us. We are persuaded, at times, that a change of attitude or behavior will affect our reputations or our prestige. However, there are probably some aspects of ego development and maintenance which we learn that are relatively independent of other people. That is, most of us develop a self-image which is relatively independent of social pressure. It is reinforced by certain kinds of personal achievement or by other acts which we perceive as consistent with the image. Thus, for example, if one sees himself as a "liberal," or an "intellectual," or a "professional," he will tend to be moved to behave in any way that a communicator can make him believe that a "true liberal" (or intellectual or professional) would behave. Pride of country or of one's family or college or hometown are, of course, related to ego needs and are often useful motives for use in persuasion.

It is not enough, of course, to recognize some of the motives or needs of your audience and to work them into your communication. It is important that you get your auditors to relate them properly with your persuasive ends. This clarification of the relationship in the minds of your audience is not only a matter of associating them in your message; it is also a matter of selecting the *particular* needs or motives of your audience which are, in fact, relevant to your particular goal. This is both a matter of presenting a valid appeal for meeting needs which you have noted and the moral and ethical basis of your persuasive message. The use of marginal or bogus appeals is the prime basis on which the entire concept of motive appeals is rejected by some. When motives are valid, however, such a basis for rejection is removed.

Overt behavior in persuasion We customarily think of the persuasive message as directed to cognitive or affective behavior in order to bring about some change in motor behavior or other physical support. It must be noted that consistency theory often works as well by the use of overt behavioral components to induce changes in understandings and attitudes. It is in such situations that experience is sometimes said to be the best teacher. The age of involvement has operated extensively at this level. It is the basis of the advice to "Try it. You'll like it." The accidental forced compliance of circumstance with some pattern of unsought and assumed aversive situations has been known both to broaden the understanding and to contribute to the development of positive attitudes.

Credibility of the speaker and the message The kind of person a speaker is perceived to be by his audience is generally known as the credibility variable. Factor studies have shown that it has four main components.[4] They may be called expertness, trust, attractiveness, and power. The audience that perceives a speaker as an expert or comes to respect his judgment is more apt to accept his recommendations than if the reverse is true. Another factor that increases the acceptability of messages is the perceived degree to which the person can be trusted. One can be both respected as an expert and perceived as trustworthy, and still not be attractive or well liked. It also helps a message for the communicator to be perceived as well liked. The degree of power wielded by a speaker in some relationship also influences the willingness of listeners to follow his recommendations.

In selecting people or periodicals to quote or refer to, be certain to select ones that are perceived as expert and trustworthy *by your*

---

[4]Gary Cronkhite, *Persuasion, Speech and Behavioral Change,* Bobbs-Merrill, Indianapolis, Ind., 1969, p. 173.

particular audience. We stress this because there are some sources which are perceived as highly credible by some persons and as not credible at all by others. Think, for example, of the extreme differences in the ways in which George Wallace of Alabama, Hubert Humphrey of Minnesota, and Bobby Seale of the Black Panthers are perceived—or *Time Magazine, Ramparts,* and *The New Yorker.* Consider not only expertness or reputation in general, but also reputation in the particular case. Some sociologists have found that for some topics, such as local issues, the problem of the best cut of meat to buy, or the best movie to see, people tend to accept most the advice of others whom they know well and who are very like themselves: a fellow student, another housewife, a fellow worker in one's office or factory. On the other hand, for national or international issues, people are more likely to follow the advice of persons with more "worldly" experience.

Though research evidence does not appear to be completely consistent, it indicates that you will be more persuasive if the audience perceives that you are similar to them. One scholar has suggested that this sort of identification is important because if the audience perceives that you are like them in a variety of characteristics, they will tend to assume that you also share their needs and goals.[5]

Social interaction in context One of the keys to successful persuasion, we believe, is finding the right time and the right situation in which to attempt it. Almost any man considers the question of the time and place very carefully when he wants to persuade a woman to marry him; just as any woman considers such matters when she wants to persuade a man to persuade her. However, when we are concerned with other kinds of persuasion, we too often forget how important time and place may be.

One aspect of time and place has to do with the audience being in the mood to seriously consider your proposal: their readiness. Another aspect has to do with their not being overly aware of or overly defensive against your point of view.

Obviously, you cannot always select the time and place or

[5]McGuire.

communication context in which to persuade. At times, you will be in a situation which simply demands that you make the effort. In such situations, if you are to fulfill your responsibility, you must simply try to create with your introduction and the rest of your communication a context which will be facilitative.

Audiences consisting of groups whose members are well known to each other tend to facilitate or inhibit the reactions of other group members through nonverbal symbols. This phenomenon of social facilitation may account, at least in part, for the fact that interpersonal persuasion tends to be more effective than group persuasion. When the speaker is alone with the listener, the only facilitation he gets is for change. When a group of listeners are together with the speaker, they may facilitate and reinforce resistance to change among themselves.[6]

Although research in the area is not completely consistent, there is evidence that if you can get your auditors to publicly agree with you, they are more likely to continue to hold that attitude or to act in the way they agreed to act. For example, if you are involved in a discussion about an election which is to be held soon, the probability of the participants in your discussion going to the polls to vote is probably increased if you get each one to publicly agree at the end of the discussion that he will do so.[7]

Persuasion is not limited to efforts to induce others to change. It sometimes happens that one can anticipate an argument for change and interfere with its possible effects by reinforcing the present attitude of an audience or by stating and refuting the anticipated argument in advance. This has been likened to medical inoculation where resistance to a disease is built up in an individual by exposing him to weak forms of the disease virus. These weak forms of

[6] Robert K. Merton, "Patterns of Influence: A Study of Interpersonal Influence and of Communications Behavior in a Local Community," Paul F. Lazarsfeld and Frank N. Stanton (eds.), in *Communications Research, 1948–1949,* Harpers, New York, 1949, pp. 180–219; Elihu Katz and Paul F. Lazarsfeld, *Personal Influence,* Free Press, Glencoe, Ill., 1955.

[7] See, for example, Harold G. Gerard, "Conformity and Commitment to the Group," *Journal of Abnormal and Social Psychology,* 68:209–211, 1964.

the virus stimulate a person's defenses without destroying them. Weak forms of the opposing arguments appear to work in the same way.[8] Even simply telling an audience that there are arguments on the other side of the issue with which they will be or may be confronted sometimes builds a certain amount of immunity to persuasion from the other side.[9] On the other hand the two-sided argument has been shown in some circumstances to be more effective than spending all one's effort on one side of an issue.

Message strategies The language used is an important part of any message. There are two aspects of language though which are didirectly relevant to our consideration of the psychological aspects of persuasion. The first of these is what communication scholars have termed "language intensity."[10] This is the attribute of language which people perceive as indicative of the extremity of a speaker's or writer's attitudes. Research indicates that strong language can easily boomerang, that you are generally more effective if you avoid the most extreme descriptive terms and metaphors.

Another important and relevant effect of the language which you use is its effect on the way in which the audience perceives you; it can clearly have an effect on how credible you appear to the audience. It may be, for example, that the reason very intense language lessens the persuasive impact of a message is that it makes the speaker or writer appear less credible and, hence, reduces the degree to which his views are accepted. Similarly, your language can make you appear more or less knowledgeable or intelligent. It can also affect the degree to which your audience identifies with you.

More is often gained by the search for an effective way of putting

[8] Arthur A. Lumsdaine and Irvin L. Janis, "Resistance to 'Counterpropaganda' Produced by One-Sided and Two-Sided 'Propaganda' Presentations," *Public Opinion Quarterly*, 17:311–318, 1963.

[9] William J. McGuire and Demetrios Papageorgis, "Effectiveness of Forewarning in Developing Resistance to Persuasion," *Public Opinion Quarterly*, 26:24–34, 1962.

[10] See, for example, John Waite Bowers, "Language Intensity, Social Introversion, and Attitude Change," *Speech Monographs*, 30:345–352, 1963.

an idea than by the perceived strength of the language as such. The slogan represents one form of this type of statement. Consider for example the conservationist's slogan: "It's not a blind objection to progress. It is an objection to blind progress." Repetition of a statement is at times better than a restatement. Be aware of these factors as you select the language with which to clothe your ideas.

Your message may take various forms or treatments. Some of the most effective messages are cast largely in narrative form. At the time of this writing the air is filled with the prophesies of success of political candidates. They are intended no doubt to reinforce the self, and the faithful, as much as to drive the entering wedge into the doubts of the faltering. Concentrate on a few points and develop them thoughtfully. Explicit statements in the long run are more effective than implicit ones. The natural language is clearer to most people than are the special languages of a particular group. Concrete statements are more meaningful to many than are abstractions. The reverse may be more true for others. People whose lives are devoted to things and experiences are apt to prefer concrete images. Those who are devoted to words and ideas may find the abstract more meaningful. Adapt your message style to your listener. More can be accomplished by doing a little over a long time than by trying to take your auditor the whole way in which you want him to go at one time. This contrast has been called the campaign versus the hypodermic needle approach.[11] It might also be called the stalagmite approach.

Relationship between attitude change and other behavioral changes

Research in recent years has raised important questions about the relationship of attitudes or attitude change to other behaviors or behavioral changes. For example, we have traditionally thought

[11]See Charles R. Wright, *Mass Communication*, Random House, New York, 1959.

that if we could change people's attitudes toward minority groups, there would be less discrimination. Recent research indicates that, in most cases, it doesn't work so simply. There are a number of studies in which the measures of attitude show that attitudes toward minority groups or toward some other general class of persons or objects have been changed, but that other behaviors toward individuals in that group have not changed.

There are various explanations for this lack of relationship, all of which have implications for your persuasive communication. One explanation is that for most of our behaviors toward another person or object there are at least two relevant attitudes. Not only is our attitude toward the person or toward the class of persons important; our attitude toward the situation is also important.[12] For example, whether the owner of a business will hire a woman as an executive depends not only on his attitude toward women but also on his attitude toward his business and toward that particular position. In persuading, therefore, you must consider all the major and relevant attitudes which affect your audience's behaving in the way you want and you must develop your communication plan accordingly.

Another explanation for some of the instances in which there appears to be little relationship between attitude and other behaviors grows out of some of the research on racial prejudice. It has been found that in some cases prejudice is not related at all to what one knows or believes about the group against which one is prejudiced, but rather grows out of other factors, generally some sort of personal frustration. One study, for example, showed that a group of college women who were prejudiced against blacks could be changed more by communication about the way in which prejudice is a psychological reaction to frustration and other personal problems than by communication demonstrating that the negative stereotypes of blacks were not true.[13] There is evidence from

[12]Milton Rokeach, "Attitude Change and Behavioral Change," *Public Opinion Quarterly*, 30:529–550, 1967.

[13]Daniel Katz, Irving Sarnoff, and Charles McClintock, "Ego-Defense and Attitude Change," *Human Relations*, 9:27–45, 1956.

other studies that prejudicial behavior is sometimes the result of
people's accepting the general social norms of their community,
rather than the result of any knowledge or experiences or personal
problems.[14]

The implication of these various findings and these various explanations for the relationship between attitudes and other behaviors
is that you must attempt to understand the major reasons why
those whom you are attempting to persuade hold the attitudes they
do or behave the way they do. You can then plan your campaign
of persuasion more intelligently. In short, as we have stressed
throughout this book, effective communication has at its base a
thorough understanding of the people with whom you are
communicating.

PROJECTS AND PROBLEMS

1 Consider a problem in your school or community for which
you believe that you have a solution. Analyze the problem and
your solution and develop a plan for getting your solution adopted
and carried out. In a three- to five-minute speech to the class, explain your analysis of the problem, your solution to it, and then
your plan for gaining adoption and execution by those involved.
Your speech should convince the class of the wisdom of your solution and the probable success of your plan.

2 Analyze the motive appeals in three quite different newspaper
or television advertisements. Describe the nature of each of the
appeals that you found (source credibility, basic drive, ego need,
social need, etc.). Evaluate the effectiveness of each for the audience to which the advertisement is directed.

3 Compare the points of view expressed about persuasion in the
chapters by Fulton and by Simons in *A Reader in Speech Communication*. (The full citation can be found in the bibliography

---

[14]Percy Black and Ruth Davidson Atkins, "Conformity Versus Prejudice as
Exemplified in White-Negro Relations in the South: Some Methodological
Considerations," *Journal of Psychology*, 30:109–121, 1950.

at the end of this chapter.) Can the phenomena described by Simons be explained in terms of the theoretical ideas described by Fulton^ Give a five-minute speech in which you develop your point of view on this question.

4 You want to bring about some changes in your home town—e.g., urban renewal, redistricting of precincts, building of low-rent housing, or starting a club for youngsters from low-income families. Explain to the class your communication plan for bringing about the change. Include in your explanation at least the following:

   a The key publics who must be convinced.
   b Present attitudes of each of these publics and the reasons for the existing attitudes.
   c What should cause each group to change.
   d Media of communication that you will use.
   e Other parts of your communication strategy.

5 Select a persuasive speech from *Vital Speeches,* the Appendix, or any other source, and analyze the way in which the speaker used or failed to use the psychological techniques discussed in this chapter. Evaluate the effectiveness of these techniques in this particular speech.

6 Present a five-minute persuasive speech to the class in which you make use of some of the ideas in this chapter to get the members of this class to accept the idea or action that you propose.

REFERENCES

Bandura, Albert, *Principles of Behavior Modification.* New York: Holt, Rinehart and Winston, 1969.

Bennis, Warren G., Kenneth D. Benne, and Robert Chin, *The Planning of Change,* 2d ed. New York: Holt, Rinehart and Winston, 1969.

Bindra, Dalbir, and Jane Stewart (eds.), *Motivation.* Baltimore: Penguin Books, 1966.

Brown, J.A.C., *Techniques of Persuasion.* Baltimore: Penguin Books, 1963.

Cronkhite, Gary. *Persuasion, Speech and Behavioral Change.* Indianapolis: Bobbs-Merrill, 1969.

Edelman, Murray, *The Symbolic Uses of Politics.* Urbana, Ill.: University of Illinois Press, 1964.

Feldman, Shel, *Cognitive Consistency.* New York: Academic Press, 1966.

Fishbein, Martin (ed.), *Attitude Theory and Research.* New York: John Wiley & Sons, 1967.

Fotheringham, Wallace C., *Perspectives on Persuasion.* Boston: Allyn and Bacon, 1966.

Fulton, R. Barry, "Motivation: Foundation of Persuasion." in *A Reader in Speech Communication,* ed. James W. Gibson. New York: McGraw-Hill, 1971, pp. 280–296.

Insko, Chester A., *Theories of Attitude Change.* New York: Appleton-Century-Crofts, 1967.

Meyerhoff, Arthur E., *The Strategy of Persuasion.* New York: Coward-McCann, 1965.

Rogers, Everett M., *Diffusion of Innovation.* New York: Free Press, 1962.

Rokeach, Milton, *Beliefs, Attitudes and Values.* San Francicso: Jossey-Bass, 1968.

Scheidel, Thomas M., *Persuasive Speaking.* Evanston, Ill.: Scott, Foresman, 1967.

Simons, Herbert W., "Confrontation as a Pattern of Persuasion in University Settings," in *A Reader in Speech Communication,* ed. James W. Gibson. New York: McGraw-Hill, 1971, pp. 316–325.

Vernon, M.D., *Human Motivation.* Cambridge, England: Cambridge University Press, 1969.

appendix
examples of
speech
communication

Some formal speeches and informal colloquies or discussions have become examples that suggest desirable methods for the student in his own speech development. This is not to suggest, however, that excellent talks, long or short, are to be closely imitated or copied, but rather that the experiences and methods of successful public and more informal commentators give clues and principles that can guide you in your own effective creativity.

How, then, are we to profit by the illustrative examples in this book, including those in the section below?

Your judgment of a communication and its speaker can well be guided by the principles and methods that make up this book.

The communicative process that you judge is composed of the speaker, the speaking situation, the audience, the speech, the channels of communication, and the overall combination of these factors. (See again Chapters 1, 2, and 3.)

Pertinent questions that may help you to explore a given communication are thus suggested:

1 Did the speaker compose the discourse attributed to him? We need to question whether a ghostwriter produced the document.

2 Did the text as produced duplicate what the speaker

actually said? If an electrical or other recording of the actual remarks uttered is available, we can compare it with the written text of the speech.

3 What was the speaking situation? Was the speaker talking in the midst of a war, economic depression, campus riot, or other event, large or small, that might have affected what was said? (See Chapters 1 and 3.)

4 What was the nature of the specific audience? What were its race, education, economic level, or other characteristics? (See Chapters 3 and 12.)

5 What was the purpose of the speaker? Was it mainly to inform, persuade, inspire, entertain? (See Chapters 2, 4, 9, 10, 11, and 12.)

6 What were the chief ideas of the communication? Were they worthwhile? (See Chapters 4, 5, and 11.)

7 What evidence or other details supported the central ideas? (See Chapters 4 and 11.)

8 What motivative elements in addition to logical substance of the discourse were apparent, and were they effectively developed? (See Chapter 12.)

9 Was the communication well organized? (See Chapter 5.)

10 Was the language effective? Was it original, interesting, clear, accurate, adapted to the occasion and audience? (See Chapter 6.)

11 Can we determine the effectiveness of the speaker's delivery? The written speech, to be sure, provides no clues to a speaker's voice, rate, quality, and other vocal features. Also absent from the script are the accompanying physical activities of the speaker. These elements can obviously be checked by the testimony of those who heard and observed the speaker. (See Chapters 6 and 7.)

12 Can we judge the total effectiveness of the given speech communication? Your judgment here will involve a study of the separate details and of the overall effect. You may judge a speech on the basis of its ideas, its structure, its appeals, its language, its reflection of the speaker's personality, its adjustment to the immediate audience, or some combination of these factors that obviously overlap.

You will need a norm by which to judge the various types and details of specific speech communications. A review of the principles of this book should help you to frame your own criteria for such evaluations, and for application to your own communicative experiences.

A New Economic Policy

RICHARD M. NIXON

Good evening.

I have addressed the Nation a number of times over the past two years on the problems of ending a war. Because of the progress we have made toward achieving that goal, this Sunday evening is an appropriate time for us to turn our attention to the challenges of peace.

America today has the best opportunity in this century to achieve two of its greatest ideals: to bring about a full generation of peace, and to create a new prosperity without war.

This not only requires bold leadership ready to take bold action— it calls forth the greatness in a great people.

Prosperity without war requires action on three fronts: We must create more and better jobs; we must stop the rise in the cost of living; we must protect the dollar from the attacks of international money speculators.

We are going to take that action—not timidly, not half-heartedly, and not in piecemeal fashion. We are going to move forward to the new prosperity without war as befits a great people—all together, and along a broad front.

The time has come for a new economic policy for the United States. Its targets are unemployment, inflation and international speculation. This is how we are going to attack them.

First, on the subject of jobs. We all know why we have an unemployment problem. Two million workers have been released from the Armed Forces and defense plants because of our success in winding down the war in Vietnam. Putting those people back to work is one of the challenges of peace, and we have begun to make progress. Our unemployment rate today is below the average of the four peacetime years of the 1960s.

Broadcast on television, Washington, D.C., Aug. 15, 1971. By permission of President Richard M. Nixon.

But we can and must do better than that.

The time has come for American industry, which has produced more jobs at higher real wages than any other industrial system in history, to embark on a bold program of new investment in production for peace.

To give that system a powerful new stimulus, I shall ask the Congress, when it reconvenes after its summer recess, to consider as its first priority the enactment of the Job Development Act of 1971.

I will propose to provide the strongest short-term incentive in our history to invest in new machinery and equipment that will create new jobs for Americans: A 10 percent Job Development Credit for one year, effective as of today, with a 5 percent credit after August 15, 1972. This tax credit for investment in new equipment will not only generate new jobs; it will raise productivity and it will make our goods more competitive in the years ahead.

Second, I will propose to repeal the 7 percent excise tax on automobiles, effective today. This will mean a reduction in price of about $200 per car. I shall insist that the American auto industry pass this tax reduction on to the nearly 8 million customers who are buying automobiles this year. Lower prices will mean that more people will be able to afford new cars, and every additional 100,000 cars sold means 25,000 new jobs.

Third, I propose to speed up the personal income tax exemptions scheduled for January 1, 1973 to January 1, 1972—so that taxpayers can deduct an extra $50 for each exemption one year earlier than planned. This increase in consumer spending power will provide a strong boost to the economy in general and to employment in particular.

The tax reductions I am recommending, together with the broad upturn of the economy which has taken place in the first half of this year, will move us strongly forward toward a goal this nation has not reached since 1956, 15 years ago—prosperity with full employment in peacetime.

Looking to the future, I have directed the Secretary of the Treasury to recommend to the Congress in January new tax proposals for stimulating research and development of new industries and new technologies to help provide the 20 million new jobs that America needs for the young people who will be coming into the job market in the next decade.

To offset the loss of revenue from these tax cuts which directly stimulate new jobs, I have ordered today a $4.7 billion cut in Federal spending.

Tax cuts to stimulate employment must be matched by spending cuts to restrain inflation. To check the rise in the cost of government, I have ordered a postponement of pay raises and a 5 percent cut in government personnel.

I have ordered a 10 percent cut in foreign economic aid.

In addition, since the Congress has already delayed action on two of the great initiatives of this Administration, I will ask Congress to amend my proposals to postpone the implementation of Revenue Sharing for three months and Welfare Reform for one year.

In this way, I am reordering our budget priorities to concentrate more on achieving full employment.

The second indispensable element of the new prosperity is to stop the rise in the cost of living.

One of the cruelest legacies of the artificial prosperity produced by war is inflation. Inflation robs every American. The 20 million who are retired and living on fixed incomes are particularly hard hit. Homemakers find it harder than ever to balance the family budget. And 80 million wage-earners have been on a treadmill. In the four war years between 1965 and 1969 your wage increases were completely eaten up by price increases. Your paychecks were higher, but you were no better off.

We have made progress against the rise in the cost of living. From the high point of 6 percent a year in 1969, the rise in consumer prices has been cut to four percent in the first half of 1971. But just as is the case in our fight against unemployment, we can and we must do better than that.

The time has come for decisive action—action that will break the vicious circle of spiraling prices and costs.

I am today ordering a freeze on all prices and wages throughout the United States for a period of 90 days. In addition, I call upon corporations to extend the wage-price freeze to all dividends.

I have today appointed a Cost of Living Council within the Government. I have directed this Council to work with leaders of labor and business to set up the proper mechanism for achieving continued price and wage stability after the 90-day freeze is over.

Let me emphasize two characteristics of this action: First, it is temporary. To put the strong, vigorous American economy into a permanent straitjacket would lock in unfairness; it would stifle the expansion of our free enterprise system. And second, while the wage-price freeze will be backed by Government sanctions, if necessary, it will not be accompanied by the establishment of a huge price control bureaucracy. I am relying on the voluntary cooperation of all Americans—each one of you—workers, employers, consumers—to make this freeze work.

Working together, we will break the back of inflation, and we will do it without the mandatory wage and price controls that crush economic and personal freedom.

The third indispensable element in building the new prosperity is closely related to creating new jobs and halting inflation. We must protect the position of the American dollar as a pillar of monetary stability around the world.

In the past seven years, there has been an average of one international monetary crisis every year. Who gains from these crises? Not the workingman; not the investors; and not the real producers of wealth. The gainers are international money speculators. Because they thrive on crises, they help to create them.

In recent weeks, the speculators have been waging an all-out war on the American dollar. The strength of a nation's currency is based on the strength of that nation's economy—and the American economy is by far the strongest in the world. Accordingly, I have directed the Secretary of the Treasury to take the action necessary to defend the dollar against the speculators.

I have directed Secretary Connally to suspend temporarily the convertibility of the dollar into gold or other reserve assets, except in amounts and conditions determined to be in the interest of monetary stability and in the best interests of the United States.

Now, what is this action, which is very technical? What does it mean for you?

Let me lay to rest the bugaboo of what is called devaluation.

If you want to buy a foreign car or take a trip abroad, market conditions may cause your dollar to buy slightly less. But if you are among the overwhelming majority of Americans who buy American-made products in America, your dollar will be worth just as much tomorrow as it is today.

The effect of this action, in other words, will be to stabilize the dollar.

Now, this action will not win us any friends among the international money traders. But our primary concern is with the American workers, and with fair competition around the world.

To our friends abroad, including the many responsible members of the international banking community who are dedicated to stability and the flow of trade, I give this assurance: The United States has always been, and will continue to be, a forward-looking and trustworthy trading partner. In full cooperation with the International Monetary Fund and those who trade with us, we will press for the necessary reforms to set up an urgently needed new international monetary system. Stability and equal treatment is in everybody's best interest. I am determined that the American dollar must never again be a hostage in the hands of the international speculators.

I am taking one further step to protect the dollar, to improve our balance of payments, and to increase sales for Americans. As a temporary measure, I am today imposing an additional tax of 10 percent on goods imported into the United States. This is a better solution for international trade than direct controls on the amount of imports.

This import tax is a temporary action. It isn't directed against any other country. It is an action to make certain that American products will not be at a disadvantage because of unfair exchange rates. When the unfair treatment is ended, the import tax will end as well.

As a result of these actions, the product of American labor will be more competitive, and the unfair edge that some of our foreign competition has had will be removed. That is a major reason why our trade balance has eroded over the past fifteen years.

At the end of World War II the economies of the major industrial nations of Europe and Asia were shattered. To help them get on their feet and to protect their freedom, the United States has provided over the past 25 years $143 billion in foreign aid. This was the right thing for us to do.

Today, largely with our help, they have regained their vitality. They have become our strong competitors, and we welcome their success. But now that other nations are economically strong, the time has come for them to bear their fair share of the burden of defending freedom around the world. The time has come for exchange rates to be set straight and for the major nations to compete as equals. There is no longer any need for the United States to compete with one hand tied behind her back.

The range of actions I have taken and proposed tonight—on the job front, on the inflation front, on the monetary front—is the most comprehensive New Economic Policy to be undertaken by this nation in four decades.

We are fortunate to live in a nation with an economic system capable of producing for its people the highest standard of living in the world; a system flexible enough to change its ways dramatically when circumstances call for change; and most important—a system resourceful enough to produce prosperity with freedom and opportunity unmatched in the history of nations.

The purposes of the government actions I have announced tonight are to lay the basis for renewed confidence, to make it possible for us to compete fairly with the rest of the world, to open the door to a new prosperity.

But government, with all its powers, does not hold the key to the success of a people. That key, my fellow Americans, is in your hands.

A nation, like a person, has to have a certain inner drive in order to succeed. In economic affairs, that inner drive is called the competitive spirit.

Every action I have taken tonight is designed to nurture and stimulate that competitive spirit; to help us snap out of that self-doubt and self-disparagement that saps our energy and erodes our confidence in ourselves.

Whether this nation stays number one in the world's economy or resigns itself to second, third or fourth place; whether we as a people have faith in ourselves, or lose that faith; whether we hold fast to the strength that makes peace and freedom possible in this world, or lose our grip—all that depends on you, on your competitive spirit, your sense of personal destiny, your pride in your country and in yourself.

We can be certain of this: As the threat of war recedes, the challenge of peaceful competition in the world will greatly increase.

We welcome competition, because America is at her greatest when she is called on to compete.

As there always have been in our history, there will be voices urging us to shrink from that challenge of competition, to build a protective wall around ourselves, to crawl into a shell as the rest of the world moves ahead.

Two hundred years ago a man wrote in his diary these words: "Many thinking people believe America has seen its best days." That was written in 1775, just before the American Revolution, at the dawn of the most exciting era in the history of man. Today we hear the echoes of those voices, preaching a gospel of gloom and defeat, saying that same thing: "We have seen our best days."

I say, let Americans reply: "Our best days lie ahead."

As we move into a generation of peace, as we blaze the trail toward the new prosperity, I say to every American: Let us raise our spirits. Let us raise our sights. Let all of us contribute all we can to the great and good country that has contributed so much to the progress of mankind.

Let us invest in our nation's future; and let us revitalize that faith in ourselves that built a great nation in the past, and will shape the world of the future.

Thank you, and good evening.

The Educated Man in the Age of Aquarius

RICHARD WHITE

"This is the Age of Aquarius, when peace will guide the planets and love shall steer the stars." Today, this prophesy from the musical *Hair* sums up the feelings of many young Americans toward their society. Its appeal is especially strong among college students. For youth is asking basic questions about the goals and methods of our society in general, and of education in particular.

I think it is a fair summation to say that the turbulence of most Aquarians is the result of principle more than passion. In all too many cases, their greivances are solidly justified. First, they reject the hypocrisy so common in America today. For example, according to traditional American beliefs, no medical care is too good for our wounded combat veterans, and no punishment too severe for the leaders of organized crime. Yet the last two issues of *Life* magazine have exposed incredible filth and inattention in some of our military hospitals, as well as the rise to power in Saint Louis' city government of men with clear ties to the underworld. Another example is the vengeance with which young people—the law-abiding as well as the law-breaking—were beaten down on Chicago streets while trying to work "within the system." Second, the Aquarian objects to the limitation of personal freedom in our society. On paper and in fact, we are one of the freest peoples on earth. But society today regulates private morality, acts to limit free expression of ideas, and makes justice depend on wealth, social status, race, or hair style. So caught up are we in the external appearance or habits of other people that we judge them by looks without bothering to consider the quality of their ideas. As one Aquarian said to me, "If they can't go beyond that, then they can't see what's happening." The final complaint of many Aquarians is the value system of a society which puts so little emphasis on matters

A commencement address at Wabash College, June 7, 1970. Mr. White was a graduating senior. By permission of Mr. White and *Old Wabash*.

of the spirit, so much on material comfort. It is a matter of shame that western man has lived fewer than 300 of the last 3000 years in peace.

Now these are legitimate objections—they deserve a fair hearing at least, if not support—and the Aquarian sees his role in society as a conscience, pointing out wrongs and bringing attention to the problems we face. But many Aquarians have gone one step further. Losing hope in America's ability to change peacefully, they drop out, creating a sub-culture based on self-interest and drugs. They treat all representatives of opposing views with scorn; basing their thinking on moral absolutes, they refuse to compromise, or sometimes even discuss, their demands. And this inflexible attitude brings an equally inflexible response: Mass confrontation, police riots, physical attacks by private citizens, rhetorical attacks by public officials.

Neither of these extremes and irritational views seems to me to be productive of good for our society. For the unbending response of one side only convinces the other that it was right all along. I have three objections to these positions: First, neither side proposes changes as often as it should and then sits down and discusses them. The average American will accept change, but you must show him that it is beneficial. Copping out, with drugs or self-righteousness, won't do a thing to help change our society for the better. My second objection is that many of these people seem to have lost faith in a system which has great potential for change—as long as a majority peacefully approves it. The McCarthy kids may have felt disillusioned after Chicago, but they should remember how they brought down an administration and redirected American foreign policy. Third, and as a result of this hopelessness, I don't think that all Aquarians or their opponents are dedicated to reason as a problem solving method. In his article, "Anglo-Saxonism and Fascism," Professor Andrew Ezergailis contrasts the Anglo-American tradition of persuasion and pragmatic compromise with the continental European view of moral absolutes, which may not be compromised. Such a contrast is visible in the refusal of many to even consider changing views they believe are fundamentally correct.

These three weaknesses lead to misunderstanding between young and old. To bridge this gap, a concerned citizen with special talents must be found. I call that man, "The Educated man." Who is this wonder worker? What is he like? To answer these questions we must first ask, "What is education?"

Many of the alienated young protest that a diploma represents sixteen years of conditioning by society, learning to jump meaningless hurdles at the command of the Establishment. For them, the three R's mean "Rules, Respect, and Rote." But we have enough examples of men who were set free—introduced to great ideas, given a deeper understanding of people, and rigorous training in logical thought—to discount this argument. A second view holds that education is what education does—lectures in class, study of notes and books, exams, and extracurriculars such as good, old-fashioned hell-raising, social and athletic events, and commencements. These activities have their value—a solid factual background, self-discipline, the ability to get along among people —but they are only forms which have been grafted onto the skeleton of education.

The essence of education, and its value, are not in such external forms, but are internal, part of the educated man himself. Education means exposure to ideas; it is the ability to live and work with people very different from us; it is the ability to draw something meaningful from daily life. But this ability must be guided by certain basic attitudes. Today, I suggest five, and though they may seem obvious to you at first, I believe there are numerous examples of action inconsistent with these principles by supposedly educated people in both the new left and the Establishment.

The first attitude is a sense of personal honesty—or if you will, honor. An Aquarian told me that he was looking for a "glittering white knight"—and I think that, as a nation, we need to have complete confidence in our leaders at all levels. Scandals involving conflict of interest or personal ethics and credibility gaps have no place in our life. The educated man must have a scrupulous sense of honesty.

Another personal trait the educated man needs is the ambition to excel. In his thought-provoking book, *Excellence,* John Gardner writes:

There is a way of measuring excellence that involves
comparison between myself at my best and myself at
my worst. It is this latter comparison that enables me
to assert that I am being true to the best that is in me—
or forces me to confess that I am not.

The person who just gets by, who doesn't try to do his best, is cheating both himself and society. For society suffers the loss of a valuable resource—his talents and skill; but he loses the excitement and sense of purpose that come from working to achieve a worthwhile goal. That a national magazine should devote an issue to America the Inefficient is an indication that this quality—the pursuit of excellence—is missing in our national life.

Commitment to our society and to the achievement of its highest ideals is the third critical attitude. In my opinion, one of the chief weaknesses of the new left is its belief that America is hopelessly corrupt. The silent majority is equally mistaken by so stressing conformity—"America: Love it or Leave it"—that it threatens the ideals for which America stands. A recent *Newsweek* poll showed that half the population opposes Bill of Rights freedoms in practice. One reader of the *Christian Science Monitor* wrote the editor to suggest a better slogan—"America: Love It and Help Make It Better!" Faith in America as a land of freedom is still justified, and the educated man should share this faith and practice it.

Fourth, the educated man uses reason to solve the problems he faces. It is very appealing to live by slogans and let your mind go to sleep, especially if the slogans are violent or emotional—"Kill the Pigs!", "Bomb Hanoi!", "Effete Snobs"—but rhetoric will give you neither wise nor livable solutions. The educated man, to use Bob Buroker's phrase of three years ago, solves problems by asking the right questions about them. Nonnegotiable demands and uncompromising orthodoxy are not his coin.

Finally, the educated man is tolerant. Nothing has torn America

more these last few years than intolerance—students who shout
down speakers or throw pies in their faces rather than listen to
them; hardhats who maul peaceful demonstrators, anyone who
uses force to prevent another from peaceably stating his views is
doing his part to destroy America. People often say that, in a
showdown, the orthodoxy of the right will prevail over the absolutism of the left—but this misses the point: no such orthodoxy, no
such absolutism should be upheld in the first place. San Francisco's
Longshoreman-Philosopher, Eric Hoffer, points out that

We used to think that revolutions are the cause of change;
actually it is the other way around: change prepares the
ground for revolution. The difficulties and irritations inherent in the experience of change render people receptive
to the appeal of revolution.

Tolerance is the midwife of peaceful change—intolerance will lead
only to repression on the one hand and revolutionism on the
other. Either way, the results are the same; broken bodies in the
streets, and flaming hatred in men's hearts. Our society can do
better than these grisly alternatives; men who are tolerant insure
that it will.

I have selected examples from the political right and left, from
young and old, from the formally educated and those with less
schooling, because I believe that education is more than a matter
of classroom learning. Rather, it is an outlook on life. Clearly, it
doesn't take a college degree to practice the qualities I've mentioned. There are as many men without diplomas who deserve
the title "educated", as there are men with degrees who do not.
The diplomas we receive do not say, "you are educated." They
only say that we're in a good position to try. And so today is not
so much a celebration of accomplishment as it is a service of dedication for all of us, parents and friends as well as graduates, to
commit our minds, our talents, our lives to the best qualities that
education offers.

For more than two weeks last month, the flag behind you flew at half-staff—mute testimony to our need for all the honest, committed, reasonable and tolerant citizens we can produce. If we fail, our loss will be all mankind's. If we succeed, we shall have an age of peace and love among men—a true Age of Aquarius.

Higher Education Begins the Seventies

THEODORE M. HESBURGH

In the twenty-five years that I have been associated with the university, as faculty member and administrator, I can think of no period more difficult than the present. Never before has the university taken on more tasks, and been asked to undertake many more, while the sources of support, both public and private, both moral and financial, seem to be drying up.

In the 314 years from the founding of Harvard until 1950, we grew in the United States to a total capacity of 3 million students in higher education. From 1950 to 1970, that number and capacity more than doubled to over 7 million students. Maybe our traditional ways of governance have not kept pace with our enlarged size and the new mentalities of both faculty and students. Maybe both we in the universities and the world beyond really expected too much of our university operation. We live in a university world of idea and imagination. But these alone will not insure peace, social justice, an end to racism and poverty.

Maybe our growth was too uneven, with the physical sciences getting the lion's share and all the other disciplines emulating the physical sciences' methodology to qualify for a larger share. This was doomed to failure for, however attractive the humanities and the social sciences are, they become singularly unattractive once quantified, mathematicized, and unattentive to values. Having sold their birthright, in large measure the mess of pottage was not forthcoming.

Maybe our problems relate more deeply than we suspect to the parlous state of the world around us—to its basic malaise, to its anomie, to its frustration and rootlessness. I suspect that we are,

This address was delivered to the faculty of the University of Notre Dame, October 5, 1970. By permission of President Hesburgh and of *Representative American Speeches*, 1970–71.

in the Western world and even beyond its boundaries, passing through an historical watershed which we little understand and which may be ultimately of more importance than the Renaissance, the Reformation, or the industrial revolution.

I doubt that anyone would be able to label our age, although it might be called the age of frustrated expectations, the age of protest against almost everything, the age of unlimited possibilities and disappointing results. It is an age that can put men on the moon yet create an impossible traffic tangle in every metropolitan center. It is an age of unbelievable wealth and widespread poverty. It is an age of sensitivity to human dignity and human progress in which there is relatively little of either, despite the available resources. It is finally an age where the hopes, the expectations, and the promises of humanity have been more rhetorical than real. Because the university lives largely by rhetoric alone, it has come to be blamed for much of the frustration. In a very real sense, the university has been oversold as the key to all human progress. There is a wide gulf between the blueprint and the reality—the word and the deed.

Given the actual state of the world around us, we in the university are little comprehended in that all of the world's anxieties are focused strongly in the university where there exists an explosive combination of young, searching minds that are invited daily to view all problems and every variety of response to them and a faculty that is problem-oriented and given to play to the generosity and idealism of youth. Also an administration that is only able to survive by responding positively and emphatically to the aspirations and hopes of faculty and students, however impossible they are of immediate accomplishment.

Into this explosive mix comes a strong cry for "law and order" from the so-called silent majority who are not anxious to face new approaches to human equality or social justice if these threaten their hard-earned gains. When the university responds negatively to this demand for law and order, which it rightly construes as "status quo," and continues to insist on stronger priorities for the nation, new initiatives for peace, for equality, for social justice,

whatever the shock to the "status quo," then we have a superex-
plosive situation. The university is judged to be subversive, it is
certainly not understood and it loses more and more the public
and private support that is needed to sustain it.

It is simply an historic fact that any group, and particularly a university community, does not understand not being understood.
What is more serious, young people in the university do not realize
how much the university depends upon the support of the larger
surrounding society. Even less do they understand that when their
frustrations about the problems of the larger community lead them
to act in anger and, at times, with violence, there is only one normal response, from that larger community, namely, counterviolence
and repressive action. Japanese university students practically
closed the principal universities in Japan for a year or so until the
Diet passed a law envisioning the permanent closing of some universities, especially Tokyo, the largest. Then suddenly the message
was manifest and the violence dropped off.

One might speculate what would happen if some American universities which suffer constant disruption were suddenly closed
down for a year or two. It might be healthy and it might be disastrous, but it could happen and it may.

It would have been incomprehensible to mention such a possibility, even speculatively, a decade ago. But it does demonstrate the
present state of affairs that it is being mentioned today.

Some have tried to describe the present situation as the politicization of the university. It certainly is true that faculties, even at
Harvard and Princeton, have taken rather unanimous positions on
the Vietnam War that would have been unthinkable a few years
ago. University presidents have also spoken out to an extent that
has brought them condemnation from the highest levels of Government and from a broad spectrum of alumni and benefactors. Students who were termed apathetic a few years ago are now deeply
involved in political lobbying, electioneering for favored candidates,
and protesting the actions of other political figures with whom
they disagree.

There is some merit in all of this, but some thoughtful university observers call it the politicization of the university and the end of that objective, other-worldly, balanced and impassionate activity that has long characterized the university. Some see in all of this the end of academic freedom and a call for repressive action.

The fact is that almost every state in the Union has considered in its legislature some punitive legislation against faculty and students —about half of which has been enacted into law. Trustees and governors have practically forced the resignation of a number of presidents, for instance in Texas, Oklahoma, and California. Feeling is running high against many highly visible universities and the witch hunters are out and at work. Both Federal and state programs of support for higher education have been reduced or tied to impossible conditions. Many private universities find themselves hard put to hold fast to the support they now have, much less to augment it. Disaffection with universities, their presidents, their faculties, and their students is simply a growing fact of life that will probably get worse.

The great majority of the best university presidents that I have known, respected and worked with over the past years are simply resigning to escape what has become an impossible task: to keep peace inside and outside the university, when trustees cry "law and order" and students condemn this concept as another form of "status quo" in a very imperfect world. Alumni think the whole enterprise is coming apart at the seams, while faculty call for even greater changes than those now taking place. Benefactors lose confidence in the whole unruly endeavor when they are attacked by students or faculty because they are accused of giving money gained through what is proclaimed to be an unholy military-industrial alliance. Parents expect a control over their children which they themselves have never been able to maintain, while the students in turn want absolute freedom and certainly no one acting in the place of their parents, however ineffective these may have been. At this point, the president, who is believed to be in charge although his authority has been monumentally reduced, begins to see that he simply cannot succeed unless the academic community is a real community—something becoming even more rare in university circles.

Many of the new experimental forms of university governance are aimed at building a stronger university community. Whether or not they will achieve this is simply conjecture at this point. In general, the trustee system has served American universities well, when faculties were allowed to decide academic matters and when students were given a reasonable voice in the arranging of their affairs. One might fault some university boards of trustees by noting that they have generally not represented the broad spectrum of the public they were supposed to represent. There have been all too few women, or blacks, or middle class, or younger people on most boards. Most of them, at least at the great private universities, resembled too much an exclusive club for WASPs (White Anglo-Saxon Protestants). But this is changing as it should, and faculties and students are having an even larger voice in those decisions that mainly affect them and their lives. Reform of governance alone is certainly not the total answer to the problems that face us.

So far, I have been mainly engaged in an analysis of the present situation facing universities in a changing world. The view, as I have thus far presented it, is admittedly pessimistic. As a committed optimist, I believe that at this time I should attempt to find a few positive aspects of the total picture.

To begin with, student and faculty unrest in our day—a worldwide phenomenon—is in large measure a manifestation of their moral concern for the priorities or the values of present-day society. One would find it difficult to fault them for those things they oppose: war, violence, racism, poverty, pollution, human degradation on a large scale.

It has been a quality and inclination of most young people, since the time that Aristotle accused them of being too vehement about everything, to see the world in absolute terms of good and evil, to be inspired by great idealism, generosity, and enthusiasm, and often to give their all, to man the barricades for causes of justice and equality. Life, problems, and solutions somehow seem simpler to the young who are yet unscarred by the acid of cruel experience. This is not all bad. Maybe the weary and cynical world today, more than ever before, needs this kind of youthful conscience to find its way out of the lassitude and ambiguity that attend so much of modern human life. Maybe the university is the only place on earth where we can bridge the generation gap by common moral concern on the part of young and old, faculty and students. Granting that students are often naive in their concern for instant solutions to very complicated problems, granting their addiction to absolute black and white judgments in matters that are often very gray, granting their lack of a sense of history, their rupture with tradition, and their inability to appreciate experience and competence, they still are concerned and are unafflicted by the anomie that is the cancer of so many of their elders.

Perhaps this calls for a greater dedication to teaching on our part, for great teaching can manifest competence without preaching it, transmit a sense of history without seeming to be antiquarian, show how much patience is to be valued just by being patient with them. Good teaching, nay, great teaching, may yet be the salvation of the university and of society in our day. It has been rather obvious that our professors have in large measure sought distinction through research rather than great teaching, through adherence to their discipline far beyond loyalty to their particular institution. The theory was that research would enrich teaching, but for all too many professors, it has largely replaced teaching. This has not gone unnoticed by the students who flock to the chosen few who still can profess and teach.

I do not believe that the university has by any means come to the end of its road, but I am willing to concede that it faces a fork in the road and must make some real decisions as to where it is going. Generally speaking, I would conclude that the university can and must remain politically neutral as an institution, although its faculty, students, and administrators are free to take their own political stance, indeed must do so when faced with national and international crises with deep moral undertones. It is difficult for a president to do this as an individual, but he must always try to make this clear to the public. I am personally against faculties taking political stances as a particular university body academic, unless the matter is of supreme moral, national or international

importance. Students are somewhat freer in all of this because
they do not have such permanent attachment to the university.
Alumni less so. Avoiding politicization in highly emotional and
deeply polarized times is not going to be easy. The threatening
loss of academic freedom or academic objectivity is reason enough
to keep trying in every way one can.

Balancing the development of research in the physical sciences,
the social sciences and the humanities may be somewhat easier
now that the golden age for research support in the physical sciences seems to be passing. Since teaching needs all the importance,
respect, and reward that we can accord it, giving it some measure
of priority may be at the heart of the solution.

The service relationship of the university to the communities that
surround it, local, state, national and international, is something
that needs great clarification for the survival of the university. In
some cases, the university has become too much of a service station expected to solve problems by its actual operation rather than
seek solutions theoretically and pilot-test them in a more microcos-
mic fashion. The university cannot become the Red Cross immediately attending to all manner of social emergencies. It is not an
overseas development corporation or a foreign or domestic Peace
Corps. It may well have strong intellectual and educational ties to
these and other service organizations, but it should never confuse
its university identity or task with theirs.

Universities should be ready to experiment with new forms of
governance, but I see no great value, in fact great loss, in confusing
the specific tasks of trustees, faculty, administrators or students.
Maybe we should proclaim more often that the prime function of
the faculty is to teach, that of the students to learn and that of the
administration to make the conditions for teaching and learning
more fruitful. Trustees can be enormously effective to the whole
operation if they appoint and protect good officers of the university, help keep the institution financially viable, and support
against any power inside or outside the institution the integrity
of the whole operation and its best priorities as they emerge from
the total community, including the alumni. Every community

needs, especially in troubled times, some final authority, some strong protector. Trustees have fulfilled this role for the better universities that have emerged in America.

One is often reminded of Charles Dickens' opening statement in *A Tale of Two Cities:* "It was the best of times; it was the worst of times." I think this can well be said of the state of the university in the rapidly changing world of our day. We can survive the worst if we achieve the better or hopefully, the best.

Remarks at the Centennial Charter Day Convocation, The Ohio State University, Mar. 22, 1970

JAMES RESTON

In the spirit of this happy occasion and out of respect for Vice President Agnew, I have taken my text for today from the Bible. It is from the 19th chapter of the Book of Luke, the first to the third verse: "And Jesus entered and passed through Jericho, and behold there was a man named Zacchaeus and he sought to see Jesus and could not for the press . . ."

If you listen to the melancholy drummers of the present time, it is hard to believe that anything can endure for a hundred years or would want to, but a hundred years should give us a sense of history and maybe even a sense of humor.

This University was founded during the administration of President Grant and somehow survived that conspicuous misfortune. It has lived through the reconstruction after the War Between the States, through five other wars, the economic depression of the nineteen thirties, and even the Michigan defeat of last December. After that, what tragedies and terrors of life could possibly prevail against it in the next hundred years?

We have gathered together with our individual memories and our common dreams to pay tribute to the men and women who have founded and sustained this institution. We do so at a time when all institutions and all authority are under attack, and it is my hope that, having come here to pay our respects to Ohio State, we shall remember that we are not isolated souls but part of a large and noble company, with common ideals and common obligations.

I would like to try to say one or two things about the spirit of

By permission of Mr. James Reston.

our country today, the role of the university, and the art of living through a rebellious era. The pessimists seem to be in full cry these days. The noble effort of America to organize the nations for peace, to find accommodations with the communist world and to create a system of collective security in the Western World is obviously in deep trouble.

The equally noble ideal of bringing the races, the classes, the regions and the generations of America into a common and equal life is now clearly being challenged in the North as well as in the South. The trend of the day seems to be toward separatism: Nationalism is rising all over the world; the old concepts of spheres of influence is coming back; there is a tribalism in Africa, defiant separation by some black leaders and some whites; students are calling not for leadership but control, taking over or dropping out into the hills and into dope; and all around we hear prophecies of instability, division, anarchy, and even Civil War...

I should observe in passing that we in the press are partly to blame for this emphasis on the negative. My generation learned our craft in the police courts and county-courthouses of America, where news was what was on the police blotter and in the court docket—that is to say, we were taught to report what went wrong —not the usual, but the unusual—the disputes, divisions and dissensions of life. No doubt this has had an excessively depressing influence on our time.

Still, in the perspective of these hundred years, we should remember that pessimism is not an invention of this generation. You ought to read some time the debates in the Congress of the United States on the Morrill Land Grant College Act, which established these state universities. Federal aid to education was denounced as a tool of the devil—still is some places—and even Mr. Lincoln, who signed the bill, had his doubts.

We think of Fred Cornell's famous "Carmen Ohio" song as a joyful assertion of our faith in this University, but actually it comes from an 18th century Spanish hymn, which is one of the gloomiest dirges in the history of religious music.

In the early days of this University, Walt Whitman wrote a little

article on the State of the Union: "Never was there," he said,
"more hollowness at heart than at the present, and here in the
United States. Genuine belief seems to have left us. The underlying principles of the states are not honestly believed in. . .
The spectacle is appalling. We live in an atmosphere of hypocrisy throughout. The men believe not in the women, nor the
women in the men. The great cities reek with robbery and
scoundrelism . . ."

So much for the Good Old Days! The main difference merely
seems to be that the old grumblers wrote better than the present grumblers. In 1870, the population of the United States was
39,818,000. Just a hundred years ago this week, the 15th Amend-
ment was adopted proclaiming that no state shall deprive a citizen
of the right to vote because of race, color or previous condition of
servitude. Women voted for the first time in the United States that
year, in the state of Utah, and President Grant, like President
Nixon today, was worrying about the economy. So everything is
not entirely new, and since we have survived and grown to over
200,000,000, it is only fair to assume that we must have been
doing something right.

Mr. Chairman, there is always a danger when you invite Old Gee-
zers to talk that they will make silly sentimental speeches. And
there is the further danger that if you invite a Scottish Old Geezer,
he will preach. I will try to behave and stick to the facts.

We are going through an awkward time in our country, and we are
going to have to do hard things with our minds. I am very sympa-
thetic with the young: they have to grapple with prosperity.
"Lead us not into temptation." We merely had to deal with ad-
versity in our generation, and having dealt with it fairly well, we
have led them into temptations beyond our worst nightmares and
certainly beyond anything we had to overcome. We have to be
fair about this, or we won't help them but merely lose them.

I listened to my old high school friend, Milton Caniff, on the
television last night recalling how he came to this University and
put down his $60 tuition to start one of the most illustrious
careers in America today. He expected so little and did so much,

not only with his artistic talents but with his love and compassion
for his fellow man. It was much easier for us then. I went to the
University of Illinois because my buddy was a football player
named Fuzzy Evans. He thought he was another Chic Harley and
came here but didn't make it. So he asked me to go with him to
Illinois. I never applied or registered in advance. We just got out
on the highway and bummed our way there and signed up. Things
are more complicated today and we have to ask ourselves, before
we get too critical and self-righteous, whether we would have been
able to prevail over the tensions and temptations life now puts
before our children.

This is the devilish thing about this time. It forces us to choose
always between complicated imponderables. This is what I mean
by saying we have to do hard things with our minds. There are no
clear choices. Who is to say what is clearly right or wrong in Vietnam, where to draw the line between the hypocrisy of the old and
the hypocrisy of the young, when to liberate our children and
when to come down hard and say "no"; how to tolerate dissent
without loitering down into anarchy; what is a Republican and
what a Democrat, neither having any reliable set of principles or
priorities, and most of their leaders being as bewildered by these
ambiguities as all the rest of us?

Almost half a century ago, Alfred North Whitehead wrote a little
book called *Symbolism*, in which he said something which may
help us understand the turmoil of this age and even help us to endure it.

"It is the first step in wisdom," he said, "to recognize that the
major advances in civilization are processes which all but wreck the
society in which they occur . . ."

"The art of free society," he continued, "consists, first in the
maintenance of the symbolic code; and secondly in fearlessness of
revision . . . Those societies which cannot combine reverence to
their symbols with freedom of revision, must ultimately decay
either from anarchy, or from the slow atrophy of a life stifled by
useless shadows . . ."

Now, Mr. Chairman, this seems to me to be an almost perfect

definition of the American condition today, with all its divisions,
strugglings, yearnings, controversies, dangers and opportunities.
I cannot remember a time, and I have not read about a time save
the very beginnings of the Republic when the American people
were grappling with the hard facts of life as they are now.

There is not a human relationship in the nation today, whether of
husband and wife, parents and children, employer and employee,
teacher and pupil, preacher and parishioner, that is not under the
most searching analysis. Nor is there another country in the world
where the fundamental problems of life are being faced so squarely.

I am not saying that we are settling these problems, or that they
are comfortable. On the contrary, it is a period of great vexation
and anxiety which is shaking our society to its roots. This is precisely what Whitehead said: "that the major advances in civilization are processes which all but wreck the society in which they
occur."

It is not, however, possible to escape from these problems or to
avoid the consequences by blaming them on politicians and governments. Governments clearly have the power to make war—and alas
they are still at it—but it is not governments that are changing the
world today. We are changing the world faster than we can change
ourselves, but it is being changed, essentially, by the fertility of the
human mind and body. The governments of the states, the government in Washington, the socialist governments of Europe and the
Communist governments of the East are all in the same boat. They
are all flummoxed about how to deal with the problems created by
the fantastic growth of population and the spectacular advances of
science.

It isn't Richard Nixon's fault, or Governor Rhodes' that the population of the United States increased by almost 25 million in the
decade of the Sixties. That is half the population of Britain, or
France, or West Germany. But the President and the Governor
have to figure out where to get the jobs, the houses, the schools,
the roads, and all the other services required for two million additional Americans every year—and the plain truth of the matter is
that nobody quite knows how to do it.

We see the problem right here on this campus with its spectacular growth. We see it in the school districts of the state, where local control provides sometimes fifty times as much money per pupil in a rich school district than it does in a poor district. We see it in the striking mail carriers, who are expected to live in New York on the same salary as a carrier gets in Chillicothe. There is no need to bore you with more examples: they are all around us. But most of them, from population to pollution, which is really the same thing, come primarily from the people and not primarily from the governments.

How are we to approach these problems? I think Whitehead has given us a key: first, maintenance of the symbolic code; second, fearlessness of revision, and I wish he had added: "Both together." For obviously we have a great many people on the right who want to concentrate primarily on maintenance of the symbols and procedures of the past, and are not very interested in fearlessness of revision. Also, there are quite a few people, many of them around universities, who want to defy the symbols of the past and toss deans out of second story windows in order to demonstrate their fearlessness of revision.

It is going to take a very vigilant electorate to keep these dual purposes in mind, for it is clear where I come from that political prejudice is now computerized. The candidates make the most careful studies of the prejudices of the voters in the various districts. They know precisely how to play on the special interests of those districts, whether to talk about Vietnam or avoid talking about it, whether to appeal by radio or television, what kind of slogans to peddle. The bull horn, the sound truck, the radio and TV are now at the command of men who know all the arts of illusionism and appeal to all the fears and demons decent men and women usually try to drive out of their lives.

I do not despair about this. The answer to the political activists of the extreme right and left is not less political action by the majority but more political action. We are not going to make the politicians give up their prejudices or their computers and we are not going to get rid of political pollution even if we get rid of the other kind. If I may paraphrase the old advertising jingle, you can take politics out of the gutter but you can't take the gutter out of politics.

In the face of all this, the universities, I think, have a great role to play. When Bill Wilcox was taking me around the campus and showing me all those wonderful new buildings—forgetting the silos by the stadium—I was reminded of a statement Thomas Huxley made when he came to Baltimore in the 1870's, just as this University was starting its first classes. He told his audience that he had looked at the magnificent prospects of America, all its power, all its energy, but he added that size was not power. The truly inspiring question, he said, is: "What are you going to do with all this? What are the ends you are trying to serve?"

You must realize that I am a Scotch Calvinist and particularly interested in this question of purpose. The first question in the catechism of the English church is the same as the first question on your income tax form, if I may refer to that unhappy subject. It is: What is Your Name? But the first question in the Scottish catechism is: What is the Chief end of Man? There is quite a difference here and it is not a bad question for a university or a nation.

We are clearly going to have a rough time on the campuses from now on. It would be foolish to suppose that the kids now in high school, watching the resort to violence in the universities and seeing force used as an instrument of policy in Vietnam and coercion used successfully even by federal government employees, are going to be less militant in the coming years.

We are going to hear more about alienation, confrontation, disintegration, separation, and pollution in the Seventies—why are the popular political words these days all so long and why do they end in "t-i-o-n"?—but it is clear that the universities, while being in the center of this turmoil and commotion are going to have to strive harder than ever to retain their value as independent and disinterested sources of judgment.

This is both a challenge and a paradox: to encourage commitment for the old goal of creating a more perfect society, and yet to retain the detachment and disinterested inquiry essential to a free university. No doubt this will be a slow hard business, but when we look over the trials and triumphs of this University and of all the land grant institutions, we have to be impressed by this country's infinite capacity to change and adapt. I notice that even Yale and Princeton have finally discovered after several hundred years that the most civilizing instrument in the world is a woman.

"Reverence to the old symbols, fearless of revision, and both together"—that I think is the key. I would like to close with a special word to the alumni. I sometimes think we celebrate the wrong things on ceremonial occasions: the child at birthdays instead of the Mother, the graduates at Commencement instead of the parents who finally stayed the course. If it is true as the disillusioned young assert that we have left them a world of confusion and hypocrisy, that the world is crazy and governments are venal, then surely it follows that more than any other generation, they will have to fall back on the family and on the company of faithful friends.

Mr. Chairman, I am grateful for your courtesy, I am glad to sing Ohio's praise, and on the whole, I feel rather hopeful about the next hundred years.

iNdEx